THE
SHETLAND
WAY

RAISED IN EDINBURGH, Marianne Brown spent many years working as a journalist in Southeast Asia and later in Britain as the editor of an environmental magazine. She now works for a community-owned renewable energy cooperative. She lives in Devon and can often be found running on the moor or attempting to tame her allotment with her partner and daughter.

THE
SHETLAND
WAY

Community and climate crisis on my father's islands

MARIANNE BROWN

THE BOROUGH PRESS

The Borough Press
An imprint of HarperCollins*Publishers* Ltd
1 London Bridge Street
London SE1 9GF

www.harpercollins.co.uk

HarperCollins*Publishers*
Macken House,
39/40 Mayor Street Upper,
Dublin 1
D01 C9W8

First published in Great Britain by HarperCollins*Publishers* 2025
2

Copyright © Marianne Brown

Marianne Brown asserts the moral right to be
identified as the author of this work

A catalogue record for this book is available from the British Library

HB ISBN: 978-0-00-8596156
TPB ISBN: 978-0-00-8596163

Typeset in Sabon Lt Pro by HarperCollins*Publishers* India

Printed and bound in the UK using 100%
Renewable Electricity at CPI Group (UK) Ltd

This book contains FSC™ certified paper and other controlled
sources to ensure responsible forest management.

For more information visit: www.harpercollins.co.uk/green

To Esme, who is, basically, the boss around here

Prologue

I was standing at the foot of the open grave when a shadow nudged into my peripheral vision. At first, I thought it was a raptor, and I squinted at it eagerly, hoping for a visitation from something rare or meaningful, a sympathetic act from the residents of these peat-layered hills of whom I knew so little. A longer look revealed the commonplace yellow beak, grey wings and reptilian glare of a herring gull. It was too busy gripping the wind to meet my gaze.

Beside me, figures zipped up against the February weather kept their eyes on the ground, their faces washed in horizontal rain. One mourner recited a well-known poem about a kaleyard and the eternal cycle of life and death, the lines 'aye some een dead, aye some een born' crumbling into the wind.

The same scene had been enacted by generations before us: a long line of wet faces, muddy feet and tight throats, stretching far back into the history of these islands to a time before the value of the sea and land was measured on a ledger. Along the shore, the tide ground the detritus of thousands of iterations of human life into the silt: ceramic cup handles, rusted nails, scraps of nylon fishing net. Beneath the undulations of grass and peat bog, ancient tree roots lay as a reminder of what this earth once was.

As we shivered between the gravestones, accompanied by the ghosts of our dead relatives, I considered the contrast of my own life with theirs: a childhood safe within the predictable perimeters of a large and pleasant city, never knowing the terror of a suddenly swelling sea, never experiencing belly-scraping hunger. I wondered what my ancestors would have thought of such an existence, and whether our shared bloodline was enough for me to claim a place by their side.

On the surrounding hills more spectres lurked. Some were little more than tussocky lumps in the nettles, while others retained the ragged remnants of a tarred roof clinging to the rafters. These were the skeletons of crofts, small rented farms of a few acres, typical of the north and west of Scotland, and the isles. The way of life for the residents of these stone shells was tough, with crofters living hand to mouth, growing crops like oats or kale and keeping a cow to survive. In solid contrast to these disintegrating structural remains, a grand building stood at the end of the bay, its many windows glinting blankly against the dull light. Voe House with its seven bedrooms and large walled garden was part of the visual language of historic inequality. As well as relying on the varying moods of the weather, and the productivity of the soil, the crofting residents were also dependent on the whims of the landlords who owned mansions like these. The landowning class could (and often did) evict tenants at short notice to make way for more profitable sheep farms, or demand a cow for the loss of a fishing boat, even if the men on board had drowned.

These were days of starvation and emigration. Eventually, legislation would introduce security of tenure, fair rents and heritable rights. Decades later, my great grandparents used this right to buy the croft they were renting – a two-room, one-storey building near the foot of a hill called Sneugie. They laid the foundations for a new chapter in the fortune of the Browns – for my grandfather, and eventually my father, to build homes on the land, both just about visible from the patch of grass I now stood upon next to their graves.

Other lives had passed too. The clouds of birds that once followed the fishing boats to the herring station, or the whaling vessels that would empty their cargo near the mouth of the bay. Now the empty seas mirror the empty skies, and the empty crofts return their heavy stones to the hills. But as things die, some are born. Just over the hill lay Sullom Voe, Europe's largest oil terminal, the existence of which helped rank Britain in the top ten oil producers of the world in the year I was born.[1]

Although the country had slipped in these rankings over the intervening decades, the global production and consumption of oil was hotter than ever, releasing into the atmosphere dangerous levels of greenhouse gases. The terrifying consequences of burning more oil had led to another phase in energy exploitation: one that would once again sculpt the landscape of mainland

---

[1] 1981. *Shetland's Oil Era* by Elizabeth Marshall. From the foreword written by then Secretary of State for Energy, David Howell.

Shetland. It had been looming on the horizon for a long time – discussed among collections of relatives while I sat wedged in a sofa during one of my rare visits, attempting to catch up on several years' worth of news at once – but it was the kind of story I had always been too busy to engage with. But what had once been a vague possibility was soon to become very real. Like the herring, the whales and the oil, this latest industry was another pattern sewn into the Shetland identity: contrasting threads of killing to sustain life. In a few years' time up to 37 monuments to a different energy era would be visible from the churchyard just a kilometre away: the top of what would be one of the country's largest onshore wind farms.

On that rainy afternoon on 22nd February 2020, I had very little notion of these layers of connection – past, present and future – or how I would become woven into them. At the time I was too concerned that as my relative completed his eulogy, I might slip on the wet, clay-rich ground and follow my recently deceased father into the angular hole.

The poetry of being buried in Voe clay would not have been lost on Dad, who was a highly respected potter and teacher. Despite having spent most of his professional adulthood working in Glasgow, he was also a Shetlander. Just a few years earlier, he had returned home to live – the first time since leaving as a teenager. He built a house and a pottery on the land once worked by his forebears. He reforested the slopes around his house with saplings – hazel, rowan, whitebeam and blackthorn, shields of white plastic protecting them from hungry rabbits. He hacked a tattie patch out of the dull green hillside and filled the grey ruins of the original building with pink-tipped Shetland kale and the saw-edged leaves of strawberries. Under the wide-open sky, he dug clay out of the ground to make pots inspired by local wildlife, history and the Shetland way of life. If my eye drifted past the bird above my head, I would be able to see the shapes of all the new life he had seeded.

A year after finishing the house, Dad died there.

In the isles, a herring gull is a 'maa', a word which in a Shetland accent starts with a kiss and ends with a sigh, unlike the wheedling cry of the creatures themselves. Even in the most putrid rubbish tip, the bird always carries the aspirated sounds of the sea. Dad had a soft spot for these charmingly charmless birds, the European herring gull being among the most common species on the isles. One of his last designs was a white serving jug with panels of grey, white and red, so cunningly placed on the lip and side of the vessel that they gave a clear impression of wings and beak. At local exhibitions he would carefully display these around one of his other popular creations – a plate with an image of chips on it. Perhaps he saw something of himself in these birds, in their shared ability both to live a rural, coastal life and to survive in the clatter and clamour of the big smoke. Also, perhaps, a shared taste for salty foods.

During Christmas 2019, the first and last that I remember spending with him, Dad recalled the story of Sam the herring gull. Sam was well known in Aberdeen in the late noughties for swaggering into a newsagents and shoplifting packets of tangy cheese Doritos. (Apparently he tried and didn't like the spicy flavour.) The bird would do this regularly and was even caught on camera, the clip making the national news.

Dad's sense of humour was something that we had in common. Our nuclear family divided when I was two, and after that my childhood relationship with him was mostly strung together with weekend visits, sleepovers and annual trips to his native islands to visit relatives. I didn't remember his presence at birthdays or Easter or Christmas. The lack of effort I perceived in his actions solidified into a sense of rejection I would carry with me throughout adulthood. But as the Voe churchyard could also testify, views change. It was only after his death that I would consider our relationship differently.

The intensity of the gull's battle with the wind had captured my gaze: the stasis between wind and animal, indifferent witnesses to the human ritual enacted below. There was something in their turbulent embrace that felt familiar. Recognition is the passage from ignorance to knowledge, Amitav Ghosh writes in *The Great Derangement*. But to recognise is to be cognisant of something you knew already but had forgotten. 'The knowledge that results from recognition, then, is not the same kind as the discovery of something new: it arises rather from a renewed reckoning with a potentiality that lies within oneself.' Poised on the lip of the grave, I was at the edge of that recognition.

Sometimes in hot weather, the difference in temperature between the warmer ground and cooler air above distorts the passage of light. That is why, when driving along a road on a hot day, you might see at its furthest point a shimmering reflection of the sky: an optical illusion. My relationship with Dad was like that, simultaneously present and absent, always suggesting something that it would never deliver. There was another similarity too; the word mirage has its roots in the French verb *mirer*, meaning mirror. While I resented his inattention, I also saw in him glimpses of myself.

At last it was time to throw a handful of earth on the coffin, and when I looked up again, the herring gull was wheeling away, propelled inland by the coastal wind. As we tugged our shoes out of the mud on the way back to the car, darkness was closing in. It was the 2 p.m. onset of evening, but there was something else, too. We didn't know it at the time, but a virus was spreading across the world towards us with every infected sneeze, cough and exhaled breath. For many it would mean death. For me it would mean confinement in a land that claimed half my genealogy, a history and culture of which I knew next to nothing about.

Beyond the bay, on the line between bog and sky, another story was beginning: a plan for a giant onshore wind farm. Many warned it would pollute water, disrupt birdlife, and damage peatlands; others welcomed it as part of an urgent transition to green energy amid an accelerating climate crisis. There was a slippery path ahead, and not just the one leading to the wake at the village hall.

As we filed away from the grave I was, unknowingly, starting out on a new road of my own, one which would redefine 'home' and alter the course of my future.

No raptor could have been so portentous. A group of gulls, after all, is called a squabble.

Part One: Separation

1

The Call

I stopped the trike against the front door and patted my pockets for the keys. Esme was still singing the Forest School song: 'Forest School is lots of fun, playing in the rain and sun.' Before I was able to turn the key, Josh opened it from the inside. He had a received a phone call, he said, his eyes wide. I wrestled with the handlebars, postponing the moment I would have to meet his gaze again and hear the news.

'Building dens and climbing trees, watching flowers and smelling bees.'

Esme was still singing away cheerily at my feet. The trike was always such a pest to get through the door frame.

'Your Dad died.'

*

Theseus hears the story of the Minotaur and decides to go to Crete.

A frog offers to return a princess her golden ball.

Gandalf instructs Frodo to leave the Shire with the Ring.

These moments are what Joseph Campbell describes as a 'call to adventure', an opening stage in the Hero's Journey, an archetypal storyline structure found across human history from ancient myths to Hollywood films. In Campbell's template, 'destiny has summoned the hero and transferred his spiritual centre of gravity from within the pale of his society to a zone unknown'.[2] I had received my call. The news of Dad's death had ruptured my familiar world and sent me in the direction of a land that while not unknown, felt to me unknowable.

In one of those tricks of memory, the rest of that day has slid out of focus, but occasional details spring out crisp and clear, as if the result of adjusting the focal point of a camera lens. The slippery surface of the seat in the airport departure lounge; kind text messages from colleagues; coffee that tasted of blisters. Then I was in the air, pulling away from the 'improved' green fields of the Devon countryside, squares of monotone ryegrass which would sprout with the occasional buttercup, dock and thistle as spring set in. Back home in our blue-and-white terraced house in a small town west of Exeter, Josh and Esme were probably in the middle of their usual Monday afternoon tug-of-war as he attempted to drag her away from her drawing and dolls' house to the fresh air of the play park. I had decided to travel north as quickly as possible

---

[2] In his famous work *The Hero with a Thousand Faces*.

to help organise the funeral. It would be a week before I saw them again.

'Grey today, isn't it?'

I had only been vaguely aware of the man sitting next to me until he spoke.

'It is,' I replied. 'Dreich.'

He was folding away a newspaper. The headline said something about a new virus spreading from China. Usually, I would have taken note of which newspaper before adjusting my chat appropriately, but my tools for talking to strangers, acquired during years as a reporter, were not to hand.

'Are you going to the isles on holiday?' he asked.

His voice had the firm rising intonation of the west coast of Scotland rather than the light crispness of the Shetland dialect. He was another Scottish southerner with local connections, although my accent was of the flatter, more generic east coast variety.

'No, I have family in Shetland.'

He hummed approvingly.

He said something about his business and how it took him to the isles every now and again, but the details washed over me. I was nodding and smiling.

'Yourself?' he enquired.

I told him where I lived and how I only managed to visit every year or so.

'Can I give you a lift to Lerwick?' he asked.

'No, it's OK, someone is meeting me.'

I wondered briefly if he imagined my ties with the isles were a lot deeper than they really were, rather than my fleeting visits as an adult, or distant memories of school holidays visiting my grannie and other relatives. I wanted to tell him I didn't usually fly because of the carbon emissions, but I was too tired.

'What brings you here now?' he asked after a pause.

I cleared my throat. 'A funeral.'

'Oh, sorry to hear that.'

'It's OK', I mumbled and turned away.

He seemed to understand my body language and asked me no more questions. I looked at the clouds outside the window, the puffs of vapour that look so solid until you pass through them. Dad had been my tie to these islands, pulling me back only to fulfil a disassociated sense of filial duty. Even when he was alive, this was an unstable connection, eaten away by resentment and a fragile desire to please. Now he was gone, I could feel my Edinburgh identity, formed in the dominant setting of my childhood, closing around the gaps. How would these islands welcome me now, imbued as they were with the memories of countless generations along my patrilineal line, now that line was severed?

Below us the grey sea heaved relentlessly, the occasional gull skimming over the edge of the waves. Perhaps at some point one of them turned its beak up from the swell to see the scar across the sky as we cruised thousands of feet above.

Soon we would be landing.

2

A Road Through Time

Sumburgh Airport is in the south of the Mainland, an island shaped like a sword hilt which gave the archipelago its name 'Hjaltland' in Old Norse.[3] Here grassland is hemmed by dark cliffs dividing the North Sea and the Atlantic. A relative had come to pick me up, making the forty-mile trip down from the village of Voe, where Dad's house was. We drove back, the windscreen wipers squeaking against the smirr. Through the driver's window on the right, the runway stretched across a flat pea-coloured landscape, which on my side ended abruptly at the water.

The airport was a different entry point to the islands than the one I had been used to as a child. After Dad left, there was a period during which he would bring me to Shetland for a few weeks every summer holiday to visit relatives. We

---

[3] Singular. This is why Shetland should never be referred to as 'the Shetlands'. For a very entertaining bit of background, I recommend reading this: https://www.shetland.org/blog/in-frequently-asked-questions

would always arrive at the ferry terminal in Lerwick still feeling the violent rise and fall of the sea even as we walked ashore. The fourteen-hour boat journey was ameliorated by the excitement of pick-n-mix supermarket salad and powdery hot chocolate from a vending machine. I never thought of the airport, apart from a story about an accident that took place before I was born. A plane full of oil workers failed to take off and pummelled straight into the freezing water, drowning seventeen people.

It seemed appropriate that I was now entering the isles by a different route – through the air rather than over the sea. I did not feel like the same person. I was in pieces, like Frankenstein's monster, sewn together from different experiences, different lives, making a way through a fractured landscape of low pasture, hag-ragged peat bog and the encroaching ocean. The road itself was well trodden. It was the fast and furious A970, a single carriageway that pumped a constant flow of traffic from Sumburgh through Lerwick and up to the top of the mainland in North Roe. Fuelled by the substantial oil fund, the smooth, well-maintained tarmac of Shetland's public roads gleamed in comparison with the potholes of cash-strapped Devon.

As the edge of the North Sea winked at me through the windscreen, I thought about the last time I had travelled this way. I was sitting in the back of the car, my hand curled around the front passenger seat as I leant forward to speak to Dad.

'It's only just dawn and it's ten o'clock!' I remarked, like a tourist.

Dad didn't respond and I thought I'd caused offence. I always worried about everything I said to him, turning the words over in my mind afterwards like pebbles. Had I said something stupid or something funny? Was he interested or was his mind elsewhere? It was his lack of reaction that always concerned me most. Thinking back on it, he was probably just exhausted, too ill and tired to pick me up from the ferry terminal and relying instead on someone else to give him a lift. I had been shocked at how thin he had become, his giant frame sunken and hunched, and his once strong, long stride reduced to a painful shuffle.

Here we were, three months later, the rain stopped and the brief February sun already dimming. As we skirted the hills around Lerwick, the spectral forms of small wind turbines spun their pale fingers languidly through the thickening dusk.

The valley opened out on either side of us, and we passed a lonely building I'd always noted when taking this route, its rather grim outlook onto the A970 never failing to inspire a sigh of pity. The name of the dwelling, 'Halfway Hoose', was a nod to its previous incarnation as an inn. It wasn't so long ago that folk would have gone overland by foot if the sea was too rough – boats were the most common means of travel up until the last century. I often imagine travellers catching sight of the whitewashed walls and glowing lights of the inn, amid the endless browns and greys, and hastening towards it. At a distance of seventeen miles between Voe and Lerwick, it would have taken at least half a day to walk, and twice that to Sumburgh. Making the journey on weary feet, bellies empty, and shouldering whatever burdens they had to carry, the road must have seemed endless. Perhaps, in the layers of peat, there still exist the imprints of their soles. It was another reminder that this journey wasn't just mine. Countless others had made it too, over the centuries.

*

The man lifts the spade a few inches from the ground and drops it again. The sharp edge bounces off a stone. He wipes his damp forehead with the back of his hand. His face is stretched too tight over the skull, the bones on his arms too prominent through the skin. He can barely stand, but he can't stop. He must lift the spade, drop the spade, lift the spade and drop it again. He must build this road or his family will have no food tonight. When he closes his eyes, he sees them: his wife, his eight children, crying with hunger. Their potatoes lie rotting in the fields. Even if they had the money, there is no grain to buy. So he does the only thing he can: he lifts the spade, drops the spade. If he stops they will eat nothing again tonight.

*

Not that long ago, only around 150 years, there were very few roads in Shetland.[4] The change began with disaster. In the middle of the nineteenth century, wet, cold weather across the Highlands and Islands brought crop failure and meagre fishing. The devastating blight that afflicted Irish potatoes was also heading east. Men, women and children, already only

---

[4] I learnt about this at a fascinating talk at the Shetland Museum with researcher James Arnaud. You can read his thesis here: https://theses. gla.ac.uk/ 83278/1/2022ArnaudMPhil%28R%29.pdf

just surviving, were starving to death. Destitution boards were set up, through which the poor were provided with oatmeal or low wages in exchange for labour to build roads. The work was tough to ensure only the really desperate would apply. Eight hours a day, six days a week, hacking stone and earth using crowbars, hammers and spades. One account of road-building on the island of Yell describes an emaciated man attempting to chip away at the rocks but too weak to do much; he hadn't eaten the previous day. When paid at the end of his shift in coins, he told the official in charge: 'We canna aet money.'

As ever, tenants were at the mercy of the landowning class. Some landlords gave more meal, some none at all. Some sought only to improve the value of their land; others embarked on a genuine effort to help their tenants survive the times. One theory suggests the programme might have been part of a wider effort to steer the local economy away from an unofficial bartering system known as 'truck' by encouraging the use of money in exchange for goods and labour. In this way, the 'gruelling work',[5] was an inroad for capitalism as it forced the population closer to a state of proletarianisation. Whatever the rationale, it transformed the landscape. Between 1849 and 1851, some of the isles' most desperate residents built 188 kilometres of these 'meal roads' across the islands.

In some places it is still possible to catch a view of one of the old tracks, soggy and narrow, lying parallel to the A970 –

---

[5] As one member of the audience of the talk described it, relishing the pun.

a shadow of a not so prosperous past. Over the years, more branches appeared, a network which was greatly improved following the oil boom of the 1970s.

Sometimes the road itself is the story.

Thanks to the extraction of crude oil, the processing of fuel, and money to construct sturdy infrastructure, the trip from the airport to Dad's would take around fifty minutes. With a terminally empty house waiting for me at the end, I was not looking forward to reaching the door.

3

Kleber

*'Since returning to live and work in Shetland, I have
been exploring the possibilities of making things
using locally sourced materials such as clay and
kleber (soapstone), as well as looking to our own
past traditions of making, our stories, culture and
environment as sources of ideas.'*

Bill Brown, 2018

In the weeks before we buried Dad, relatives would drop by
Kirkhoose to say hello. Someone had picked up a jigsaw puzzle
at a charity shop and left it on the kitchen table. In the quiet
moments between bursts of small talk, folk would often drift
over to the table and slot pieces of the puzzle together. First
the coastline, then the landmarks and finally the sea: it was
a picture of the British Isles. During these strange dreamlike
days, we sorted through the death admin, a novel task I found
surprisingly laborious. Shortly before the funeral, Josh and

Esme arrived from Devon, taking the ten-hour train journey from Exeter to Aberdeen followed by a night on the ferry.

We ordered the cakes, the casket, the death notice, the obituary, then the day arrived. Pictures of him were perched on the edge of the stage, fragments of his life captured and framed: pulling a mackerel out of the sea on a fishing line; sitting at a potter's wheel; reading to his grandchildren. I did not have many photos of my own to contribute. Esme was pleased with the black-and-green tartan dress I had bought her from a high street shop in Lerwick. Despite the gold-coloured thread, it felt suitably dour for the occasion.

Soon the rows of fold-up chairs were filled with bodies – old school friends, neighbours, relatives, local artists – and messages were read out from former students and fellow ceramicists all over the world with admiring words about the man they had known and loved. I sat on the front row as people came up to share their tributes. One story in particular hooked my attention. It was by a man called Callum Moncrieff, an old friend of Dad's. It was strange to hear of their friendship and how much my relatives knew and liked him. I couldn't remember having heard his name before. Callum spoke in Shaetlan, the dialect which weaves together Scots, English and Old Norse. I didn't understand many of the words so I concentrated on the sounds and the humour. Instead of being a passive listener, I imagined myself there, wandering invisible alongside the two men as if I were the ghost and not Dad.

*

It is a fine summer's day as Bill and Callum, a potter and a sculptor in the sunset years of their lives, rustle through the cotton-grass on their way to Gossa Water on the outskirts of Lerwick. The treasure they are searching for is something that they both need in order to mould their thoughts into the material form through which they can interact with the world.

Clay.

Clutching a rucksack and fending off the black clouds of midges with the reek of his pipe, Bill strides with the energy of a clear purpose. The clay he seeks is very particular, durable and strong enough to hold together the potter's 'holy grail', a heat-resistant cultural jewel known as 'kleber'. Kleber mixed with clay can, as Callum says, 'deliver an alchemy, a hybrid dat wid suture vision, form, an da midder tongue'.

The plan had been laid through chance conversations snatched on the ferry from Lerwick to Aberdeen and back again as they crossed paths over the years. The greying pair know from having studied geological maps that what they are looking for lies nearby in a vein beneath their feet.

From the start, they tread in the footsteps of dead soldiers, starting at Sandy Loch reservoir and following Cunningham Way, a road which carries the name of an army officer detailed there during the Second World War. In their parents' time, these hills were a line of defence for the isles against their enemies. Still the bones remain: a spotting tower, trenches, bunkers and barbed-wire pickets.

Today it is peaceful.

The path takes them to the smaller loch of Gossa Water, which feeds a feisty stream and waterfall. It is a 'trowie place' where unseen things can infect the imagination. They have been walking some way, a line of muddy water soaked up into the hems of their trousers, when they come upon strange shapes in the soggy ground: a collection of metre-high concrete pyramids. What are these strange-looking structures that stand out from the landscape, scattered like a giant's toys: the remains of alien spaceships, or artefacts from another geological era?

The two men know what they are. These are dragon's teeth, tank traps, left on the edge of this lochan. Reinforced concrete designed to stop the approach of oncoming vehicles so their occupants would be within the exact range of the gun battery, to be shattered to bits – here in this quiet place.

In the end there was no land invasion, no lethal strategizing. Their only use was for the raingoose, measuring the length of water for takeoff before hunting fish in the sea, or the bonxie eyeing a sick lamb for the kill.

The men press on and at last find themselves at the edge of the cold, clear water. From his bag, Bill pulls out a folded-up shovel which, after some required assembly involving wing nuts (Callum is very impressed 'ta say da least'), Bill plunges into the wet ground. It sticks. Bill heaves. He heaves again. He heaves again, not realising that all the energy he is transferring into the shovel is about to return to him with some force. The shovel comes out of the ground with a great thop *and Bill finds himself flying backwards about to meet the squelch of wet clay . . . only to be saved by Callum's outstretched arms. They take a minute to recover from this sudden embrace and near-wet experience and Bill picks up the crumpled remains of the shovel.*

'A lotta damned guid dat wis,' he says, *and tosses it into the water.*

The waders flap from their hiding places, and perhaps a trowie hand, the skin green as moss, closes over a boulder as the pair ripple the stillness with their laughter. Not entirely thwarted, they roll up their sleeves and fling handfuls of the sticky clay into plastic bags to take home, promising to return another time with a pair of old trousers, tied up at the legs, which they would fill with more clay and leave to drain. It would have been quite a sight for a passing walker to come across, a pair of disembodied breeks left lounging on a rock, the moulded material inside creating a disconcerting animacy. It might even have become the source of legend.

They thought they would have time to come back, but they never did.

'Some day aa'll geeng auld breeks in hand an secure a guid skelp o yun slester fae Gossa Water,' Callum says to a hall filled with folk saying goodbye to Bill. *'Aan da memory o dat boy's adventure will sustain me till I bring some hame.'*

*

After delivering Dad's coffin to his ancestors in the graveyard, we returned to the hall to chat and eat the food close family had helped prepare earlier in the day: egg sandwiches on white bread cut up into triangles, bannocks with 'reestit mutton',[6]

---

[6] A Shetland delicacy made from mutton still on the bone which is salted and dried. Traditionally the meat would be from a home-killed sheep

cream cakes and iced buns from the local bakery. We drank tea and coffee from industrial urns, poured semi-skimmed milk from metal jugs, filled glasses from boxes of wine and plastic cups with blackcurrant squash. Piling our plates with shameless volumes of food, we walked around an exhibition of Dad's work spanning fifty years, carefully curated by my eldest cousin, who had made a call-out to relatives to select the most representative and meaningful pieces. It was a relief that the weeks of organising were over at last.

A red-striped tea-cake stand dominated the display on one of the many fold-up tables that we'd arranged in a corner of the village hall. Dad had made it when he worked in Glasgow, 'the cultural home of Tunnock's tea cakes' – those chocolate-covered marshmallow 'biscuits' that are mostly just a bite of sugar that seems to evaporate in the heat of your mouth like a cloud. Each level was shaped to mimic the form of the iconic wrapper and at the top, a small ceramic tea cake gleamed under the strip lighting. It looked good enough to eat.

'If you were asked to design an item of confectionery that would chime perfectly with the Scottish psyche, you could hardly do better than come up with the tea cake,' Dad had written. 'This piece was inspired by the challenge of straightening out the thin foil wrapper without tearing it – and who hasn't tried that? Having eventually succeeded, it seemed a natural progression to scan the wrapper, turn it into a silkscreen print and use it to make this cake stand in

---

and hung over a peat fire on a reest, a wooden framework laid across the rafters of a croft.

celebration of a cultural icon.' I could all but hear his voice when I looked at it.

Funerals are a good way to get to know the recently deceased, to celebrate the connections you already have and to discover new ones. When philosopher Julian Baggini attended his own father's funeral, the church was packed: 'It was not that he had dozens and dozens of very close friends,' he wrote. 'It was that, over the course of his life, he had become part of the lives of many people in his village, usually in small ways that were nonetheless significant enough to motivate them to come out to remember him. This community had lost a part of itself, and they were grieving for that.' In this way also the small village of Voe on the Mainland of Shetland mourned the loss of Bill Brown.

Another plate, this one like a slice of salami, red clay shot through with chunks of soapstone. It was disconcerting to see his fingerprints still visible, fired into the matte surface of the piece, while his hands grew cold in the graveyard down the road. It was Shetland clay, and I wondered if he had collected it out on the hills around the house, or if it had been the clay he collected with Callum out on Gossa Water. Clay strong enough to hold kleber.

Kleber has been called Shetland's oldest industry. A metamorphic rock, made mostly of talc, it is almost greasy and so soft you can scrape shapes in it with your fingernail. It became coveted for use in cosmetics, industrial lubricants and for its resistance to high temperatures, hardening when placed in a fire – handy for making crockery a thousand years ago. People call it steatite, soapstone, and 'kleber' in Shetland, a word with roots in old Norse. Though soapstone items such as armlets, amulets and beads made in the Bronze Age have been unearthed across Shetland, it was the Vikings who excelled in kleber-craft. Familiar with this material in Norway, the Vikings chiselled circular chunks out of it, shaping them into a tactile smoothness to form fishing weights, moulds and, of course, plates.

A millennia after the Vikings, another craftsman took his daughters to an archeological site in Cunningsburgh, in the south of the Mainland, to gaze at a cliff wall with round shapes chipped out of it by hands so long dead they were now mingled with the dust of ancient volcanoes and plankton in the tracks of our boots. We stared in awe at the metre-wide rings carved into the stone like a trow's doodles – the remains of a Viking kleber quarry. I remember losing interest long before Dad did.

*

It was the day after the funeral that we began to realise how serious the situation was. News of the spread of a novel coronavirus had been trickling through the radio, but we had been too distracted to really listen to it. In the lull after Dad's burial, however, we found ourselves paying closer attention to what was happening. Italy had just imposed a lockdown to stop the virus spreading. Cases were being reported across Europe and people in the UK had started to die.

We didn't know yet just how infectious it was – could you catch it from a cough, a sneeze, or a hug? From touching the same door handle or brushing past someone on an escalator? The thought of the long journey back to Devon with our four-year-old daughter seemed foolish – but what about our clothes, toys and books? We'd packed thinking we'd only be staying a few weeks, maybe a month at most. What about our friends, our house and jobs? Despite all of this, I couldn't take such a risk with Esme's health. Josh worked from home, and as the editor of a small environmental magazine I was mostly desk-based anyway. We'd have to leave our friends, but we had my family in the near vicinity and somewhere we could stay. We decided just in time.

'Let me be blunt,' we heard Scotland's First Minister Nicola Sturgeon say on the radio: 'The stringent restrictions on our normal day-to-day lives that I'm about to set out are difficult and they are unprecedented. They amount effectively to what has been described as a lockdown.'

Across the country, people would only be allowed to go outside to buy food, exercise once a day or go to work if they could not do so from home. We would face the UK's first lockdown in Kirkhoose, the home Dad had built overlooking the ruins of his grandparents' croft, across the road from the house of his childhood, a home his own father had built. At meal times we would look out at the view of the inlet from the dining table and see the graveyard where his body lay. We would cook in his kitchen, sleep in his bedroom, wash in his shower, water his houseplants and never get around to tiling his bathroom.

*

Sitting in the office chair, I swivelled slowly from side to side. Now it was just the three of us: Josh preparing dinner in the next room and Esme playing with the hats and scarves Dad kept in a large bowl in the hall. To my right, shelves were stacked with more papers, more ceramics, boxes of belongings Dad never had a chance to sort through following his return to Shetland. Folded in a corner were his pyjamas. Old bank statements and invoices covered the desk, some dating back to the 1980s. I had been attempting to organise them, but after a very short time had lost the will for it and was instead staring through the curtainless window to the darkening landscape beyond. There would be plenty of time to sort out the documents. Too much time.

In the spotlight of an anglepoise lamp, I looked at Dad's things gathering dust. For the first time in my life, he was everywhere, not only in the photos and plates on the walls around me but outside in the moss, the stream and the rocks. He was scattered across the landscape like jigsaw pieces. I would have to find out where they fitted before I could understand my place in the puzzle.

A squawking noise snapped me out of my dwam and the door fell open. Esme tumbled inside, her grin two rows of neat little baby teeth. She flapped her arms up and down and shuffled across the wooden floor. 'Look at me, Mumma, I'm a bird.' She did indeed look disconcertingly avian and it took me a moment to understand why. I spotted what was on her feet: long floppy black fingers. A pair of Dad's woollen gloves.

4

Wi' Tauchts o' Kale

'This fateful region of both treasure and danger may be variously represented: as a distant land, a forest, a kingdom underground, beneath the waves, or above the sky, a secret island, lofty mountaintop, or profound dream state; but it is always a place of strangely fluid and polymorphous beings, unimaginable torments, superhuman deeds, and impossible delight.'

Joseph Campbell on the first
stage of the Hero's Journey

Instead of entering under the rotten lintel, Dad and I stepped over a row of collapsed stones and found ourselves in a secluded walled garden. It was the summer of 2019 and he was giving me a tour of his new house, including Green Knowe which was the roofless ruin just outside it. It was in this building that we now stood. I knew nothing at all about our family connection there and could hear some impatience in his voice as he answered my questions about Scottish crofting rights.

Knowe is a magical word. It means mound or hillock in Scots and is, according to the dictionaries, often associated with faeries. I guessed this building was so named because of its position on the slope near the base of a hill which formed the opening to a long valley. Its magic for us was not so much the idea of mythical creatures, but the passing of time. Several generations ago, the building was home to eleven people, including Dad's father, who was born there. It was difficult to imagine so many people crammed into this small space now.

After moving into Kirkhoose, Dad had set about transforming the ruined building into a new home – not for humans but for horticulture. In such a windswept landscape, the shielding power of the walls, however rickety, was not to be wasted, and he'd created a walled vegetable garden. As we looked around, I spotted the rich greens of strawberry and potato leaves, the thickening stems of a currant bush preparing to bud and the jagged edges of lovage. In the corner, a great pile of dark brown bladderwrack decomposed dutifully, emitting from its moist depths the soft tang of the sea. Dad gestured to a patch of colour by the wall – a froth of yellow.

'That brilliant display of flowers is actually cabbage,' Dad told me. 'It's Shetland kale so it's kind of dark, purply green. It tastes a bit different from your factory kale.' He rustled his plastic packet of tobacco and pinched a whiskery morsel into his pipe. As he flicked the lighter and inhaled the fumes, he gave the kale an affectionate look. 'I wasn't really intending to let it flower but it just has.' The sweet reek of smoke seeped into the air. 'I was thinking we'll just see what happens.'

What happened was this: a year later, Dad was dead and because of a global pandemic, Josh and Esme and I had replaced him as residents of Kirkhoose. When raking through the kitchen drawer in search of tape, I discovered the hard kale seeds, rattling in an envelope like tiny cannonballs.

*

From the top of the rounded hills, you could see the curve of the horizon – miles of open sea stretching into miles of open sky under a circular sun. Gentle, soothing curves. From the windows of Kirkhoose at the bottom of the valley, this was not what we saw. We were inside a box inside a box inside a box: the room, the house, the fence around the croft. It was week three of lockdown and the routine was getting tedious. Josh worked in the morning, wrestling with the sketchy internet, and I did my job in the afternoon, editing and commissioning articles.

All the things we had previously taken for granted were now shoved into sharp focus: our friends, local play parks, Esme's favourite toys or books. Our only excursions beyond the surrounds of Kirkhoose were when Josh or I drove to the supermarket in Lerwick to follow a trail of socially distanced arrows from aisle to aisle, carefully taking from the shelves only the allotted ration of toilet roll or a packet of rice. Like most other people in the country, we were cut off from our familiar connections and fenced into an unnatural enclosure of isolation. We never forgot, however, that unlike most others we at least had lots of open space to sweat out the stress, haunted as that land might have been.

Children tend to enjoy being around other children, and we were painfully aware that however hard we tried, we could never be convincing four-year-olds. So we tackled each day as it came, trying to create interest and variety as best we could. I didn't know it yet, but on this particular day we would encounter an unexpected presence.

Light leaked through the makeshift shutter in the bedroom – a square of cardboard ripped from a box containing bags of lentils I had panic-bought in bulk. Dad never got around to buying curtains for any of the rooms. We would never get around to buying them either, or to eating the lentils. Outside the sea absorbed warmth from the intensifying sunlight – already the air pressure was beginning to change. There was no wind yet, only a dulled *pee-wit* of oystercatchers and *clunk*, *clink*, *splash* of Josh washing up last night's dishes downstairs. He'd already been up for an hour. He was a lark and I was an owl, which meant passing the baton between us for work or parenting was a little bit easier.

Josh was in Dad's study by the time Esme and I got downstairs. On the table were the slightly stale bannocks I had made the morning before on Dad's griddle. I cut up some apples and Esme chose which Cosmic Yoga we would watch online to wake us up. I preferred the *Star Wars* one. Her favourite was Mimi the Mermaid.

'Hey, let's find a den for Mimi in the field,' I said in my daily attempt to get her outside for fresh air before my shift in the office. We could carry on planting the saplings I'd found potted up in the ruined croft.

'No, this is Mimi's den,' she replied, collecting cushions from the four corners of the room.

'But the moss and rocks can be like coral, Mimi *loves* coral, it's so beautiful. You can find all sorts of creatures in it.'

'Mimi likes the sofa.'

I sighed and turned my attention to the breakfast dishes. It was like collecting well-water with a sieve. No matter how many times we washed up, there always seemed to be dishes in the sink. My hands twisted an old sponge around the whorled inside of one of Dad's cups. The sponge squeaked against the ceramic surface and bubbles fizzed on my skin.

All around us lay a reminder of the living and the dead, generations stacked as far as the eye could see. Beyond the remains of Green Knowe, there was another building of Brown family significance. This one was a dark grey bungalow, built just after the Second World War. My grandfather built it, and, along with my grannie, raised their family here. Brush the layers away and you could reveal even more distant history – periods of human interference that shaped the landscape. A long, long time ago, there had been a forest here.

'Mumma, can I have a biscuit?'

'You haven't eaten your breakfast.'

'I want a biscuit.'

'No, eat a banana.'

'Aww.'

A lemon geranium sat on the windowsill in one of Dad's flower pots, a piece he finished shortly before he died. The plant flopped over the side of the pot, desperate for water and unable to reach for the light. I rubbed the leaves and sniffed the citrusy scent on my thumb. I knew how it felt.

I grabbed Esme's coat and went to the door.

'Let's go out.'

She remained unmoved.

'Come on. Let's go to the ruin and dig for bones.'

'Bones?' She looked up from her game.

'Yes, you never know, we might find the bones of some of our ancestors.'

I liked to encourage this rather ghoulish side to her personality to complement the princesses and unicorns. In the time since Dad had died, I had begun to see (or needed to see) his interests reflected in my daughter. A wonder for the natural world, language, music, and particularly history. She even liked pickled herring, a detail I pounced on with an unnatural level of enthusiasm. Like most children, she loved stories. A good yarn was almost always guaranteed to get her outside. The promise of finding the remains of our long-dead relatives was perhaps not the line of investigation I had intended, but it seemed to be working.

She packed a bucket with an orange plastic spade, a bouncy ball and some wool. We were ready to go.

*

The plant unfurls with rounded blades like a bud opening. It has a delicate spectrum of colour, sometimes green with pink veins, sometimes green with a white midrib, and sometimes entirely purple like a birthmark. Its tough leaves taste peppery, popular in mutton stew. The roots soak up water, while its leaves reach up to capture the sun's light and absorb carbon dioxide, converting it into oxygen and glucose – air and energy. In the summer, bees suck nectar from the spray of yellow flowers and green pods emerge, stretching outwards until their skin crisps and they turn dark brown. Fingers pluck away the brittle packets and thresh the seeds by rubbing them between calloused palms. In this way, the next crop is harvested, another cycle completed.

Eighty grams of raw kale contains 26 calories, 2.7 grams of protein, 3.3 grams of fibre and 88 milligrams of vitamin C.

*

We were exploring the miniature jungle inside Green Knowe when Esme pointed to a collection of stalks that stood out taller from the rest.

'What's that, Mummy?'

I probed my memory, sure the answer was there, but it felt like a blank spot in my brain. I concentrated for a minute. The metre-high plants were growing soggy at the top of the stalks as the cells decomposed. It was obviously a cultivated vegetable, as Dad had used this spot to grow things, and it had to be tough enough to withstand the climate here. Then I remembered.

'It's Shetland cabbage, darling.'

But Esme was already distracted by the rhubarb.

The forlorn-looking brassica of Esme's curiosity had an

impressive history of helping generations of Shetlanders to survive. I had learnt a few things about Shetland cabbage since the tour of Dad's makeshift walled garden. It is the oldest known Scottish variety of kale. No one knows who brought the plant's ancestor to the isles, or exactly when, but as this domesticated vegetable grew, like the human hands that stripped its leaves, it adapted to local conditions: cold, windswept, salty. For the next few centuries, crofters would eat the heart and give the tougher leaves to the beasts (cows, maybe a pig) and so sustain their families through the dark winters. It was a light ballast against hunger, one which would keep them barely above subsistence level.

As people found ways to live in the landscape, so they also changed that landscape. To shelter tender seedlings from the scything wind until they were strong enough to be replanted in kaleyards, crofters built circular walls of stone known as a crö. The most famous of these belonged to Auld Maunsie, whose small building adorned a hill in Unst. Maunsie was a typical crofter, down-to-earth, fond of mutton broth and boiled kale; not so fond of the rabbits that tried to eat his kale. He was the subject of one of Shetland's most famous poems, written by Basil R. Anderson[7] – the same one read at Dad's burial. In these verses, a community of nineteenth-century crofters comes back to life.

> Auld Maunsie's crö wis fair ta see,
> A tooer an laandmark ta da ee.

---

[7] Anderson himself was the son of a fisherman, who drowned at sea when he was a child. He died at the age of 26 of tuberculosis, which he contracted after moving with his mother and siblings to Edinburgh.

Maunsie's crö, in the shape of an 'honest O', becomes a symbol for the people living around it, and 'as is the way with symbols, the more people read them, the more meanings they accumulate', as Mark Ryan Smith writes in *The Literature of Shetland*. In the poem, a fisherman uses the crö as a landmark to steer north to the haaf (deep-sea fishing), and a schooner is pointed towards the kaleyard to avoid being stuck in a bay. From sunrise to sunset, neighbours judge the time of day by the position of the sun over the crö. Betty Bunt scolds her daughter for not getting the tatties ready as 'the sun is by Auld Maunsie's Crö', and Auld Elder Rasmie uses the kaleyard as a symbol to repel evil. The circular walls reflect the circle of life. As Auld Maunsie ages, so does his crö, until at last, he is too decrepit even to eat mutton broth. As he dies, the walls fall in, crushing an unfortunate pony. A raven 'craas' and eats the pony's eyes.

But the consequences of Auld Maunsie's 'touchts o' kale' do not end there. Folk are 'fey to raise a ghost', and decline to state his name in case his spirit returns to haunt them. So the stone structure becomes known as 'Ferry-ring' and the crö passes into the world of folklore and myth. At the end, like the crö itself, the poem comes full circle. Anderson's verses are also part of the cultural landscape, those invisible contours that shape so much of how we see the world and our connection with it. A verse of the poem is carved into Dad's headstone.

Esme was in the rhubarb. A moment ago she was Tintin, but now, she was a fairy on an archeological dig. The deep pink stems, and the large leaves unfurling into a promise of a giant umbrella – a perfect habitat for fairies.[8] I was scraping the soil nearby with a gardening fork, attempting to clear some ground to plant garlic. I'd ordered the cloves the previous autumn after asking Dad what he'd like for the garden, before he'd started to get really ill. The plants had only recently arrived at the door. Even now, two months after his death, I still wanted to impress him and claim for myself a kernel of his attention.

Esme was pouring soil into her old wellies, cracked beyond repair despite repeated rescue attempts. Beside her she arranged a pile of treasures, interesting roots and the occasional piece of broken tile.

I thought about how this place would have looked a century ago, when my grandfather lived here with his many siblings, under a taekit (thatched) roof and the patriarchal eye of my great-grandfather. They kept animals in a byre at the end of the building. The boys would sleep in the barn in the summer for the space.

Esme was holding something in her outstretched hand. 'Look, Mumma.' It was white and smooth. I peered at it. 'Is this a bone?' Her rising intonation betrayed a tremor of hope. I took it between my finger and thumb and brushed the biggest chunks of dirt off it.

'I'm afraid not, darling.'

'Aww.' Her disappointment stung me.

'But it's just as interesting. Look.' The dislodged soil revealed a delicate blue pattern. 'It's a piece of pottery.'

---

[8] The angelic, winged variety, not the more sinister faerie found in Scottish and Irish folklore.

Her eyes widened. 'Granpa Bill's?'

'I don't think so, this looks a lot older. Part of a plate maybe.' My brain quickly made connections that might render this object more interesting. 'It must have belonged to the people who lived in this house.'

'My ancestors?' There was unadulterated awe in her voice now.

'Yes! Maybe your great-grandfather ate from this. Or your great-great-grandfather.'

'What about my great-great-great-great-great-grandfather?'

'Oh, I don't know where he lived. Probably not here.'

'Oh,' she says. 'I think it was a plate.'

'Yes, maybe a plate.'

'I want to find the rest!'

I enjoyed a shiver of relief. We had a new quest.

5

Alien Invaders

After turning several shards of slate, I noticed a streak of white goo, as if someone had sneezed and smeared the mucus across the flattened earth. I sniffed. It was odourless. To my limited knowledge, it did not look mycorrhizal. We continued to dig, my own hands slightly more hesitant than before. I had suspicions, but dared to hope that I was wrong. We raked through the soil, Esme commenting on this or that curiosity she unearthed nearby. No more pottery, but it wasn't long before we found something else.

It was grey and glistening and about fifteen centimetres long. I stared at the ribbon-like form with revulsion for a few seconds. A jar and a piece of paper was my usual method for dealing with stray creatures, even the hornets that stalked wasps on our grapevine in Devon, but this was different.

'Look at this,' I called to Esme, and she hurried over.

I scooped it up with a small stone, careful not to touch it. It flailed, revealing its orange-beige underside, a creature unfamiliar with predators. I wondered what it could be thinking, if it was capable of thought.

'What's that?' Esme asked, her voice full of wonder. It was the kind of wonder I tried to nurture even in those high-octane moments with surprised house spiders or over-friendly seagulls. Encircled by a war on nature, I needed my daughter to be a warrior against extinction.

I sighed. 'It's a New Zealand flatworm.'

She peered at it and poked it with one of her pebbles. It instantly contracted (in fear or pain or neither). Usually I discouraged her from harassing wildlife, but this time I didn't stop her.

'Is it a worm?'

'Not an earthworm. It's a flatworm. It eats earthworms.'

'It eats worms?'

We watched the grey slimy thing stretch across the stone, glistening like liquid clay. Crumbs of soil stuck to its body.

'Yeah. That's why Mummy doesn't like it.'

'Why?'

'We need earthworms to break up the soil for plants. They eat the earth and then poo it out, leaving those castes you see on the top sometimes.'

'I like worms.'

'Yeah, me too. So do hedgehogs and birds and lots of other things.'

'What eats flatworms?' she asks, tossing her pebble back into the half-demolished wall.

'Nothing. It's quite new here and nothing knows how to eat it, or if they'd like it.'

'It would taste disgusting.'

'There's that too,' I replied.

I had read about New Zealand flatworms and long dreaded meeting one in person. The scourge of gardeners across the UK (and an emerging menace to farmers), these slimy invertebrates can decimate precious earthworm populations.[9]

They ingest their prey by wrapping themselves around the unfortunate earthworm, excreting a mercifully anaesthetic enzyme from their body, which dissolves the worm from the outside in. These 'alien invaders'[10] can then shrink in size (down to as little as ten per cent of their original body weight) and hibernate for up to a year until there are enough juicy worms to eat again. Without the aerating influence of earthworms, soil can become compacted and lose its nutrients. In other words, flatworm-infested ground might not be much use for your veg patch, your field of corn.

Thanks to the booming global trade in horticulture

---

[9] They are, nonetheless, fascinating creatures. When a flatworm needs to reproduce, a hole rips open on its back, releases small eggs, then immediately heals over again. The eggs are actually rather pretty. Often compared to a blackcurrant, they are pleasingly smooth and black, jewel-like in their perfection. Each contains six or seven little baby flatworms. In his regular gardening column in the *Glasgow Herald*, Dave Allan recommends trapping flatworms to keep numbers down and disposing of them in very salty water (in my humanity, I might prefer the potentially less tortuous pestle and mortar method). However, even this level of dedication will not eradicate it. 'I'm afraid your only long-term solution may be a visit to an estate agent,' Allan suggests. Adults can reach up to twenty centimetres in length, but loom far larger than this in my imagination.

[10] Described in the fascinating book *Invasive Aliens: The Plants and Animals from Over There That Are Over Here* by Dan Eatherley.

precipitated by colonial expansion in the nineteenth century, and a taste among gardeners in the global north for 'exotic' plants, New Zealand flatworms have been hitchhiking their way across the world for over half a century in plant pots.[11] Unlike other creatures that have arrived on Shetland's shores through direct or indirect human intervention (Arctic hares, frogs and sycamore trees for example) these flatworms are 'invasive' because they have no notable predators and can spread quickly, causing measurable negative impacts. All it takes is for a well-meaning gardener to share a cutting in infected soil for the flatworm to escape into its new territory and get busy dissolving a fresh supply of precious earthworms.

I can't count the number of books I've read that express (quite rightly) the wonder of watching wildlife as a means of connecting with the natural world and managing anxiety. I have read precisely zero books, however, that advocate this approach with invasive flatworms. Perhaps this is because those of us living in countries that enrich themselves on the exploitation of people and natural resources see too much of ourselves in the creature. We live in a system which wraps itself around the natural world and extracts its life juices, leaving behind a field of knackered soil.

We watched it for a few moments. Then, without a word, I took another rock and ground the flatworm firmly into the smooth stone, only stopping when it had become a grey paste.

---

[11] First recorded in Belfast in 1963, and in Edinburgh two years after that, according to Eatherley's excellent book.

'Can I?' Esme asked, and took a turn at the grindstone. Under the motion of rock against rock, before long the flatworm looked like little more than an opaque slug trail. Even then I was not entirely convinced it was dead.

Esme had gone back to her excavations; I stared at the trowel on the grass but couldn't concentrate. Familiar waves of panic radiated across my chest as adrenaline flooded my bloodstream. The cry of a gull scraped the stillness with sharpened clarity. The remaining stones in the walls of the croft looked more shoogly, as if with the accidental brush of a hand they could tumble down and bury Esme beneath a patchwork of granite and blooms of yellow lichen. They were large, cold and heavy with the weight of countless lives. I got to my feet and called her away from her game with the lure of a chocolate digestive. I had to get away from my flatworm shame, the lurking dangers of the ruined croft, the kale plants that had been left to rot, the knowledge of bones under my feet. I was living in a land of the dead and I had to shut the door against the ghosts.

6

The Bookcase

Rose is an ancient creature, a trow born from the molten core of a volcano; her skin the colour and texture of granite. She is the sometime resident of the hollow at the bottom of the field that stretches up the slopes behind Kirkhoose. There is a scooped-out dip lined with a carpet of sphagnum moss, tussocky cushions and the occasional length of wire left over from some fencing. This is Rose's 'summer house', her home during the season of light nights, orchids and oystercatchers. She can often be found here sipping dew from mussel shells.

One day Esme and Rose were having tea together when a large shape alighted at the edge of the hollow. It was an eider duck and it had news from the North Wind. Some humans were poisoning the river. It was leaking into the homes of the eider and other sea birds that nested there. Rose was the only one who could help them . . .

It was to stories like this that Esme, stretched out on the bed in the spare room, would gradually let go of the day. Her breathing would slow and deepen, her head growing heavier on my arm. After gently extricating myself, I would pad down the curved wooden staircase to the sitting room below. The soft thud of sock on wooden stair would be the bridge between the two rhythms of Kirkhoose: one set by the unpredictable energy of a small child, and the other by her resting state. It was at these times, suddenly caught in the new stillness, that I would find my gaze sliding along the spines of the books on Dad's shelves: encyclopaedias, dictionaries, books on economics, language, natural history, ancient history, Scottish history, and one that I'd given him on the history of the AK-47. I would select one and open it, imagining Dad's hands on the covers, his large rough fingers teasing apart the thin pages. It was as if I were inside his mind, pulling out his thoughts and interests to examine and try to understand.

Folklore of the Shetland Isles by John Spence, first published 1899

The old-world ways of the Shetlanders have given place to a new order of things. Our domestic, social and industrial life is conducted on different lines. Hence it is evident that even the remembrance of the times of our forefathers will pass away forever with the present generation.

One of the creatures described in this book is the trow. These mythical beings are descendants of the Norse trolls, but have shrunk in size to fit the mounds and cairns of the low islands of Shetland. They resemble Scottish faeries – not the delicate sprites of children's picture books, but mischievous pixies that live in hillocks, play the fiddle and like to lure humans into their world with music. Through language, they live in people, vegetation, and even the weather.

Trollmolet – troll-mouthed, surly or angry
Troll-slaget – to have a badly shaped figure
Trollamog – an insignificant and malicious little person
Trows' kairds – ferns
Trowieglive – foxgloves
Trollie wadder – persistent drizzle
Trollamist – a particularly dark fog

They have a sinister side. They snatch away women and children to take with them to their world, replacing them with changelings. In the story 'Mind the Crooked Finger',[12] a voice resounding from the ground warns a man that the trows have their eye on his wife, who has a crooked finger, and their newborn child. So he lights a candle, and takes down a Bible and a knife. As soon as he opens the book, a terrible noise thunders from the byre, rattling, stamping and bellowing. With steely determination, and his family at his back, he walks to the outbuilding and opens the door, throwing the Bible inside. At once the sinister noises stop. All that remains is the uncanny likeness of his wife that the trows had left there, which 'haed

---

[12] The story as told in *The Folklore of Orkney and Shetland* by Ernest Marwick.

every joint an' pairt of a woman'. Being a pragmatic sort, he takes the likeness back into the house and uses it as a kind of table on which to saw wood.

The Folklore of Orkney and Shetland by Ernest Marwick, 1975

Even today, practically every district in Shetland can provide its trow story. It is true that several other mythical creatures – whom the Norse inhabitants of the islands would have distinguished – have dissolved into the trow, and that ever since the coming of printed fairy tales the trow has acquired characteristics which do not properly belong to such an unruly being.

I remembered mentions of trows from my childhood holidays to Shetland. They blended in my mind with the trolls of the Norwegian folk stories that Dad translated at bedtime during weekend visits. I found an English translation on the internet and read these to Esme too. These were precious, intimate moments I knew I would remember as Esme outgrew them (and perhaps Dad did too as he watched his daughter become an adult). They are, however, the static version of such stories as they were once told, with no print or paper prompts: storytelling 'at its best it was an art, with a technique to be learned and conventions to be observed', Marwick wrote. 'The tradition, as earlier generations understood it, is sadly decayed, but some authentic tales have been saved for us by people whose instinct has been to pass them on exactly as they were told to them, with a scrupulous attention to words and word order.'

Without a teacher of my own, the stories I narrated to Esme about Rose followed no particular rule or convention other than having a beginning, middle and end. They would change with every telling, often with Esme's own suggestions woven in. By reinventing in this manner, perhaps I was breaking traditions in a way that would have met with ancestral disapproval. This sense of betrayal tended to intensify the later I read on into the night, the bare windows allowing the lamplight to burn a hole in the surrounding darkness for all in the valley to see, yet reflecting back at me only an image of myself. Once, as I was leafing through a book on Iron Age pottery, I was struck with a feeling that I was being watched. It was a sudden sensation, as if I were fixed by the glare of someone passing close to where I sat. Without thinking, I got to my feet, turned off the light and went into the darkened hall. As the door clicked shut, I felt a surge of relief. My immediate thought was this was not Dad.

Our 'Rose' was anathema to the malevolent beings that stole babies and bewitched cattle. She acted as Esme's mentor, a guide through this strange new terrain of low moor and stony beach. For me, the friendly trow was a tool through which to introduce the looming catastrophes that would define my child's life: climate breakdown, species extinction. I wanted her to be aware of them but not to be overwhelmed. Rose was the bridge between imagination and reality, a way to navigate this territory while keeping one's feet. She was also a way for me to soften the edge of my own anxieties over her future.

There was a different tale of ancient creatures that I wanted to tell, of the Faustian pact we made over their liquified bodies. The riches that had been promised by the black gold – of plentiful food, luxurious homes, and a sense of power – could become as emptied of value as faerie coins, vanishing and leaving only dead leaves. This tale is of a curse, enacted by the ghosts of these fossilised algae and zooplankton as they look down upon an increasingly haunted biosphere, spectral vapours that slowly suffocate the world beneath.

But that story was not one with which to kiss a beloved child goodnight.

7

The Knock

It began with an experiment. Esme wanted to make a potion so we scoured the kitchen looking for non-essential ingredients: we could certainly spare some of the lentils that lay in unopened plastic sacks, stockpiled in the dry room, and there was a packet of out-of-date yeast in the fridge. So we dumped them in a small plastic bowl together with some ancient blue food colouring. The plan was to wait and see what happened. For the next few mornings we would thunder down the stairs to check. The results were interesting: every day the orange and blue goo would move, expanding as the lentils absorbed the colouring and the yeast, rather unexpectedly, began to activate. One morning there were bubbles, and then the now-blue lentils started to become mushy and gruel-like, oozing with a deliberation which almost suggested sentience. After a while it really started to reek so we shoved the bowl outside the door and forgot about it. It was naive, really, to bring something to life like that and not expect there to be consequences.

Like the blue lentil mush, as living things we were also a combination of our environment and genetic code. Our interactions with the world around us shape our way of thinking, but it isn't a one-way track, we are not the only agents in the landscape.

As the blue mush was blowing bubbles at us from the plastic bowl, I was exploring the croft from the height of a four-year-old. Earning bruises and some scrapes, we'd bounced over the deep moss on the slope of Sneugie. After the first few times I remembered to put us both in waterproof trousers. At the lower end of the croft, we'd counted the small trout in the trickling stream that wound down from the rising green and brown slopes of the Kergord valley, snagging on boulders like a wedding train. Once a foul smell led us to the rotting carcass of a dead lamb. Down at the silty shoreline, we'd found otter footprints, and the grey spiny form of a scorpion fish under a stone. When I told a relative about this later, she was perplexed – a scorpion fish? For a moment I thought we might have uncovered something rare and exciting until I showed her a photo.

'Oh, a plucker,' she replied. 'They're very common here.'

While life in miniature had defined our experience on the peripheries of the Kirkhoose croft, the area immediately outside the door had been the site of many dramas too. A bucket of tadpoles that we'd taken from a pool in the old quarry had expired in the heat, and some magnificent monkey flowers had sprouted outside the door of Dad's workshop, their seeds perhaps lifted in the wind to find a home in the gravel. The doorstep had been the source of other discoveries too. Over the months of lockdown, relatives and neighbours who had heard we were staying in Kirkhoose had dropped off gifts, boxes of toys and books, to keep our daughter entertained. We never saw these items being left; it was still forbidden to mix with others. In the moments when I felt overwhelmed by Dad's presence and absence inside the house – a negative image of the presence-absence I had been used to as a child – it was these small acts of kindness that kept me grounded. The Tintin books from my cousins, the small set of drawers filled with beads and coral and other treasures from another relative, and some games a neighbour had left in a storage box. For the first time I began to think about the invisible network holding everyone together, despite our isolation. That we had become part of it.

But there were other changes that we hadn't anticipated. One came in the evening with a knock.

Josh heard it first. He was sitting in the front room on the sofa reading a book while sunlight poured across the rippling stretch of the North Atlantic to be encircled in the arms of the bay. There was a noise and his ears pricked up.

Tap.

Tap tap.

There it was again.

He heaved himself out of the sofa and went to the door. It was a glass door and when you arrived in the entranceway, you could usually see who was waiting outside. But the scene was empty. He pushed down the handle and stepped outside into the cool evening. Nothing, apart from a distant flapping of wings.

It was the opening of so many horror stories: the empty doorway, an unearthly sound of something there and not there: a presage of some thing's imminent return. In *Folklore from Whalsay and Shetland*, John Stewart describes 'a typical ghost story': It is twilight and an old man stares with horror at the bedroom window of his isolated home. His daughters run outside to see what has frightened him and catch a fleeting glimpse of a female figure neither of them recognise – yet they know all the women in the neighbourhood. It is known, however, that the old man had once been a sailor and had disappeared for ten years, leaving his young family to survive on their own. 'It was currently supposed that he had bigamously married a wife in Australia,' Stewart writes, 'and had remained there until the call of home became too strong'. The daughters clearly had a good idea what this visitation was about. 'Now, father, if you have anything on your mind, say it,' one asks. 'Yes, but what if it's too late,' he replies.

A few days later, the tapping on the front door returned. It was always when we were downstairs that we would hear it, and by the time we reached the door whatever it was had gone. It became a bit of a family joke, but my amusement did often turn to suppressed anxiety – what could the thing be and why was it so keen to come in?

The denouement took place when I was on a video conference one afternoon. Josh had taken Esme down to the shore and I was alone in the house. There was a lull in the meeting and I heard it – short, sharp, like something hard meeting something brittle.

Tap.

I excused myself and quickly got to my feet, no time to think. If a ghost wanted to come in, I'd better answer the door and get it over with. What I did see, the furious eye that glared through the glass, was no less surprising. A huge feathered creature with a blue mask: a black-backed gull with lentil gunge smeared across its face.

Tap tap.

It was battering its own reflection in the glass with its beak. Esme called the bird Captain Partridge. It came back nearly every afternoon to take more of the fermented lentil gunge from the bowl outside the door. That bird was hooked. It was also really angry that another black-backed gull might be trying to steal this treat, even if that bird was in fact itself. Finally, once the last scrapings had been cleared off the sides, Captain Partridge stopped coming to visit. Sometimes though, when we saw those tell-tale 'M's and 'W's soar across the sky, we imagined one of them might look down on Kirkhoose with a craving for blue lentils. It was a cool reminder that unknown experiments have consequences.

8

Raingoose

Habituation had mostly acclimatised me to Dad's home, but not every day was a good day.

Fog blotted the view of the sea from the window, holding us inside, a trollamist. Esme and Josh were lost in a game of Uno, but I couldn't concentrate on my cards. I needed to get out and go somewhere.

As thick cloud settled in the intimate crevasses of the drainage ditches, visibility was very low. At least the road would be quiet. Before the pandemic, this stretch was usually beset with speeding vehicles taking advantage of the brief straight that cuts through the croft. Walking along it could be a hair-raising experience and I still saw the sense in being as visible as possible. 'See you in a bit,' I hollered and pulled on a safety vest. Dad had insisted I wore it when I made a similar exit out of the house into the darkness of the previous Christmas. As I trotted out of the driveway in the dull light, I exuded a faint luminous glow.

So much can happen when you're alone in the fog.

I wasn't really alone, of course, and that was perhaps the problem. I knew I would pass several habitations, houses on the right overlooking the road, and farms on the fields sloping down to the left. Many were the properties of relatives and distant relatives, all of us connected at some point on an ancient, broad-canopied family tree.

This valley, the main land route from the village of Voe to the village of Aith, was known for a time as Broon's Brae because of the number of Browns born and raised at Green Knowe. My immediate family shed the 'Brown' through artistic choice or marriage, and after Dad's death I was the last one left. As my trainers smacked against the tarmac, I felt a shade of regret that I hadn't given Esme my surname, or a version of it: it hadn't seemed important at the time. I thought of the long lines of Browns who had sweated and bled into the landscape under my feet, their thread-like roots helping to hold together the texture of the soil, and wondered if they would be angry that I had tried to leave them behind.

One foot in front of the other; it was more of a fast walk than a run. My muscles laboured and an ominous ache radiated from my right Achilles tendon. The incline was relentless and unforgiving, exacerbating the effort of every step. Not only that, but the obscured view offered no distractions. The pattern of the fencing repeated as I pounded past. I could be running on the spot or running back through time or into another reality. Not so long ago local people would have done this journey through necessity, not choice, bent under baskets of peats, or wool or other goods.

*

The tightness in my calves recalled me to the hard, steep reality of the tarmac.

In the film *The Others*, the protagonist, Grace, is trapped inside her home with two sickly children on the island of Jersey in the wake of World War II. She manages to leave the house only once, but soon finds herself surrounded by mist which thickens with every step she takes away from the gates. Disoriented, she begins to panic, spinning around, not knowing where she is. A dark shape in a trench coat lumbers into view – a husband, who she believed to be dead. Through subtle changes, her home has become unhomely, shrouded in the 'uncanny' feeling made famous by Freud.

Fog conceals. A familiar scene becomes unfamiliar.

In his essay of the same name[13] Freud described the uncanny as the feeling 'when one is lost in a forest in high altitudes, caught, we will suppose, by the mountain mist, and when every endeavour to find the marked or familiar path ends again and again in a return to one and the same spot, recognizable by some particular landmark.' We should know where we are, but we don't, so we feel 'the sense of helplessness sometimes experienced in dreams'. It is in a dreamlike state that Grace found the key to her unhappy fate. 'The uncanny thing is nothing else than a hidden, familiar thing that has undergone repression and then emerged from it,' Freud writes.

My pace was more of a jog now and I was distracted by

---

[13] https://web.mit.edu/allanmc/www/freud1.pdf

the sensations the mist was dislodging in my mind. There were more twists and turns than I remembered when I'd been out here on a clear sunny day. I was sure I'd passed that stile already. And those scrunched-up lager cans tossed out of a car window by an idle hand, hadn't I seen them five minutes before?

I was approaching the back of the hill now, the small body of freshwater known as the Loch of Gonfirth. It was a beautiful but eerie place.

To drive my thoughts away from the effort of my legs, I recalled a story I'd extracted from Dad's bookcase: it was about a crofter and a mysterious pony. The opening scene began to take form, filtered through my own imagination.

*

It is a grainy dusk, as if the sunshine was too sleepy to leave the land in much of a hurry. A between-worlds kind of light: winter and spring, day and night, natural and supernatural. It is the period after a dry winter when the peat is ready to be cut. Stepping out through the door from the warmth and fug of the fire, James fills his lungs with evening air. He is cosy in his boots, his woollen hat, jumper and socks with their itchy but comforting insulation. In his toughened hands something glints and jangles: a piece of metal which chills the skin of his fingers and palm – a steel bridle. He needs the bridle to catch the horse to carry the peats the following day.

James is surprised that he had forgotten, so he thinks, what a beautiful animal this white pony is. It is larger and stronger than he remembers. Perhaps he could sell it to traders who seek stallions for use down the coal mines far away in Scotland, England or Wales. It is these thoughts – of the money and what could be bought with it and how it could alleviate the grinding struggle to keep his family fed and warm every day – that are swarming in his brain as he reaches the stallion's head. The beast snorts and stares and calculates. So distracting are these ideas that James fails to see in the distant haze of evening another white horse, shorter, sturdier, looking at him with a puzzled expression from across the water.

It is the work of just a moment. With a practised flick of his hand the bridle is over the horse's neck – but this is not what he expected. Instead of submitting in its usual docile fashion, the animal pulls back with a fierce power, snorting and whinnying. James holds fast to the rein – what is going on? The pony is pulling him along with a terrible strength down towards the water, his hands seem stuck to the flank, he can't tear away. The eyes roll, the gums froth. Where does this power come from? This is not natural. His feet are forced forwards, step by desperate step and soon his imprints in the muddy turf are filling with water as they approach the edge of the lochan. With a pang of horror, he realises this is no pony at all, but a njuggle; a creature in horse form that likes to trick people onto its back before thundering into deep water and tipping them into a watery doom. But James is not going down without a fight. He braces himself, tugging with all his strength on his landward rein. And so they struggle in a deadly tug of war, a pull and push and pull and push of mortal consequence, until at last, with a tremendous roar, the njuggle sinks to the ground. James steps back, panting, his skin imprinted with the steel form of the bridle. As he flexes his hands and their colour begins to return, he looks down at his feet and his eyes widen with horror. There on the grass is not a pony but a gelatinous form the colour and texture of solidified mutton stew. He pokes it with the tip of its boot; it quivers like a jellyfish.[14]

*

Njuggles are a bit like kelpies in Scottish folklore. As a child I loved reading about these great black horses that hung around the shoreline looking suspiciously damp and sandy and dragging a trail of seaweed from a back hoof. They liked to transform into tall, dark-haired, handsome men and lure young women onto their backs before thundering with them into the sea and a watery grave.[15]

There are several place names that contain 'njuggle' in Shetland. Njuggleswater in Scalloway, Nukrawater in Whalsay. People did not travel much by road, in that old Shetland when they were named. However they would still be out on the moor, whether to drive sheep, collect rushes, or cut peats. This was a time before fences, of common land where livestock, including horses, roamed the fields freely. 'I guess this is why the njuggel was able to do its dastardly deeds, because

---

[14] A re-imagining of a story in *The Folklore of Orkney and Shetland* by Ernest W. Marwick (1975).

[15] For some fascinating facts and stories about njuggles, this blog from the Shetland Amenity Trust is great reading: https://www.shetlandamenity. org/place-names-of-the-week-njuggls-and-sh%C3%B6pilties

it seemed just another horse!' curator of the Shetland Museum and Archives Ian Tait said in an interview.[16] 'However, when you got near to it, its unusual form was seen, especially the flowing tail, which was supposed to be circular in shape. It was an attractive animal that'd make you pause and take more notice than you'd normally do when encountering any other horse.'

*

I was behind Sneugie, the hill at the back of Kirkhoose, and the road was almost level. I knew the loch was on one side, but I could barely see the edge of the road. A noise grabbed my heart. An unholy mixture of vixen's scream and muted trumpet, tapering off with the sigh of a deflating balloon. 'What the hell is that?' I said aloud, startling myself. The wail wheedled through the air again.

I tried to orient myself, but there was that cry again, and a splash.

A muddle of images filled my mind:

a white horse throwing a figure into the black edges of a lochan and the body smashing through the surface with a sound like broken glass

the abrasive noise of sawing as a man balances a piece of wood over the moulded likeness of a woman with a crooked finger

---

[16] https://www.shetlandmuseumandarchives.org.uk/blog/the-most-deceptive-of-creatures-the-njuggel

unfriendly eyes watching as I take a book from Dad's shelf

I wanted to run. Not for fun, or in a crazed effort to get fit. This would be adrenaline-driven, instinctive, and would probably see me pelting over the hills into the peat bogs, slowing only when mossy soup began to suck my ankles. But an unexpected thought broke free from my subconscious and I paused. I was alert and tense, still listening, but I was distracted from my desire for flight by the memory of something comforting. A distant encounter floated back to me.

I was sitting in the front of Dad's van, parked at the edge of the loch. The sky was clear but there was a breeze disturbing the surface of the water. He was holding a pair of trusty RSPB binoculars to his eyes and gazing fixedly at a point in the distance. 'Ah, there it is,' he said, and passed the binos to me. 'You can just about see it.' I peered through the eyepieces, adjusting the focus wheel. It always took me ages to get it right. At last I swung the barrels left and right, trying to find what Dad was pointing at. 'It's just at the edge, can you see it?' Frayed gems of grass, grey sky, water the colour of burnished steel – there! A tiny island scooped away from the side of the loch. I kept my hands steady. Yes, there it was, just for a second. The silky silver plumage hinted at the zebra stripes on the back of the neck, the distinctive red splash on the sturdy throat and a glint of ruby eye – it was a raingoose.[17]

---

[17] Shetland's raingoose has two lives: one in the open sea, and one inland, where it nests in lochans to breed. The male tends to return close to where it was hatched, and the females disperse further afield. Their plumage also transforms to match this change in lifestyle. But they are

This is a landscape where the slightest change in weather on land or sea might result in a one-way journey to oblivion. Ground that can give way under your feet, devouring your body from the toes up; wind that can whip the heat from your vital organs; gales that can turn a boat over into the surf. To survive, people looked for patterns that could tell them what to expect when the wind changed, when the full moon rose, when the clouds closed in. They translated a language from the land, sea and air and the living things around them.

I was by no means the only one to have noticed the eerie timbre of the red-throated diver's call, like a lost soul in a desert. In North America, their alternative name 'loon' speaks to associations with lunacy and the moon's cycles. The sounds it makes when travelling overhead before it begins a descent to the sea or a loch has been translated by locals as: 'wear-a-weet, weer-a-weet . . . waur wadder, waur wadder' (beware of rain coming). With a name like 'raingoose' (derived from the Old Norse *regn gas*), it is not surprising to learn its associations with changes in the weather. Short cries were thought to herald a dry spell but long, plaintive wails presaged a downpour. As others often point out, in Shetland, rain is never very far away. But in the not-so-distant past when predicting the temperament of the skies could mean life or death for the crofter or fisherman, these kinds of signs were extremely important. One Shetland proverb underlines this point, probably referring to when birds

---

not always elegant; like other water birds, when they walk, as their legs are set far back in their bodies.

go inland in the spring to breed and when they return to the
sea in the autumn.

> If the raingoose flees ta da hill
> Du can gang to da haaf whin du will;
> Bot whin shö gangs to da sea,
> du maun draw up du'r boats an flee

> When the raingoose flies to the hill,
> you can go to the deep-sea fishing,
> but when it goes to the sea,
> you should draw up your boats

The guttural *craa* of a raven woke me from my daze. I was
standing in a layby and began to feel the lack of blood in my
fingertips and the chill of cooled sweat around my torso. It
was time to go. I launched off again, keeping to the right-hand
side of the road. The fog was still thick, but it felt lighter than
it had a moment before. There was something ascending the
road towards me, a strange yellowish-green light. I slowed to
a walk, but still it came, closer and closer until it was almost
upon me. I felt my chest tighten – what new shade of horror
was this?

'Oh!' we cried in unison. 'You gave me a fright!'

It was a neighbour from across the valley. She was wearing
a luminous yellow jacket and trainers and was up there for
her regular exercise. We stared at each other for a moment,
catching our breath.

'Thank you for the box,' I said, referring to the gift of

secondhand toys we'd received on the front step. 'Esme was delighted.'

'It was no bother,' she replied, and after a few more words of cheer about the fog and the hill and our worries about Covid, we continued on our separate ways.

I hoped my 'thank you' in the fog could express the depth of my gratitude.

9

Tang

It was one of those mornings when the sea was as still as glass, mirroring the shoreline in the water: two worlds aligned. Passing traffic was becoming more frequent, but it was still safe enough to wobble the wheelbarrow around the bay for our weekly pilgrimage to the petrol station. I didn't bring the hand sanitiser now to wash my hands after opening and closing the gate, but I did wear a mask in the shop.

Esme agreed to come on the condition that I pushed her up the spine-wrenchingly steep incline at the end of the journey, and on the promise of ice lollies and shop-bought tattie scones, delicious straight from the packet or toasted and dripping with butter. My reward was a copy of the *Shetland Times*. Our figures moved slowly through the stillness, accompanied by the distant whoop of curlews and the rumble of the barrow's wheel. In the bottom of the wheelbarrow a trowel slid about. This was for the potted plant we would buy outside the shop for Dad's grave, a ritual of the last few weeks. The flowers were colourful place markers as we waited for the headstone.

Later, our six pansies and a yellow primula sat waiting as we scooped holes out of the turf on Dad's grave. The grass was healing the scars council gravediggers had left all those months before. Only the primula would take root and survive into the next year. Many of the graves belonged to immediate relatives, and others more distant, stretching back over a century. The view from this contemplative spot would have been quite different a century ago, overlooking a scene of industry steeped in colonialism and exploitation that stretched across the globe.

In the 1920s, Olnafirth – the ribbon of sea that carved into the edge of Voe – was a bustling hub of noise and activity as the bodies of giant mammals were hauled ashore to fuel global industrialisation. On the north side of the bay, before it narrowed out, stood Olna Whaling Station, the last of four, that operated between 1904 and 1929. It was run by Norwegian businesses after their country banned the practice off its own shores. Whales were eviscerated for oil to fuel the processing of jute, a flowering plant grown by peasants in British colony Bengal. Mixed with whale oil, the fibres were extremely tough and were widely used for making packaging materials like sacks. These same sacks were the ones used to carry cotton from the American South, grain from the Great Plains and Argentina, coffee from the East Indies and Brazil, wool from Australia, sugar from the Caribbean and nitrates from Chile.[18]

---

[18] https://www.open.edu/openlearn/history-the-arts/history/dundee-jute-and-empire/content-section-3.1

Photographs of Olna whaling station at the time reveal a direct window into the past: men in flat caps carving up the giant deflated carcasses.[19]

Although Shetlanders hunted whales for generations, this way of making a living is unthinkable now. Indeed, attitudes towards whales have changed entirely, with social media sites allowing the real-time tracking of whales as they traverse the seas around the islands. On the Facebook page Shetland Orca Sightings enthusiasts post photos of minke whales, dolphins, basking sharks and other species. Times are gone when a crew of men would haul aboard the skewered body of one of our planet's largest mammals, the water churning with blood, to be dissected for lamp oil, industrial lubricant or use in explosives. The whaling industry has been usurped by a different treasure from the deep – fossil fuels. But as I was to discover, while the story of whale hunting was an old one, it persisted as a haunting reflection of the present.

We were sitting on a bench in the graveyard when I opened the paper. 'Ofgem approves interconnector cable plans', proclaimed the front page.[20] For someone unacquainted with local politics, this was not hugely gripping, and it took me a few flicks through the pages to return to it. 'Ofgem has approved plans for a 600MW subsea interconnector cable to the mainland, paving the way for the 103-turbine Viking Energy windfarm.'

---

[19] https://www.youtube.com/watch?v=yN3WELlgFfo

[20] https://www.shetlandtimes.co.uk/2020/07/16/ofgem-approves-interconnector-cable-plans

Wait, 103 turbines?

'Mumma, can I dig a hole in Mam's grave?'

Esme was beside me, trowel in hand. It took me a moment before I realised what she was asking me.

'No, no, don't do that,' I replied as gently as I could. 'Why don't you pick some daisies for her?'

'Mam', Dad's mother, died nearly a decade before Esme's birth, but my daughter has attached herself to her great-grannie through my stories of the kind woman who smelled of bottled flowers, was an expert knitter, strong singer, and a master in the art of bannock-making. Esme had absorbed my descriptions of itchy jumpers and warm bannocks and jam with delight, even when confronted with a plate of my own rubbery attempts. For now, the suggestion of a homage to Mam was enough to keep her happy for a moment. I read on.

The energy regulator has approved the plans after a consultation earlier this year, and said they will proceed with the cable on the condition that they are 'satisfied' by the end of this year that the project will go ahead. They admitted that the majority of the responses to their public consultation, held after they announced they were 'minded to' accept the plans earlier this year, were negative. The company say they will address the concerns of those that responded negatively to the consultation by the end of July. The news comes almost a month after SSE Renewables announced they would be pledging £580 million to the project.

A lot of turbines, a largely negative public consultation and £580 million in investment from the subsidiary of a multinational energy company. My journalistic instincts were whetted.

Esme was exploring between the gravestones. As long as they didn't look too unstable, I resisted telling her to be careful. Instead, I took the chance to wheech out my phone and type in 'Viking Energy windfarm'. There was a map of the Mainland with plotted dots marking the route of the 155 metre-tall turbines. I found Voe on the map and traced my finger along the line. There was Dad's house. I lowered the paper and stared at the hills on the other side of the bay, hills that couldn't be higher than 200 metres themselves. I'd heard relatives talking about the wind farm for years, but had never paid much attention. It seemed to be a story immersed in the squabbles of local politics. Anyway, Shetland had been Dad's home ground, not mine. I was also of the opinion that any switch from dirty fuel to renewable must be – generally speaking – good news.

The burning of oil, gas and coal was producing greenhouse gas emissions at record levels with no signs of slowing down. We were set for catastrophic levels of global warming in my lifetime. I was editor of an environmental magazine. My job was to point out the connections between human activity and environmental degradation, to shout 'we are nature defending itself' from the magazine stands and to explore routes out of the crisis (the most obvious one being to stop consuming so many fossil fuels). But Shetland was no longer a faraway land that I associated with a distant parent. Looking out across the bay and the brown tide of seaweed, appropriately called 'tang' in the Shetland dialect, the view felt part of me. Having grown so familiar with every contour of these hills and the minute seasonal changes in ecology, the thought of it being threatened in some way startled new emotions in me. An image of the cool lochan, the mist, the nest and the ruby-red eye of the raingoose flashed in my mind. What would happen to the birds on the hills, those that needed to fly from their nests to the sea to gather food; would the sixty-metre blades slice into their flight path? While the call of the raingoose was an omen for bad weather, the absence of their call promised something far, far worse.

Across the bay, the reflection of the still water doubled the shapes above it: wind-furrowed ridges in the slope, the blacks and browns of the peat, the dull green ryegrass peppered with sheep. The pastoral scene looked down at its own doppelgänger, awaiting its fate.

Esme was getting restless so we left the graveyard and went down to the shore to see what creatures we could find under the rocks. The tide was on its way out, revealing beached rafts of glistening seaweed and shards of detritus that had been hauled in by the waves. A few generations ago, this would not have been such a good place for guddling. With no septic tanks, the houses around the bay released their waste straight into the sea. Even with the distance of seventy years, one former resident still wrinkled her nose when recalling the cloying smell of sewage from her childhood. Mercifully, all that remained of those days were the pieces of broken pottery folk chucked down here before black-bagged bin collections. Other beach treasures included the rusted skeletons of ancient engines and scuffed plastic crates that had escaped the floating salmon farms and sailed the waves back to land. Sprinkled over the crisping border of marine vegetation was the smaller plastic waste. Eroded to smooth shards or beads, there were few hints to the past lives of these chunks of rubbish. Even further up was the bright orange remains of nylon rope or fishing nets, so deeply enmeshed into the bank it was impossible to pull out despite our best efforts.

Our game consisted of Esme identifying promising-looking stones for me to lift and hold up while she kept watch for life underneath. A good stone was one that was quite flat and wasn't too deeply embedded into the silty mud, but sat on top of it, allowing creatures to shelter underneath. No fear of flatworms here: it was far too salty. So far, we'd found several small crabs, a butterfish and some purple anemones with their tentacles contracted like mini jellies. I had replaced the last stone and the commotion caused by our violent intrusion into the world of the shoreline creatures was beginning to quieten. Esme was watching a whelk tentatively emerging from its shell. I got up to stretch my back and took a deep breath in, inflating my lungs with the wholesome, sour smell of rotting seaweed. Something had shifted. I was no longer a disassociated onlooker; I was in the scene, the scene was part of me and it felt nourishing. A chill had entered the valley and I thrust my fingers into my pockets. They brushed something damp, and with a yelp I drew out my hand. On my palm was a gritty shard of pottery, the pink pattern still faintly visible under a skin of red-brown algae. Amid the excitement of witnessing another realm of life, Esme had been quietly filling my pockets with treasure.

*

There was a dragon by the window. It sat among papers and books on a shelf in Dad's study. Head-to-tail it was about a foot long, crudely shaped out of red-brown clay, glazed and fired. One foot was missing. Every time I took a seat on the swivel chair at the desk and waited for my laptop to wake up I would cast it a glance and it would look straight back at me, a moment of quiet puzzlement. I was sure we knew each other, but I couldn't remember where we'd met before.

The night after our beach walk, I was sitting in the office staring into space when Josh came in with a cup of tea.

'How are you doing?' he asked.

'OK.' I pushed the chair back from the desk and took the cup. Like much of the crockery in the house, this was one of Dad's, an old specimen from the 1990s with a pattern of comma-like curls across it.

We paused for a moment, saying nothing. Esme was in bed and the rhythm of the house had stilled with her heart rate.

'Do you think I should sort through Dad's stuff?' I asked at last, suddenly feeling the weight of the things on the shelves and in the drawers.

'Only if you feel like it.' Josh put his hand on my shoulder. 'I'm going to read for a bit. Don't stay up too late,' he said and closed the door gently behind him.

I sat, feeling the tea's heat radiating through the ceramic base, a pleasing, almost painful sensation. Around me, the rich darkness of the moonless night was finally closing in, turning the curtainless windows into a mirror, reflecting me back at myself. I scanned the objects and book spines as if I were exploring the inside of Dad's brain. With a shock, I finally remembered where I'd seen the dragon before. Long ago, in the ceramics department where Dad worked, a child had stood at a stained workbench rolling shapes out of clay: a tail, and thumb-printed scales. I had made this dragon and here, next to his desk, Dad had kept it.

10

Home

'Not infrequently, the supernatural helper is masculine in form . . . The higher mythologies develop the role in the great figure of the guide, the teacher, the ferryman, the conductor of souls to the afterworld.'

Joseph Campbell on the supernatural aid
(or mentor) stage of the Hero's Journey.

'What do you think about this wind farm?' I asked Josh.

We were trundling along the Hoga Road with the wheelbarrow, this time filled with cushions, a sleeping bag and Dad's down-padded jacket, which would occasionally release a trickle of white feathers into the still air. Poking out was Esme's little pink face. She had finally drifted off to sleep, something she found difficult to do in the sunlit nights.

It was 10 p.m. and the particular milky twilight of a Shetland summer evening known as the 'simmer dim', a time of year when it never really gets dark. The weather had held us captive most of the day, a clear sky but the kind of 'brunt wind' that felt like it would dent your eyeballs, as Ted Hughes once wrote. In the wake of this violence, the evening quiet was almost otherworldly.

'I don't know,' he replied. 'Where exactly would it be?'

I pointed to the top of the valley behind Kirkhoose. 'There, and it will stretch out across about a third of the Mainland.'

Josh raised his eyebrows. 'I mean, the world does need more wind farms, but yeah, that's big. What's your take on it?'

'I haven't decided yet,' I answered.

I have always liked the elegance and slow grace of wind turbines. There were several on my way to work in Devon; white giants that loomed into view over the contour of the low hills, their blades revolving with lazy power. Up in Shetland, wind turbines were also an established part of the terrain. The Burradale 'ladies' (five 43-metre wind turbines named Mina, Betsy, Brenda, Sally and Karen) had been a landmark on the outskirts of Lerwick since the 2000s. 'Burradale's production figures show just how special and powerful the wind around Shetland is,' I had read on the Burradale website. I could well believe it. Even the sweetest summer breeze here was enough to give me windburn.

There were, however, very obvious differences between these and the 103 Goliaths proposed by Viking Energy. While the work of the ladies of Burradale was reserved exclusively for the local population, the Viking wind farm was set to power just over 475,000 homes. With only around 10,000 households in Shetland, nearly all of this would be exported to the UK electricity grid. All very well if Shetlanders were getting something out of it. Here the bigger picture came into sharp focus: the climate crisis. The last four years had been the hottest on record, and even Shetlanders were noticing it as tomatoes withered pathetically in overheated polytunnels.

Across the world, this heat was setting off more extreme weather, droughts, flooding and hurricanes. We were on a trajectory that would see many parts of the world uninhabitable for humans within our lifetimes. 'The world is on fire,' diplomat Christiana Figueres said. 'Do we watch the world burn, or do we choose to do what is necessary to achieve a different future?'

To douse the flames, emissions must fall by half by 2030 and reach net-zero – removing as many emissions as are produced – no later than 2050. Over a hundred countries had pledged to do so, including the UK. Scotland had promised to achieve this by 2045. How could it be done without renewable energy projects of this scale?

The last of the day was seeping back into the horizon as we approached Kirkhoose. Josh carried Esme to bed without waking her. I chucked the cushions into the house and put the wheelbarrow back in the workshop, releasing a breath of clay-dust when I opened the door. I went into the office and flipped open the lid of my laptop.

What exactly was Viking Energy offering in terms of its ability to fight global heating? The website claimed it would be cutting 500,000 tonnes of carbon dioxide emissions each year. In 2018, Scotland generated emissions of around 41.6 million tonnes of CO_2e.[21] If, as promised, the wind farm was fully

---

[21] https://www.gov.scot/news/scottish-greenhouse-gas-emissions-2018/

functional by 2024, it would cut the residential contribution by 1.2%. This would be an important contribution to the Scottish government's 'race to zero'.

We were talking about the fate of the human race here, yet in the newspaper article I had read, the majority of responses to the public consultation on the crucial interconnector were mostly negative. Why was the project apparently so controversial? Aesthetic objections were one thing, concern over the destruction of habitats and deep peat a far more troubling one. Around seventy kilometres of road would be built, carving access into the heart of the peatlands. Many birds relied on these quiet, undisturbed areas to raise their chicks, and the species of most concern was the raingoose. Researchers saw the birds breeding on around 70 lochs and lochans on the site between 2003 and 2008.[22] Or was this also part of a far older story, of a centralised power extracting riches from far-flung provinces? Like other colonial powers, Scottish lairds had leeched profit from the Shetland tenants living on the land for centuries. If so, then – combined with how the islands have profited from the fossil fuel industry over the years – it would be a tight knot to unpick.

It was getting late. To have a break from the back-lit laptop screen, I let my eye run over the walls. There were a series of photographs, Blu-Tacked together to form a panoramic view from a hill and the edge of the surrounding bay below. Each photo, taken on an analogue camera, was slightly overlapped

---

[22] https://www.vikingenergy.co.uk/archive/environmental-impact-assessment-2009/technical-appendices/appendix-11.1-birds-technical-report-7.3mb

like a badly cut jigsaw. I recognised them from Dad's bedroom in Glasgow, and here they were again, tacked to his office wall, familiar as old wallpaper. I recalled the montage but not the fine details. This time, something caught my attention and I stood up to have a closer look – the lines of the peat hags – those eroded wormholes, the shape of the bay. This photo was taken from Sneugie. A memory shook free in my mind – bouncing down the slope on the heather, wind slapping colour into our cheeks. There was something I hadn't noticed before about the photo. In one of the rectangles, a small figure was framed in the distance, terrible haircut and ill-fitting 1980s clothes. It was me.

Over the last few weeks I'd tentatively started to sort through Dad's things, finding amongst them the dusty, mouldering remnants of lost childhood. I found an old cushion cover I'd made in primary school, Mam's old knitting belt, and a tape-recording I'd made for him of me playing the piano. It was a surprise to find these things here, as if excavating a familiar ruin and finding buried treasure.

Throughout my life, I had heard only one side of the story, and seen Dad as a distant figure. But I was learning that while I had believed in a story of rejection, he had kept parts of me close to him. The realisation that there was another view of my own history was beginning to change how I felt about my place in the present.

My eyes flitted back to the photos of Sneugie. It had been taken thirty years ago but if I went up there now, the view would probably be much the same. For a moment I imagined what the view would be like in another thirty years. Standing at the top of the hill, what would a grown-up Esme see? Lines of wind turbines, perhaps, exporting energy across the ocean to Scotland.

I decided to search for old news articles about the wind farm. There was one by the *Guardian*'s Scotland correspondent from 2012 which caught my eye. 'Shetland Islands to host "world's most productive" wind farm,' it said. The project would lead to earnings of £30 million a year for islanders and Shetland's wealthy charitable trust, and would become operational in 2017. Hang on a minute. I skipped back to the Viking Energy website to read: 'The islands would receive around £2.2 million in community benefit every year'. The definition of 'community benefit' had clearly changed quite a bit over the course of eight years. Was this what had caused the delay? Or was there something else going on as well? At that moment, I remembered a scene from ten years before. I was sitting in Dad's top-floor flat in Glasgow, yellow afternoon light drifting in through the window. Far below us, traffic tore along the M8, creating a sound like waves on the shore. We were drinking strong coffee from a thermos flask. He was talking about a vast wind farm that was to cover mainland Shetland with turbines. The story sounded complicated and was hard to follow. Dad did not sound like he was in favour of it.

He clicked the saccharine dispenser over his cup, his blue eyes flicking up at me as he disturbed the surface of the coffee with a spoon.

'You should write about it,' he said.

'Hmm, yeah, maybe,' I replied.

Sitting at his desk a decade later in the enveloping gloom, I realised that yes, maybe I should. I looked up the opposition group Sustainable Shetland on Facebook and sent them a message asking to meet.

*

It wasn't until I opened the door that I realised we had met before. Frank Hay, a retired maths teacher, had been one of the many friends and admirers who had made the trip to Voe Hall in the ice-edged wind and rain to pay their respects at Dad's funeral. Although there was not a big age difference between them, their paths had not crossed much until Dad's retirement and his return to Shetland. Here, in Voe, they had got to know each other, and shared mutual concerns about the wind farm.

We sat down at the kitchen table, still unconsciously socially distancing, and his blue eyes looked out at the bay over the edge of one of Dad's mugs as he prepared to tell me 'the whole sorry tale'. I listened in the still room as Frank unfurled his side, punctuating the stillness of the room with the soft clunk of ceramic on the plastic tablecloth.

What Frank described was a quest for power, or, more accurately: energy. It began in earnest with the discovery of black gold in the North Sea, a moment in history that had altered the fate of the islands. When that pot had started to run dry, a few canny folk had started to look elsewhere for top-ups. What could Shetland offer in vast abundance that set it aside from the rest of Britain? A glance out of the window at a landscape cowed by the force of the weather provided the answer: wind. That was over twenty years ago, so what had happened since? Frank spoke slowly and deliberately. It was easy to imagine him in front of a classroom. Even then my furious note-taking struggled to keep up with my thoughts, that familiar feeling of sensing a potential story, looking to fill in the gaps of who, what, why, how and when.

Frank recalled a complicated picture of public meetings, letters to the local newspapers voicing concerns over health, bird life and even carbon emissions because of the peat. There was a host of allies and enemies – politicians, journalists, landowners, farmers, artists, homeowners, birds, even the hills themselves – pitched against one another in battle. According to Frank, the community was at war with itself. This was an epic story, but as a journalist, I was very aware that I was hearing just one side of it. If I was to have any hope of understanding what had happened, I'd need to hear from other actors in the tale.

Outside, the wind had hushed for a moment and thin grey light diffused through the cloud cover. I imagined our position on a digital map, little dots on the edge of a bay, on the edge of an island in the middle of the ocean, a patch of blue on a globe. Just twelve miles north from the sitting-room window was Sullom Voe, one of the largest oil and gas terminals in Europe. Just a few miles south, on the edge of the hills, would be the top of a line of 155-metre wind turbines. As Frank talked, it became clear that this was not just a story about Shetland, or even Europe. This was a story with global importance and here in Kirkhoose, we were in the middle of it.

Frank drained the last of his tea. He had to go, but as I had been learning, Shetland goodbyes were rarely hasty, so we continued to chat for some time before he got to his feet.

Lunchtime was fast approaching as I waved him off. Despite the dull sunshine, the wind was picking up, cold and inhospitable, and I was quite prepared to stay inside with the company of the underfloor heating. The phone rang; it was Josh telling me he and Esme would be returning from their trip to the playpark very shortly.

'OK, see you at home,' I replied, ending the call with surprise at my own words.

The ruined croft, the stream, our relations and attentive neighbours – for the first time I realised I really did consider this place to be our home.

*

July had become August and school would be starting soon. Across the country, life was settling back into its old routines. Traffic was starting to fill the roads once more, cafés had reopened and we could even go for a trip down the high street to visit the wool shop. But this 'normality' also felt to me like foreboding. The closer we came to returning to 'normal', the sooner we would have to make a decision. What were we to do – stay in Kirkhoose and enrol Esme in the local primary? She already had friends at the playpark and Shetland was asserting itself in the way she saw the world – replacing 'small' with 'peerie' in her everyday vocabulary. But our own house in Devon had been empty for over half a year; we couldn't simply leave it. And I couldn't very well commute to my office in Southwest England from Shetland. So eventually we decided that now was the time. We would pack our things and make the journey from the extreme north to the extreme southwest of Britain, over eight hundred miles, in a borrowed, slightly battered car, which we intended to sell on at the end of the road.

Before I had Esme, whenever I prepared to leave the place where I was living, there was always a period of adjustment. It was an uncanny time when I would suddenly become hyper-aware of my everyday rituals and how soon they would become only memories. I was already nostalgic for them, even as I was in the act of doing them.

Leaving Shetland was not like that. I didn't want to let go. While I looked forward to returning to the protective canopy of ancient oaks and beech that hemmed my adoptive town in Devon, I knew I would long for the smell of tang and the soft peep of oystercatchers. I would miss my immediate and distant relations. I would miss being 'placed' by the people I met on the road. My connection seemed too fragile to survive such a separation, like a badly constructed drystone dyke, the stones threatening to topple at any minute. I had spent many months getting to know Dad and realigning my relationship with him. All the same, I didn't feel like I had the right to stay in Shetland. I was still not 'Shetland' enough.

We had to hold Esme down to stop her wrestling free from the car seat. Unlike her parents, conditioned to repress strong expressions of emotion, she was kicking and screaming: 'No, I don't want to go. I don't want to go.'

My close relatives stood outside the house, lips tight, waving stiffly at our departing car. Through the passenger window I watched as we pulled away from Kirkhoose, the home Dad had built and died in, the ruins of Green Knowe and birthplace of my grandfather, past the grey bungalow Olnagarth where Dad had grown up.

For a while we followed the edge of the sea holding the bruised light of the summer sky until at last we turned away south to join the main road. It had been over seven months since I had made the journey in reverse, and although on the surface the land looked the same, the way I viewed it had changed forever.

I would return, this time for a bigger reason. I would tell a story of home that was not just about me, but everyone else living in this climate emergency.

Part Two: Initiation

11

Crossing the Threshold

Greyhope Bay seemed like an appropriate place to be that day. I was looking out at the South Breakwater Lighthouse in Aberdeen harbour. It was only around 5 p.m., but this was northern Scotland in October so the sun was already beginning to set. The light cast a glaze of gold on the long grass; the kind of afternoon that heralds longer nights ahead. I was thinking about where I was headed.

Two years had gone by since Esme, Josh and I had left Shetland. Our four-year-old infant, who loved to dress up and play Tintin, had grown into a seven-year-old schoolgirl and was now to be found either getting up to mischief on her scooter in the skate park or burrowed into the sofa, lost in a book. She no longer said 'peerie' for small, and instead inflected her sentences with the rounded vowels of Southwest England. Tracked alongside her growth, the passing of these years was easy to measure, but I was also different.

My ties to a town on the fringes of Dartmoor's temperate

rainforest, as far from the sea as Devon can be, were fragile and breakable. But with the anchor of a small child and the forced inertia of subsequent lockdowns, our lives had centred on school and friends. We got to know the nearby bends of the river, the rope swing and the climbable trees. We got to know people through their troubles and joys, and so wove ourselves into a settled life.

Many times I found myself longing to go back to Shetland, to wipe the smirr from my face as I looked out across the voe from the top of Sneugie; to drop in on relatives for a cup of tea; to hang my name on the family tree. But to return there to live would be to stake a claim on land that I still felt wasn't really mine. I was both an insider and an outsider, and until the two parts of me were reconciled, the idea of an island home felt far away.

In my mind, I saw on the horizon monumental figures – Mina, Betsy, Brenda, Sally and Karen, the turbines from Burradale wind farm – spinning energy from the air like miller's daughters. These heroines were to save the human race from climate chaos, but what price would we pay for it? As they spun, they seemed to be drawing out energy from the earth too, from the peat and the soil, occupying the landscape with their industry; land which was no longer an abstract place to me. If I closed my eyes I could see the undulations of the Kirkhoose fields and feel the moss under my feet. The journey was unfinished and I couldn't walk away. It was as if, back in Kirkhoose in the summer of 2020, Frank Hay had been inviting me through a door – one that wouldn't shut until I went through.

In just a few hours, I was due to sail to Lerwick on the overnight ferry and begin interviewing people. It was a full-time commitment; I had quit my job at the magazine to fulfil it and left Josh and Esme in Devon while I sought out key characters to piece the story together.

Now, sitting on the dock and waiting for the next stage of my journey, a blizzard of worries filled my head: no job; returning to an empty Kirkhoose without Josh and Esme; what family would think about my new project; if anyone would agree to share their side of the story. My excitement at returning weighed precariously with trepidation.

'I can't believe I'm doing this to myself,' I muttered.

The grey sea heaved and swelled. There was something odd about it, but I couldn't tell quite what. I scanned the water restlessly, like a lookout in a crow's nest, and finally allowed my mind to tear away from the storm within and focus. There were distant black shapes lifting out of the waves and crashing back in again, a dance of joyful acrobatics. I stared harder. It was a pod of porpoises.

'A porpoise in life,' I thought, and I could imagine Dad standing next to me, rolling back on his heels as he used to do, pinching some tobacco from a packet between his fingers and giving an amused 'humph'.

*

The house would be cold and dark: an unhomely home. At once empty of people and at the same time crammed with the memories of them.

It was the moment before sleep that I was dreading the most. That time when, lying on the bed, staring at the ceiling, thoughts settle like falling snow. When there is no conversation, no light, no screens, no cups of tea, no showers to distract from them. Just the unfathomable language of the house, creaking and clicking, and the black night pressed against the window panes outside.

The key was under a stone by the door, a jangle of metal treasure.

Two years.

Of course, the house wouldn't be the same. The stuff we had collected, the second-hand toys, children's clothes, books, bags of lentils, had all been cleared away. So too were Dad's things, ceramics, books, a fiddle – these were also gone, rehomed, binned or boxed away. Kirkhoose was home to someone else now – a tenant. She was away so the house belonged to me for two weeks.

The light was low, so unlike Captain Partridge the angry black-backed gull, I did not see my double taunting me from the glass door. A dark thought intruded into my mind: If I knocked, would someone – or something – answer? There was nothing for it. I pushed the key into the lock and turned.

The entranceway still had the earthy, almost granular smell I remembered, but the familiar photos and plates were no longer on the walls. There was no bowl overflowing with hats, scarves and orphaned gloves; and none of our shoes were in the cupboard. I dropped my bags in the hall. The heating had been off and it was really cold – although I had never been hardy in low temperatures anyway. Flicking on the kettle, I rummaged in the cupboard for a tea bag and then had a look around.

The living room was now home to a piano, and the bookcase was rammed with titles that despite being mostly unfamiliar, looked like the kind of thing Dad would have enjoyed reading, even the ones in Cyrillic.

I had first come across Jen Stout on Twitter while we were living in Voe. She was a journalist working for Radio Shetland, a native of Fair Isle and with a strong interest in Russia. This impressive woman was also, I was to learn later, a keen grower of kale and maker of sauerkraut.

'I'm renting a holiday let, have to leave in April for tourists,' she wrote in a message to me on Twitter shortly after we had left Kirkhoose and returned to Devon. 'I'm so despairing of finding anything to rent that I might leave.'

I'd heard this anecdotally from a lot of people in Shetland. An increase in interest from 'sooth' following the pandemic (people armed with cash and a strong desire to live somewhere rural, quiet and beautiful) and a lack of affordable housing stock mirrored the plight of many rural communities across Britain. I'd been to more than one village in Cornwall where the local shop only opened in the summer, the pub had closed down, and the buildings lay lifeless until the owners appeared in the holiday season.

The idea that the rental crisis could force a talented reporter to leave her homeland nipped me as I wrestled with my own conscience. At a time when young people couldn't afford to stay on the islands, did we have the right to claim a piece for ourselves? While I lamented the loss of local journalism, if I made the wrong decision, would I be actively participating in its further demise?

As soon as I asked her if she wanted to move in, I knew it was the right thing to do. This would be her base, her home. She prepared the ground in the ruins of Green Knowe and planted kale, weeded the strawberries and dug in potatoes. Scrolling through her photos on social media loosened thoughts of different shapes and textures; while it was heartening to see life continue at the croft, part of me felt left behind, even jealous that she was there and I was not.

In the time since we had left Shetland, the world had changed too. No more masks, no more lockdowns, no more free lateral flow tests. There was something else: a war in Europe, displacing millions, killing thousands. Jen, with her language skills and attachment to the people of Ukraine, was in the country reporting on it. She didn't need the house. It was all arranged, she even lent me her ageing Nissan, Ronnie.

While Jen and I were heading in different directions across the globe, our stories were connected.

As a major supplier of natural gas to Europe, the Russian invasion had shifted the balance of two of the pillars[23] holding up the energy system: security and affordability. The crisis had brought into ever-sharper focus the need to move away from oil and gas and invest more in renewables, like wind. The role of renewable energy generated by and for the community had never been so important and it stoked my desire to get the story of the Viking Energy wind farm.

While the kettle exhaled into the quiet room, I searched

---

[23] The third pillar in this so-called 'energy trilemma' is environmental sensitivity.

the cupboard for a suitable mug. But as my hands hovered over Jen's crockery, I found myself resisting the selection. In a sudden movement, I was walking out of the kitchen, into the hall and back outside again, key in hand. In the workshop I unlocked doors, felt for light switches. At last, on the cool dusty shelves of the loft, I found what I was looking for: one of Dad's cups with curled handles and Bernard Leach-style commas. Ten minutes later I had returned to the dining table and was sitting with the freshly scrubbed cup between my hands. Already the house was beginning to feel warmer.

12

Listen

Sound waves are what happen when motion displaces particles in a solid, liquid or gas, making them vibrate: like a fist thumped on the table, the tide coming in, a digger claw dragged across peat or vocal folds rubbing together.

Humans are very skilled at finding patterns and deciphering codes, like mapping the stars to navigate sea and land, or heeding a warning from a raingoose about a gathering storm. But sometimes we train ourselves so well in the art of deciphering that our expectations drown out reality.

My interpretation of one particular conversation changed very much over the course of time. It took place on a clear and still day in June, 2019. Dad had recently moved into the newly built Kirkhoose, and we had come to visit. He had less than a year to live, but we didn't know at the time that he was even ill. I'm not sure why I decided to record him; there was no news agenda, no deadline or commissioning editor. I had a vague idea that I could do a radio story about Dad's return to the croft, with the pair of us discussing its history as we walked around. Even if no editors were interested in running it, the recording would be a nice thing to keep for Esme. In the end, instead of a story about his return to the ancestral croft, I would write about his unexpected departure.

As we walked together, I heard in our voices a strained awkwardness: his irritation at my constant questions, my annoyance when he would suddenly wander off to look at a bush or tree that he'd planted. During these moments, the space Dad had recently vacated would be filled with the surrounding environment – sheep baas and whooping curlews – while I gritted my teeth, perhaps resentful that I was no longer the focus of his attention.

I kept the recording of Dad talking about the croft on my laptop and forgot about it. That was, until seven months later, trapped by lockdown in February 2020, when I was sitting on the edge of the camp bed upstairs in Kirkhoose. I scrambled with the mouse, desperately hoping I hadn't deleted the file. Then with a shudder of relief, I found a folder: 'Dad talking about croft'.

Play

'My Da was a great fan of anything that had an engine . . .'

Stop.

I could feel myself calming down, as if his voice was arms wrapped around me, but I couldn't listen to more than a few words. When my breathing had regulated again, I wiped my cheeks and closed the laptop.

It wasn't until years had passed before I could open the file again. This time I had a different purpose in mind. I would transcribe our conversation and use it as part of my research into the wind farm.

Transcribing a recording can leave me feeling like an

interviewee has held me hostage in their head. I listen with deep concentration to the intimate sounds of their voice: a thin stream of white noise released between tongue and teeth or a hum held behind pursed lips. My thoughts stretch around each word, every vowel and consonant, every conversation marker and cleared throat. The sounds reverberate in my skull for hours afterwards.

So it was when I transferred Dad's voice into a script in an electronic document. Something else happened too. Since our walk through the croft, so many things had changed: a global pandemic had shrunk our worlds to the size of a room and then back again. It had forced me to fill the space Dad had once occupied and then close the door behind me and say goodbye. As I listened to the recording, the susurrating grains and grasses from that afternoon in 2019 evoked different feelings in me. They whispered of calm evenings; pushing Esme in the wheelbarrow; a stroll on the moor; chats with a neighbour after a day's work, Captain Partridge knocking on the front door. I was no longer the same person who had walked next to Dad those years ago, holding the microphone, trying to read his body language and stressing about his responses. Now it was as if I was in the breeze buffeting around him, free to imagine sounds of the past he evoked with his stories.

Pause / Rewind / Play / Pause

I didn't pick up what I had been expecting: tension, awkward pauses, irritation. What I heard was the sound of ripe fields by the sea and a cheerful conversation between a father and his daughter.

*

'My Da was a great fan of anything that had an engine so he was into cars and stuff very early on,' Dad says, his long-legged strides disturbing the greenery. 'He had a part-time taxi so that meant he met a lot of folk.'

'And you said he built that waterwheel on the stream to create electricity?' I ask him, holding the microphone close enough to his face that I can capture his words clearly.

'Yeah, I think he spotted that the waterfall down there was ideal. When there was a lot of water coming down it would go round the second one. It's a good drop. It meant you could get in there with your concrete and make piers for a waterwheel to sit on. At some point he got hold of an old mill wheel. How the hell he got it there I have no idea. It was about a twelve-foot-diameter wooden wheel. Just after the Second World War when it wasn't that easy to transport things like that. So they must have actually rolled it from the road down to the burn with enough helpers to do it by hand.'

Pause.

The rolling and creaking, the shouts as the wheel picks up speed over the rough ground. What did they shout? Get out of the way, hold on, keep going?

Play.

'It must have been quite a sight,' I say.

Dad chuckles.

'Yeah. The neighbours helped. They did little test runs. Apparently Mam had been out one night; when she came back she discovered Da and one of our neighbours had actually sawn up all the spoons and made a kind of model waterwheel to figure it out.'

We both laugh.

'They got a lot of ex-Second World War stuff, all the wire would have come from Graven where the RAF station was. Since Da was in the RAF, he was stationed there so he would have known where everything was and [got] first dibs on the stuff. Oh, look, there's a frog!'

Dad's voice grows fainter as we bend down to look. He points to some movement in the vegetation.

'Just there,' he says, but the frog had gone.

We're walking again.

'I didn't know he was in the RAF,' I say.

'He was a driver, mechanic. He was amazingly lucky because he spent a lot of it here. He was home. Apparently the generators were out of old Catalina flying boats. There's a long shed at the house there,' Dad says, pointing to Olnagarth, the house across the road from Kirkhoose, where he grew up. 'The far end of it was a kind of Dr Frankenstein workshop with these big switches, you know the ones, flash, bang. Lots of dials and meters and things.'

'Brilliant. So what did it power?'

'They had the house wired up for lights. That was really the big thing. Before anything else, people would get lights.'

We are walking across the road now, and Dad is examining the embankment.

'I just spotted that broom there, see the broom? We planted that a year or two ago.'

The flowers of the gorse-like plant are a pinkish red colour, unlike the usual yellow.

'So lights were the biggest priority. In the days of oil lamps

– just a revelation, switching on a light. That would have been in the late 1940s.'

'Before you were born.'

'Before I was born, yeah. There were various other gadgets as well. Mam had a clothes iron for instance. It was hard to regulate, you know, the flow of electricity. So if there was a real rainstorm, and the wheel was working, it was going flat out. So they had to keep the lights going all night and switch everything on that could be switched on to absorb it all.'

Pause.

The sound is thunderous as the sky empties its weighty burden onto the land. The radio blares, and all the lights in the house burn through the dark.

Play.

We continue to walk and talk, our exclamations and laughter punctuated by the deep, vibrating calls of the sheep in the neighbouring fields.

Stop.

Rewind.

Play.

' – just a revelation, switching on a light.'

*

It was this line that stood out, bright and significant, and I listened to it over and over again. It seemed to act like a marker in my story, a clue as to how all the different pieces might fit together, and where my journey might be headed.

13

Wha Is Du?

Cut the trees to burn the wood for energy.
Dig the bogs to burn the peats for energy.
Hunt the whales to burn the oil for energy.
Drill the seabed to burn the oil and gas for energy.
Convert motion from wind into energy.

The car lurched and creaked over the potholes like a boat at sea. This had to be it, although the directions were returning from my memory a bit mangled with the effort. Go past the two wind turbines on the hill, keep going north until you see the sheep crö and wheelie bins by the roadside. Lots of trees.

The turbines were easy, masts rising out of the hilltop, but I had no idea there'd be so many mature trees around here, so many sheep pens and so many wheelie bins. I had turned right at a crossroads marked by a lonely telephone box. There had been no time to wonder why it was there, or the many calls that may have been made from it on this road. I was too busy deliberating over the right – or left – way to go.

My first few days had been spent visiting relatives and settling in, checking messages and making calls. My calendar filled with dates and locations, a dot-to-dot picture I hoped would make sense by the time I boarded the ferry home. In the weeks before my trip I had called Frank again, and he'd given me a list of notable characters in the wind farm debate: a balance of 'for' and 'against'. Over the course of my stay, this list would expand to a collage of players in ecology, history, business, farming, art.

Meanwhile, the news on the car radio was all about U-turns. 'Kwasi Kwarteng has resigned as chancellor of the exchequer,' BBC Scotland informed me for the third, or perhaps fourth time that day. Just weeks before, the mini budget had reignited fear that fracking could return to the UK, and they were lifting the seven-year moratorium on onshore wind projects. I wondered what the latest news from the turmoil in Westminster might mean for that, and how it could ignite the political will to invest in the infrastructure needed to accelerate the transition from fossil fuels to renewable energy, but I needed to concentrate so I turned it off.

The track ended and I pulled the car into a short gravelled drive. Through the glass door I could see fresh paint and masking tape on the walls. This place, the home of one of the most influential actors in the story of the Viking Energy wind farm, should have been more impressive somehow, with more character – perhaps some colourful timber cladding and painted rocks outside the door. This one appeared still to be under construction. There was a static caravan opposite and

I could see a shadow moving about inside. With a pang of nerves, I knocked on the house door.

Drew was a former director of Viking Energy, the company set up on the Shetland side to partner with energy giant SSE on development of the wind farm. He was also a local councillor during the crucial years of the project's history. On the 'Who We Are' page on the Viking Energy website, information about the structure of the company is illustrated with a photo of three men shaking hands over a pile of papers – 'signing the partnership agreement at Busta House in 2007'. His short clipped beard is fading to grey on the chin and his glasses look slightly tinted. He wears a green tweed jacket and dark tie as he leans across to shake the hand of the SSE chairman on his left. In another photo I found online he is in the same jacket, but at an angle where his left ear is visible – he wears a gold earring.[24]

'I will be delighted to talk, Marianne, and certainly entirely on the record,' was the reply I received to my Facebook message. 'I knew your Dad well at school. He was in lodgings near mine and I sang in the choir with your granny. Let's sort a time and you can come to wirs for a yarn.'

And so, as I stood outside the static caravan waiting for the door to open, I prepared myself to cast on a new thread in the story.

The man standing in front of me was a lot taller and younger than the image I had in my head.

'Hi, I'm looking for Drew Ratter.'

'Who?'

---

[24] https://www.shetnews.co.uk/2013/08/01/viking-energy-health-impact-report-welcomed/

'Drew Ratter?'

'Oh. No, you've come to the wrong house. You need to go back down the road, keep going past the phone box and turn right at the trees.'

Ah. I'd gone the wrong way at the phone box.

*

The beard was greyer and bushier, but the Drew who answered the door looked very much like the man in the 2007 photo. He'd forgotten I was coming.

'Come in, come in,' he insisted as I attempted to take off my boots at the door.

He led me into a room with floor-to-ceiling bookshelves and a collection of toy trucks and building blocks on the floor.

'I went to primary school with Bill's cousin' he said, arranging himself in a large armchair in the corner. I took a seat in a squeaky leather one opposite him.

'And as I said, we used to sing in the church choir in North Mavine, your grandmother and my mother and various people over the years were in that. We sang mainly Sankey hymns – famous American evangelists. Good, rousing songs.'

I could imagine him having a powerful singing voice.

The thought took me back to a time sitting next to Mam in the small parish church in Brae, sucking a boiled sweet, while around me the space reverberated with song. It was a scene reminiscent of one by Haldane J. J. Burgess, a celebrated nineteenth-century author from the isles.

'In the singing of the women you could hear the echo of the

breezes that had blown in from the North Sea in the spring . . . and in the men's voices you could hear the roar and rumble of the sea'.[25]

I liked to sing too, and had belted out a slightly flat version of 'Abide With Me' in that same church nearly two decades later for Mam's funeral.

'Anyway, you are here to know how Viking Energy got started.'[26] Drew's cheery matter-of-fact expression pulled me back to the present. We were both sipping glasses of water. I already regretted not asking for a cup of tea.

Drew had been on the council at the time the idea of Viking Energy started to germinate. It was 2003 and he was chair of development when local businessman Angus Ward approached him with a proposal to create a large community wind farm on the islands. Angus was one of the men behind the Burradale wind farm – the collection of turbines on the hills behind Lerwick.[27] Burradale was relatively small, serving Shetlanders only. With this new project, it was clear the two men were thinking big right from the start. They wanted enough turbines to generate a volume of electricity that could be exported to Scotland 'to make as much money as possible, which the community could then, through its various constituents, make up its mind about what it did with it,' he said.

---

[25] *Tang: A Shetland Story* by Haldane J. J. Burgess, 1862-1927.

[26] For a very helpful timeline on the history of the wind farm, I recommend this Shetland News article: https://www.shetnews.co.uk/2024/09/03/short-history-viking-energy-wind/

[27] Shetland has a local grid – around 1,650 km of overhead lines and underground cables, run by grid owner SSE.

I'd been warned that Drew could be a bit of a fidget – almost as if he had so much energy that he needed to be doing lots of things at once to avoid blowing up. Living up to his reputation, he wheeched out his phone and there was a brief pause while his fingertips tapped away at it. At last he put it aside and looked up.

'To begin wi', we put £10 million in to facilitate development,' he said. 'We always knew we wouldn't be able to complete it without a utility partner of some kind. Not with something of this scale.'

'What kind of scale were you looking at?' I asked him.

'Something in the region of 240 megawatts.'

That was big. With one megawatt enough to supply around 1,000 homes,[28] that surpassed by twenty times the needs of the islands' ten thousand or so households. It had to be this productive in order to justify the cost of building the undersea cable that could export this energy to Scotland. So what about this utility company? Ahead of our meeting, someone had told me that Viking Energy's relationship with SSE started in a toilet in Inverness, but further details were sketchy. I was curious to know what Drew would share with me.

'Well, I was on the board of the Highlands and Islands Enterprise back then and we had the chief executive of SSE speaking to us for something,' he said. 'Somehow or other we found ourselves washing our hands in the toilet together and we just got talking. That was in Inverness. I was really impressed.'

---

[28] https://www.nrc.gov/docs/ML1209/ML120960701.pdf

So that was the famous toilet scene. I imagined Drew catching sight of the other man in the mirror and seizing the opportunity to talk business over the sound of the trickling taps. He gave the impression that chances did not often elude him.

'So, anyhow, we were discussing how best to go about this. I invited him to come to Shetland so we could talk it through and so we did. He said what we should do is form a fifty–fifty joint venture, which was fantastically unusual for a company on that scale.'

The plans were set in motion at a council meeting in 2010, when members voted to approve a 127-turbine wind farm.[29] It was a date that was to go down as a landmark in the project's history. Despite a sixty-nine-page paper from the council's own planning department recommending that the project should not be approved, councillors voted in favour by a majority of 9:3. As well as the planning department, the RSPB and Scottish Natural Heritage had raised concerns about the project and the impact on fragile bird populations.

'Did the project address these concerns?' I asked him.

'They were addressed, but I'm not close enough to the fine details. I'm always a helicopter-view kind of guy, strategic rather than detail,' he replied.

I would need other people for the 'fine details'. I recalled

---

[29] The original consultation was for far more. In 2008, Aaron Priest, project manager of Viking, was quoted in the *Guardian* as saying: 'We consulted on 192 wind turbine sites last year, but were always going to reduce that. We're now down to about 155.' In 2010 Viking reduced the figure again after 'making changes to address concerns.' http://shet.news/z393a

the name Jonathan Wills on my list of folk to speak to. He had also been a councillor at the time and had attempted to get his colleagues to vote against the project as the move could have triggered a public enquiry. I'd been warned that he was 'quite a character'. I wondered how he would compare to Drew.

'Do you think a public enquiry would have helped to—' but Drew cut me off before I could finish.

'I know what you're going to say – no.'

I laughed. 'What was I going to say?'

'You were going to say "would it have helped to unite the community"? No, I do not. I think the people who were hostile to it – it would have made no difference whatsoever.' He drummed his fingers on the table. 'It can only be my opinion.'

'Well, that's why I'm here, for your opinion.'

'Well, it's that.'

The mobile phone perched on the glass table by Drew's elbow emitted a tinkling tune. Drew snatched it up, his face faintly illuminated by the screen.

'Oh, can I take this? It's important.'

He wanted to get a heat pump installed through a government loan scheme.

'My hope is to get it for very little,' he said, after he hung up.

I sat back with a scrunch into the leather seat and considered what I'd just heard. So the plan had been that SSE Renewables would share in the profits of the wind farm along with Viking Energy LLP – a joint venture between Shetland Islands Council and Angus Ward's wind farm business, Burradale. SSE would construct a 600MW undersea cable for the energy to be exported to Scotland and would also provide other technical expertise. For their part, Viking Energy would lease the land on which the turbines would be constructed. Once the wind farm was up and running, a community benefit fund of £20 million would be dished out across Shetland for the maintenance of the arts, sports and other activities currently supported through the oil fund.

Further south, the rotating blades of the Burradale Ladies turned on the hills behind Lerwick, like the enchanted spinning wheel that spins straw into golden thread. There was another harvest, one that ended while Drew was growing up. An old way of life that was difficult to imagine now. Yet these two eras still had things in common.

*

It is Andrew Smith and his crew who first spot them, out near the island of Mousa. Around three hundred pilot whales cut the surface of the waves with their fins, exhaling streams of water from their blowholes. Here is a promise of food, of light in the winter and money from selling the blubber for oil. It is autumn 1888, a time of poor harvests and hunger.

Men and boys wade waist-deep in the shallows, which billow with clouds of red. Into the churning water they thrust peat-cutters, shovels and knives to pierce the flesh of the thrashing bodies. Smattered with blood and tidelines of salt, they plunge their white-cold fingers in again to drag the corpses to the beach. They take their knives and in an orgy of blood and flesh, separate the blubber for oil, and the meat and the bones. All will be used at home or sold at auction for a celebratory sum of £450.

There is a problem. He is John Bruce Jr, the laird of Sumburgh, a man 'detested' by most crofters. This is his land, and if any money is to be made from living here, he will demand a cut. Lairds in Shetland have 'immemorially claimed as their right a portion of the whales stranded or brought to the shores adjoining their lands'.[30] It is a custom of immense antiquity – established before Shetland was ceded to Scotland by Norway in 1468 – that when a pod of whales is called in to the shore, the landowners will claim a third, or even half, of the profit. 'They got it because we had to give it,' says L. Robertson, who was a tenant in Hillswick on the Busta Estate in 1838 when a pod of three hundred whales was chased onto the beach. 'Possibly it was through fear. I suppose if we had objected to giving it, the proprietor could say we could leave the property, and we had nowhere else to go at that time.' Because of this 'right' to claim the profits, Bruce Junior takes the fishermen to court.

This is 1888, a time of poor harvests and hunger – but also of agitation. Just two years before, Scotland passed the Crofters Act, part of which advocated for fair rents. It is an act which frees peasants across the country from the tyrannies of tenancy. It has emboldened them against other injustices.

So here they are at the Court of Session in Edinburgh when the Lord Chief Justice proclaims his judgement: not guilty. 'While the custom is distinctly proved,' he says. 'I hold it also

---

[30] https://www.casemine.com/judgement/uk/5a8ff81a60d03e7f57eba14b

to be provided that it was not the outcome of a consenting community, but a practical tax frequently protested against and submitted to, not willingly but as a choice of evils.' It seems to him a thoroughly one-sided arrangement, in which the proprietor received a great deal and gave practically nothing whatever in return.[31]

Whale oil burns brightly and doesn't smoke. After whaling is banned on local shores, ships take Shetlanders to Greenland and South Georgia where the crew scale the mountainous corpses with pickaxes and ropes. They hoist the body up by the tail, and using knives, flay the flesh of blubber for processing into oil. The Antarctic industry is artificially prolonged by the Second World War. It's a hard and dangerous life, but good money.

Forty years later, and folk took a different view.

'A lot of people said they couldn't live without whale products, but we can,' said John Adise, recalling stories from the whaling industry in an interview in 1984.[32] Even then, people knew we could change our habits, even the habits of lifetimes.

Where was this 'consenting community' when it came to harvesting the wind? How could such fruits be divided amongst them, and if the people whose ancestors lay composting in the soil did not want such a farm to be built – what then?

*

[31] https://paperspast.natlib.govt.nz/newspapers/ST18900729.2.23
[32] https://www.tobarandualchais.co.uk/track/88330?l=en

By the time Drew was a young man in the 1970s, a different kind of fuel was being extracted from the depths.

Shetland's entanglement with fossil fuels had started to gather pace amid the race to discover oil and gas reserves in the North Sea. Among the spoils was the Brent oilfield, one of the biggest, located to the north-east of Shetland. Like many other fields owned by Shell in the area, it was named after a type of seabird, the Brent Goose.[33] Situated in convenient proximity to all this activity, the islands offered a convenient place to transfer the liquid gold, which travelled via pipelines from oilfields and was then transported onto tankers and shipped across the world.

For a far-flung community of fishermen, crofters and knitters, this was to be a dramatic change in fate, and Shetlanders were quick to make the most of it. In 1976 a deal was brokered with the oil industry over the building of the terminal.[34] The council was allowed to negotiate directly with the companies using it, and to keep the fees. A fund was set up to administer these substantial oil monies, managed by the Shetland Charitable Trust.

I could measure the impact of the deal on my own family in swimming strokes.[35] In Dad's day, growing up in the fifties and sixties, children rarely learnt to swim because there was only the sea to swim in, and as that was pretty cold, the prospect wasn't terribly appealing. But by the time my cousins were

---

[33] https://www.snsbi.org.uk/Nomina_articles/Nomina_32_Young.pdf

[34] https://web.archive.org/web/20110608075859/http://www.bp.com/
liveassets/bp_internet/globalbp/STAGING/global_assets/downloads/U/
uk_asset_sullom_voe.pdf

[35] I realise this is a bit of a cliché when it comes to describing Shetland's relationship with oil, but there you go.

growing up in the 1980s, there was a flashy new swimming pool in many villages and school lessons meant you had to learn whether you wanted to or not. For children around my daughter's age, the third generation of bairns to enjoy the bounties of the oil boom, the snazzy playparks and leisure centres remained in good repair. The Clickimin Leisure Complex, named after a broch on the outskirts of Lerwick, ranked among my favourites. There were so many things to do (including a 'river-rapid ride' with geysers, airbeds and water cannons), I almost never got around to actually swimming.

There was an end in sight, however. Oil production was drying up and the council had realised that their bonanza would not last forever. One source of energy was showing no sign of running out – wind – and councillors started to eye renewable energy as a possible source of income. But the wholesale price of electricity is hard to predict, as it depends on the price of fossil fuels, as well as factors like the weather, currency movements and political events. In 2007, when Drew was smiling for the camera at Busta House, the price of electricity was £31 per megawatt hour. A year later that had jumped to £70.

Government subsidies, known as Contracts for Difference, support businesses to navigate this volatility. Renewable generators apply for a contract by submitting a bid to an auction. The first one ran in 2014. At the beginning, Drew told me, the people behind Viking Energy were confident their bid would win and so ensure juicy financial returns on their investment. In 2012 then energy minister Fergus Ewing gave Viking the go-ahead to build 103 of the turbines, dropping twenty-four of them following objections from the owners of Scatsta oil airport.

'If we'd got going when we were supposed to and completed by 2012, the Shetland Charitable Trust would probably have sold half of its immensely valuable share,' Drew said.

As well as reaping the dividends from the remaining 25%, selling the rest would have enabled the trust to make further investments in the community.

It was not to be. Closer to home a storm was brewing. Sustainable Shetland had mobilised and was preparing to challenge the decision on the legal stage: first a judicial review, then an appeal, then an appeal against the appeal, which the wind farm's opponents lost.

Viking emerged victorious from court, but the drama had sent the project off course. Drew said that the delays caused the project to miss out on an array of government subsidies. By the time the wind farm finally received the official thumbs up, 'there looked like a notional return on capital of 2%,' he said. 'SSE decided to proceed at that.'

So faded the dream of a fifty–fifty partnership that 'would have made Shetland Croesus-rich'.

The wind farm backers were 'bitterly disappointed, obviously'. But the £10 million investment was still worth the returns, especially with the price of power as it is, he insisted. 'On the whole, we're in a much better place than we might have been but we're certainly not where we could have been. Try speaking to Angus because he has a very good understanding about the nuts and bolts of this and was very grieved about it all,' Drew said, his fingers tapping an impatient beat on the table again. 'I mean, I was grieved about it but you can't take any of this kind of stuff personally, you just move on.'

His remark made me think of a buoy out at sea, always bobbing to the surface regardless of the strength of the waves.

Drew left public life in 2017 'to do stuff I want to do'.

I noticed again the toys scattered across the floor: a glimpse of his life behind the public platform.

'Our grandchildren and their father live with us,' he added. 'Maisie is four. We lost our daughter when Maisie was born.'

There was a brief pause while I considered the enormity of what he had just said.

'But anyway, that's just one of these things that happen,' he continued. Now retired from politics and business, he was 'outside' the key decision-making for Shetland, but he maintained 'good connections'. And that, he said, was where we were today.

Where we were today – the morning's news broadcast replayed in my mind. As well as the political turmoil on the front benches, there were rising energy costs and grocery bills. Judging the state of the road ahead, we needed to be buckling in for a bumpy ride. This knowledge that prosperity was a precarious thing was never far from the surface in Shetland.

'We could actually become poor very quickly,' Drew said when I raised this. 'I'd actually quite like Shetland not to. We had five thousand years of poverty. We've only had about fifty years of prosperity and we'd very much like that to continue.'

Drew was born in 1952 and grew up on a hillside in Ollaberry, near where we were sitting now. 'We got electricity when I was about six,' he said. 'But we were too high up on the hill to get enough water to have a bathroom. We just had a cold tap which sometimes dried up in the summer.' His father was 'able at all sorts of jobs', working on the road as a foreman and other things. His mother worked on the knitting machines.

'Do you remember the transformation when the oil came? How quick was it?' I asked.

He stretched his feet in front of him and sighed. 'I always say when I'm tour guiding: in 1974, everything changed.'

*

When the men return from the whaling, deep sea fishing at the haaf, or the merchant navy, their sea legs not yet acclimated to the still of the land, this is where they come. When the herring boom's gutter lasses[36] finish work, their aprons glittering with scales from the silver darlings, the croft is home.

Croft work is hard work: looking after the beasts and the bairns, knitting, cutting peats. A bit of fishing, a bit of labouring. While the men are away, women are in charge. The kettle is always by the fire, the beasts inside or outside depending on the season. Everyone is in the same boat on a croft, dried fish and reested mutton hanging from the rafters. A picture of life for centuries.

These squat stone buildings are hard to keep homely: the taekit roofs and the peat fires need tending. The soot is sticky, a black stour that touches everything. Inside, the two rooms are dark and smoky. The 'but' end where the family sleeps in wooden bunks and cooks on a griddle over the fire, and the

---

[36] https://www.shetlandarts.org/our-work/past-projects/refresh-now/a-life-of-wir-choosin

'ben', where they entertain guests. These buildings are not a crofter's property, not assets; there are no title deeds. When a family leaves, another moves in. This is the crofting life, where money has little meaning.

Later, in 1974, everything changes again.

The oil is here, and with it jobs. Jobs piloting tankers into Sullom, jobs at the camps where thousands of workers need to be fed and their lodgings kept clean. Crofting people are used to hard work, and now they have jobs for money. In Ollaberry, Drew's sister buys the family's first colour television. In Brae, one man tells a reporter from the New York Times about how 'the money culture is getting its grips on Shetland' and how some of the traditional way of life will go.

'We're really being rushed into the twentieth century in a mad scramble,' he says.

Crime has never been a problem on the islands before, and people are worried the workers will cause havoc with that. Now folk turn their keys at night. But change is coming whether people like it or not.

'What is out there is so big, so vast, so important, it could never have been resisted. It's far too important,' the man adds, portentously. 'This is Britain's economic salvation.'[37]

Now people are too busy for crofts, cold and small, that sit on the ground and suck the damp and chills up into the walls and the soles of your feet and your blood and your lungs.

It's a dying life, the crofter's life.

---

[37] https://www.nytimes.com/1974/11/09/archives/north-sea-oil-to-transform-the-shetlands-economic-salvation-north.html

*

'Do you think the community itself has changed since the oil came?' I asked Drew.

'Well to some extent it changed and to some extent it didnae. People here, rural people, are still intensely social, if we're speaking among ourselves. For example if we meet someone, we'll say "well, wha is du?", meaning "well, who are you?" "Oh, yes, yes, you're so-and-so's daughter and so-and-so married such-and-so".'

It wasn't as if people were asking who you were exactly, but where in the Shetland family tree you belonged, he said.

'We like to maintain those networks in our heads. There's nothing in any way hostile about it. You just want to place people.'

I thought of this like a mycelial network of roots spreading across a map of Shetland, tiny threads intertwined around each other. There was Dad and Mam, and there was Drew.

'You know about Shetland folk, they just talk about people the whole time,' Drew added in his straight-talking way.

Much like the rest of Britain, folk might talk about you, but they would be unlikely to say anything unpleasant to your face. For the most part this seemed to work out fine, but the wind farm appeared to have disturbed this etiquette. What was it like, I wondered, when one of the most important actors in the making of Viking like Drew bumped into someone deeply opposed to it – say, in a small shop or a pub? Would there be harsh words and raised fists? Or would this rage be pushed under the surface, suppressed with tight lips, a frown or cold nod? The latter seemed most likely. As a child I had always found Dad's reluctance to express his feelings openly very frustrating.

'If I meet them in the Co-op or Tesco we always speak exactly the same as we always did,' Drew told me, referring to 'some of the most vigorously hostile people' who were against the wind farm.

In fact, he went on to say that he didn't believe Viking had divided people in the way some said it had. One close friend of his, he said, was 'almost dementedly hostile' to Viking, but it had made no difference to their relationship. It wasn't a view that fitted easily with the expensive court actions, angry opinion pieces in the newspaper, and the passionate comments that continued to accumulate on Sustainable Shetland's Facebook page.

I wondered what Drew might say about me after we waved goodbye – to his wife and other folk on my wind farm to-meet list. I needed him to introduce me to other actors in the story.

We rose to our feet, a bit stiff with sitting still for so long, and he chatted about a retreat on Fetlar that he wanted help promoting in a good newspaper. It was not the kind of writing I did, but as I stepped out of the door I could hear myself saying in a tone very similar to that of my father, 'Oh right, well, that's interesting' instead of giving an outright 'no'. We would need to meet again after all.

Outside the house, my ears met with the electronic beeps and trills of a flock of starlings. There was a small murmuration which congregated around Kirkhoose, shape-shifting their way around the bay. I loved their irreverent chatter – particularly one bird behind the ruined croft that liked to practise a very convincing imitation of the neighbour's barking sheepdog. The birds gather like that as a form of safety in numbers, outmanoeuvring hungry predators like peregrines with their collective aerial stunts. If one bird went missing, how might this affect the choreography? Did starlings notice when a member of the flock died or joined another group?

It reminded me of something Drew had said.

"Community' is a very fraught word,' he'd told me in his upbeat, scratchy voice. 'To me, the only definition is a group of people that if one of them disappeared, they would be seriously missed.'

That was a nice way of putting it, but what else was woven into this 'community'? The whales, the raingoose, the gossiping starlings – what would happen if they disappeared?

The road led back along the hill, along the edge of the glittering sea. The front tyre met the flattened corpse of a rolled-up hedgehog. I thought of the network of threads connecting people on the isles and I knew it was far deeper and more intricate than I could imagine. If someone asked me 'wha is du?', and heard my answer, what kind of pattern would they see?

I held these thoughts in my mind, trying to organise them as if looping yarn over knitting needles. I had an understanding now about how the wind farm had taken form, but Drew's view on how the project had impacted the community had taken me by surprise. Was there really no long-lasting division? I needed to speak to someone from the other side of the debate. For that I would have to pay a visit to Busta House.

14

Bodies

It wasn't the contents that took me by surprise: the parcel tape, screws, some useful-looking elastic bands and a nest of other odds and ends. It was the smell. Shortly after Dad's death I had been looking for a pair of scissors, and decided to poke around in an item of furniture I hadn't yet paid much attention to: an old sewing machine table. I tugged open the ornamental handle. The drawers were quite shallow and there were no runners so it took a bit of shoogling and noise to get the drawer out without jamming it.

The strong scent caught in my sinuses, triggering almost tangible memories: the mild irritation of a scratchy woollen jumper against my face, the cold seats of Dad's van, a saucer brimming with the soggy ends of crushed roll-ups. I knew the source and rummaged through the assorted things to find it. There it was, a wooden bowl and plastic mouthpiece, the same shape and size as every other pipe he'd smoked. I picked it up and sniffed it, recoiling a little at the smoky acridity. Staining the sudden rush of childhood memories, I remembered the phlegmy cough and shortness of breath that presaged his hospital admission and, later, the diagnosis. So many things existed in this small brown pipe, so pleasing in its rounded form, so deadly in its effect: comfort and pain, protection and dread.

The X-ray showed two lumps, one in each lung, tell-tale clusters of cloudy whiteness like inverted shadows. Stage four. Soon it was painful for him to lie down, to walk, to move at all, even to breathe. At last he got an orthopaedic bed. Morphine. Oxygen mask. When the nurse said he might have six months he sounded relieved, but the end came only a few weeks later.

Cancer was not the only alarming presence on the X-ray. There was another shape too, ghostly and dangerous. It could have been his heat-resistant gloves, protecting against the thousand-degree temperature of the kilns. It could have been the lining of the kilns themselves. All those times he poured his imagination into moulds and thumbed cup shapes into clay on the wheel, the fibre-like dust of asbestos had entered his body, irritating the lining of his lungs and causing scarring.

As I'd looked at the X-ray, I couldn't help thinking about my own flesh and organs. All those moments I breathed in particles disturbed from the floor of the workshop, burrowed my face in his plaster-stained jumper, inhaled the tobacco fumes that failed to escape through the crack in the car window. I wondered about those moments and whether Dad's work and his rollups had left a mark in my own body.

*

Noise = unwanted sound

'The frequency, complexity, and meaning, as well as the loudness of sound all have implications for how noise is perceived.'

from 'Report on the Health Impacts of Wind Farms Shetland 2013' by Dr Sarah Taylor

Play
    Rustle of a plastic packet.
    Scrape of a disposable lighter.
    Sook to inhale.
    Puff to breathe out.
    Pause
Listening again to the tape, these sounds are like props in a theatre: the gun over the mantelpiece in the opening scene.

*

'We explored ideas related to our pain, and the visible devastation of the landscape,' Roxane Permar told me, spreading strawberry jam onto a buttered scone.

'We considered the complexity of pain, the many kinds of pain and how it is variously felt. Through writing, film and image-making we sought to find ways to articulate this while engaging in processes of mending and healing, treating the scars in the landscape left by human violation and destruction.'

Roxane was an American artist who, after her first visit to

Shetland in 1985, had become hooked on the place, prompting her to return every year for extended periods of time. I'd come across her work through a blog by climate charity Platform on the Viking Energy project and the exploitation of the wind as a source of private, not common wealth.[38] She was describing the creative process behind a project called 'Landscape in Pain' for which she had printed postcards of the construction site of the wind farm, lines of red traffic cones stretching across the fields like rough medical stitches under a smoky sunset. The scarred contours evoked a sense of loss and grief. 'How can we achieve sustainability in our lives, and leverage renewable energies, without causing harm?' she asked.

Part of the reason I had been drawn to her work was that she had been inspired by her own recent experience of grief. In 2020, the same year Dad died of lung cancer, Roxane's mother was dying of dementia. She used to go to Philadelphia four times a year to see her mother in the care home, but Covid restrictions had meant they could only communicate via video link.

'I watched her die on FaceTime,' she told me.

She couldn't invite me to her house so we decided to meet at Busta, a former stately home now serving as a hotel and restaurant. We sat at right angles to each other on small upholstered sofas. An electric-pink bulldog clip held up her fluffy white hair, a stylish brown cardigan complementing the colours.

---

[38] https://platformlondon.org/2022/01/18/cambo-viking-energy-the-common-wealth-of-wind-in-shetland/

'What do the cones represent to you?' I asked, pouring tea from an elegant metal teapot that tended to spill its contents over the table if you were impatient with it.

'They symbolise the intrusion of humans in the landscape, kind of like blood,' she said. 'It took a long time to get right because it was really difficult to take a photograph that carries that change that I felt.'

For Roxane, the system of roads and turbines required for the wind farm constituted a violation of the environment. She wasn't bothered by the structures, despite their monumental size, but she was concerned about the sound of the blades as they turned.

In response to a request from the charitable trust, NHS Shetland had published a study on the health impact of wind farms in general, which showed 'a clear relationship between the level of noise and the proximity of houses to wind farms', according to local media. That was in 2013, but Roxane didn't feel Viking Energy had paid proper attention to it. Intrusion of sound had driven her out of London in the 1980s, seeping up through the floorboards from the takeaway pizza restaurant downstairs. Like many incomers to Shetland, the artist had come here seeking peace and quiet.

Wind farms create sound both through the mechanics of the turbines and the movement of air over the blades. As well as sound, there were other health-related issues that she worried about. One of these was the flickering effect as the 55-metre blades disrupted the flow of sunlight, and also the pollution of microplastics released into the air through the wind's erosion of the blades over time. She felt Viking Energy had not adequately addressed these concerns either and so she was organising a series of lectures from the authors of some recent research to raise public awareness.

The title Landscape in Pain immediately evoked a feeling that this was a living landscape, rather than a remote wilderness untouched by humans.

'I love the Kames, the main construction site of the wind farm,' she said. 'I get really angry with the folk who think it's empty, bleak. It doesn't matter what happens to it. It's full of experience and history that we can't imagine.'

The Kames are three parallel valleys that pass through the centre of the Mainland. The main road, the A970, follows the middle one. According to the Viking Energy map, this is where a line of eleven wind turbines will stretch. The turbines would transform the wind into energy, which would flow through a capillary-like system of cables to the converter station and then under the sea to Scotland.

Unlike Drew's stories of the tough crofting life, Roxane's relationship with the landscape was more spiritual. Before she moved to Shetland and started a job teaching at the University of the Highlands and Islands in Lerwick, she would make regular visits to the isles. On one of these trips she discovered her favourite place, a ruinous Bronze Age burial cairn on the island of East Burra. She described coming upon the collapsed cairn one evening in August. I could imagine the kind of light she might have encountered, low and warm, drawing sharp shadows onto the dips and rises of the hills around. In the centre of the cairn there was a pinkish granite stone that 'glowed in the dusk', Roxane said, her soft

Pennsylvanian accent occasionally clipped with the hint of a Scottish vowel.

'One of the things I felt very deeply there was that connection with the past, the human connection,' she added. 'It was built by people thousands of years ago, and it gave me a sense of being part of a continuum, just kind of passing through; there's so much between the Bronze Age and now. I just loved that sense of thousands of years being visible, the physicality being concrete and tangible I feel is important, I love that.'

In a zip-portfolio bag with a handle, Roxane would pack an A1 drawing board with sheets of thick etching paper taped over the edges to stop the wind from snatching it away. With this she would head to her favourite place in Shetland to draw. To the south she could see Fair Isle, in front of her East Isle and West Burra. On the left were the Clift Hills.

As she talked, I wondered if over the millennia folk had used the cairn to tell the time, or navigate their boats into land like the characters of Basil Anderson's poem 'Old Maunsie's Crö'.

Roxane took a sip from her tea. 'But in the future, if you look north, you will see the Viking Energy Wind Farm turbines because even though they are relatively far away from Burra, they will, I'm sure, be very visible.'

By gouging roads into the fields and inserting kilometres of cables, were we indeed inflicting 'pain' on this living system, or was this naive anthropomorphism? Was my visceral response to Roxane's postcards a deep-felt empathy with the land, or more of a projection of my own experience of loss? Were these two separate things?

According to Drew Ratter's definition, a community was 'a group of people that if one of them disappeared, they would be seriously missed'. What if the community extended beyond people, encompassing the sky, the sea and the land itself? What if we were all part of one living organism?

I leant back in my chair. Connection with the past was important to both Roxane and Drew, but through different lenses – the more spiritual contrasted with the pragmatic. Only the latter could make room for the wind turbines. Even so, there seemed to be a remarkably solid common ground between two such opposing views. Where they diverged was that Roxane wanted to protect the landscape by conserving it, whereas Drew was open to changing it so the hardships of the past could not revisit the inhabitants of the future.

There was another tangible monument to Shetland's history, but this one more recent, and we were sitting in it. It was Busta House itself, a symbol of oppression and tragedy, and now a fancy hotel. Its presence represented some of the opposing forces that seemed to constitute the Shetland identity (and many more places besides) and that was the relationship between laird and tenant.

Busta House

'There an old saying, Professor Jones, in Shetland, that were just two nights aa da the year when the Shetlanders slept well. And that was the night that he

was able to pay his rent to his laird so he couldna evict him on rent arrears. The other night was when he had tekkit [thatched] his roof.'

George Gear speaking to Prof. Michael
Jones and Venke Olson in 1986

To read reviews and articles about Busta House hotel, you might think the building was alive. It is described as 'charming', 'romantic' and 'proud'. Each of its twenty-two rooms have 'individual character' just like the smaller, now-uninhabited Shetland islands after which they are named. Under the whitewashed integument, the granite stones and stuffed armchairs exude personality. It is the oldest inhabited house in Shetland, home to a ghost and a large collection of whisky.

The windows of the hotel offer a complicated view onto the world. The fanciest room is Linga, where the laird once slept. It is around three hundred years old, has a dark wooden four-poster bed, sea views, tasteful blue upholstery, and costs around one hundred pounds for the night. Further south, the isle of Linga also has a price tag. At the start of the pandemic, the island went up for sale for the same amount as a two-bed flat in London – 'perfect for anyone looking for a fresh start'.[39] Exchange one property for another – in this case an entire island. An 'unspoilt' location, according to agents. The blank windows of the derelict cottages on the island tell a different story.

-----

[39] https://www.countryliving.com/uk/homes-interiors/property/news/a2969/linga-west-shetland-island-for-sale/

In Busta's Long Room, where shoes thunk on the shining wooden floor, the dim lighting is homely and intimidating, just as every stately house should be. Two portraits face each other over the distance of the room, hanging over opposite fireplaces. One, with a powdered face and wig and a soft jawline, is Thomas Gifford. As principal merchant of Shetland in the mid 1700s, he extracted value from his tenants through woollen hosiery, salted fish, butter and animal oil. As magistrate, he wielded power over them through the law. Lady Busta, Elizabeth Gifford, looks younger, with a smooth, high forehead and arched brows. She 'could bear no contradiction from no-one, but she was a bright woman', said one woman who knew her.[40] 'Her appearance commanded respect from everyone.' This room is the heart of the house, the portraits of the Giffords like two ventricles pumping energy into the inanimate structure. Lady Busta was in her late teens when she married and over the next nineteen years gave birth to fourteen children of whom five died of smallpox. Only one child outlived her.

They were six men: the man hired to handle the boat, the four Gifford sons, their cousin and his dog. They disappeared after rowing the boat across the voe on a Saturday night, likely for a dram or two. The accident – if it was an accident – left no heirs to the estate. The eldest man had fathered a son, but no one could figure out if he had married the child's mother before his sudden death. The scandal set the course for the fate of Busta House to eventually leave Gifford hands several generations later.

---

[40] *The Story of Busta House* by Marsali Taylor.

Photographs display the house's more recent influential connections throughout history: retired major Sir Basil Neven-Spence, second owner of the house after the Giffords.

In 1975, a year after Basil's death, the Shetland Islands Council bought the Busta Estate for £200,000 for possible oil-related developments, according to the *Shetland Times*.[41] Since then, it has run the day-to-day affairs of the estate, like rent collection, and hired private lawyers to deal with legal transactions. In 2024, it will be the location of eighteen Viking Energy wind turbines. Perhaps it would be fitting if here, on the walls of the Long Room, hotel staff added another photo, that of Drew Ratter in his green tweed posing for a photo with SSE chairman Sir Robert Smith as they signed off the Busta House Agreement. Frozen in time, their cheery handshake would become a gesture that would change the course of Shetland history.

The Coffin

Around five months before Dad died, another funeral took place in Voe, but this time the coffin itself was empty: physically empty, at least, although the space inside was bursting with symbolic meaning. I'm glad I wasn't there in person, only reading about it years later in online news articles, because even from that distance, I wasn't sure what to make of it.

---

[41] https://www.shetlandtimes.co.uk/2010/02/17/review-ordered-into-management-of-council-owned-crofting-estates

The day looked cold, calm and overcast. Around a dozen people gathered for the procession, many reflecting the low light in hi-vis jackets: four lugging the box between them on poles strung with ivy, and two holding a banner saying: 'Extinction Rebellion, Rebel for Life.'[42]

I can imagine the feeling, nervous and alert, as they walked the five miles down the A970, along the ridge of hills called the Lang Kames: the banner pulled tight as they stepped over the uneven ground and the metallic rush of traffic as it sped past. As public opinion seemed so divided over the wind farm, not all the passers-by would have been sympathetic.

When the XR funeral procession reached Lower Voe, they turned off the main road and followed the sharp bend to the pier. Here, they set down the coffin and got busy setting blocks of wood for a pyre.

'We have walked together to show this land how much we love it and that we will do all that we can to protect it,' one organiser, Pete Bevington said, his hand tucked into his black waistcoat pocket. 'Let us hold a vision in our minds of an energy future for Shetland that does not involve the desecration of nature of which we can all be proud.'

One mourner sang a song, another read a Ted Hughes poem, another played the fiddle. A spark was struck, hands held the breeze back from the kindling, and slowly flames began to dissolve the coffin's varnished veneer, sending a plume of black smoke into the air.

---

[42] This was a local branch of the global (but decentralised) XR movement.

The gathering was a Lament for the Lang Kames, and the coffin represented 'all that will be lost' if the wind farm went ahead. The group supported renewable energy projects which would cause 'the minimum amount of harm to the land, its wildlife and its people,' one report quoted Bevington as saying. The strong insinuation was that this did not include Viking.

The 'funeral' took place before Viking had won the Contracts for Difference auction and the future of the giant wind farm was still in the balance. Bevington had settled in Shetland thirty-one years earlier, after falling 'in love with the wild landscape, the lively, hospitable people with their dry sense of humour, the powerful community spirit. The sheer energy of the place,' he wrote in a piece for the *Shetland News* ahead of the Lament. At first he'd welcomed news of the wind farm 'to remove our dependence on a dirty power station in Lerwick', but then the familiar concerns over the vast scale of the plan, and a perceived lack of community engagement turned him against the project.

'It feels as though Viking Energy has brought nothing but grief into our lives – so much anger, so much frustration, so much division even among environmentalists like us. It's incredibly sad,' he said.

For the protestors, the coffin not only represented the life of the land, but was also a container for people's anxieties over what the future might hold. Burning it was a therapeutic act to heal the rift. If I had driven past or seen the funeral from Dad's window, I can imagine myself telling relatives about it afterwards and all of us displaying some of our own dry sense of humour, reinforcing our familial ties with shared suspicion of outlandish forms of self-expression.

Just down the road, the final touches just coming together, the latest residential adornment to Lower Voe – Kirkhoose – stood shiny and new on the hillside. At the time of the coffin's funeral, however, Dad was not at home. In September 2019, he was wrapping up a trip to see us in Southwest England. In the space of just a few days, we walked along an old china-clay quarry run by the Devon Wildlife Trust and spotted a great-crested grebe on the aquamarine water. We watched *Avatar*, three adults and a toddler squeezed onto our two-person sofa, and remembered with horror the upcoming sexy scenes – too late to turn it off. We heard news of my maternal grandfather's death and went to the pub together to toast his memory with a whisky. It was the first time I could remember going to the pub with Dad for over a decade. He stopped for rests and took naps, but I didn't think much of it. He coughed, but I blamed it on his pipe-smoking. We laughed and he had to clutch onto the side of the chair to recover his breath. I see all the clues now, but back then, they passed me by.

On our last walk together his breath rasped, and he couldn't go further than the entrance to the woods. He said he had to get back to his house in Shetland and left Devon early. My chain of thought went like this: he was bored of our company so he'd gone home. I didn't know that when he got home, he would drive himself to hospital to receive treatment for pneumonia and an X-ray would reveal a shadow.

Just a few months later, I was with a relative in the family undertaker Goudie's choosing a coffin. Dad would have liked the pine one with the pale blue lining, she said. I let her make the decisions as I really had no idea what he would have liked. I asked the undertaker if I could see the corpse. 'I'm not sure I'd recommend it,' he said. Dad's body had been in the boat to Aberdeen and back again for a post mortem. There would be a strong smell, discolouration. He wouldn't look like himself.

It was clear to me even then why I was disappointed. Viewing the body would have meant a degree of ownership, a last experience. But Dad had never been mine. He belonged to other people. I had solved the problem by moving abroad, far away from the politics of family life. I spoke to him around once a year when I returned for a visit. Our physical distance masked an emotional one that stretched halfway across the world and back.

In his final weeks, a relative nursed him. She made sure he was taking the morphine and checked the oxygen tank. She watched him as he stared out of the window, the low winter light glancing off the new contours of his face, while dark shades filled in the hollows. She fed him kale soup and watched him chew, sprays of stock seasoning his beard. She found his body and called the ambulance. The morning after he died, I watched her pour the contents of the soup pot away into the garden as if she were emptying her own heart out with it. That was when my envy turned in on myself – a sharp and shameful feeling. Though hard to admit, I was jealous she had seen and touched his body while I had been eight hundred miles away preparing to take Esme to forest school.

There was one comfort, in a folder on my computer, kept safe behind a password. I still had his voice. While someone else could listen to the words and imagine his lips moving, the conversation would only ever be between him and me.

15

Running Out of Time

There was no path so I followed the fence up the hill, disturbing a red grouse, a species introduced here in the early 1900s so folk could shoot at it. It had been raining and dips in the fields were waterlogged. I'd already sloshed once into the ice-cold water as far as my ankles, a sensation that provoked me to yelp with surprise into the valley. There was no one else around, but I knew people could see me if they wanted to. In my yellow running jacket and bright blue trainers, I was easy to spot from the houses scattered around these exposed slopes. I may have already been in someone's eyeline and they may have already been wondering what on earth I was doing.

My answer, if anyone had asked me, was that I was on my way to explore the top of the Lang Kames, the line of hills just visible from Kirkhoose. Between our departure in 2020 and my next visit in 2022, the colours and contours of the scene had remained the same save one very prominent detail: the arrival of a silvery trail on the distant hills. This was one of the maintenance roads that would serve the turbines on the northern edge of the wind farm – the top of the vertebrae.

I consider myself to be relatively fit, but thirteen hours of sitting on my arse in a variety of vehicles on the 800-mile journey to Shetland, plus a rough night on the ferry, had taken its toll. Pushing myself up the final incline, I was knackered. Up on the hilltop and away from the shelter of the valley, the wind immediately slapped my face, punishing me for my audacity in climbing so far.

Fences sutured the patchwork of fields, angular divisions between fertilised grassland, heather and bog. On the tops of the hills was the common grazing, where neighbouring crofters were allowed to leave their beasts to fend for themselves. The sheep up here were tough, sheltering against the peat banks to protect themselves from the worst of the briny wind, giving the animals the alternative name of 'woolly maggots'. The hags, whipped by the elements, formed tunnels and islands in the soft ground, with drying-out heather and other vegetation desperately clinging to the hems. It was here amid the quiet freshwater lochans that the raingoose liked to hang out. Long ago it had been covered in trees, until those earlier inhabitants of the islands chopped them down for fuel.

On first sight, the strange patterns that look like creases in a blanket give the landscape an otherworldly quality. But rather than being wild and untouched, deep peat hags like this are a sign of environmental degradation. Healthy peat bogs, which are made up of layers and layers of decaying sphagnum moss and other plant life, need to stay wet in order to store carbon. By pressing the sphagnum moss, sheep hooves can squeeze the water out of the sponge-like structure, leaving the bogs vulnerable to drying out. This sorry state is also a result of climatic pressures, the salty air whipping layers off the top over the years. Instead of being a carbon store, the landscape becomes a carbon emitter, releasing the gas into the atmosphere.

I had to climb down before I could climb up again, and in the absence of a path I often found myself bouncing down the heather with the wind only to find myself at the perimeter of an impassable pool or sloppy peat. I would gasp for breath as I had to retrace my steps with a face full of weather.

The grass shone like filigrees of silver in the low autumn light. Back down the slope I could see the burnished metallic ribbon of the Olnafirth. The change in terrain happened suddenly as I clambered over a small peaty cliff. There it was, the wide pale road that would service the wind turbines. I jumped over the ditch, leaving my footprints in the churned black soil. A green trailer of some kind was propped near a circle of rubble, around two metres in diameter. Whatever was inside the circle was covered over with a white tarpaulin, creating a stunted cone shape. I realised this must be the base of one of the turbines. Everything was quiet. It looked like a massive layby.

For the first time properly that day, I began to run.

It was pleasant to let my feet go without worrying about hidden holes or tussocks that might damage my ankles. The surface gave slightly and did not feel as jolting to my joints as tarmac. There were no vehicles coming my way. This was a Sunday, and the road ahead looked very quiet. I passed diggers on either side, frozen for the weekend, seemingly in mid-motion as they scraped the construction rubble into piles. I saw great wooden cable reels that looked like a giant's sewing kit, and, at times, on a stretch of the road not yet covered over, lines of the cables themselves encased in plastic tubes, reaching under the ground: green, yellow and black. Claw marks of diggers scarred the soupy brown peat.

It wasn't until I turned around that I realised how windy it had become, like a giant hand pushing me back along the Kames away from Kirkhoose. To be up here in the full force of the elements was to experience 'the sheer energy of the place', as Extinction Rebellion activist Pete Bevington had said. To survive, humans have made the most of this energy, metabolising it in many different forms. To feed their bodies, Shetlanders have consumed the landscape in the form of kale, mutton and fish. To warm their homes, they have burnt peat. So why not harvest the gigantic energy of the wind? But any harvesting can be problematic. For a waterwheel they needed a war to provide the necessary parts; for whale oil you need lots of dead whales; for fossil fuels you release dangerous volumes of carbon, poisoning ecosystems from rainforests to oceans. So what would be the cost of wind power – destruction to peatlands, impact on house prices, disruption to the breeding sites of rare birds? Would this transaction be worth it?

Even though I was going downhill, running against the weather was hard work. My thighs burned and the nail on my big toe was pressing against the end of my shoe. It would probably be purple by the time I reached the house. I enjoyed this kind of pain. Tearing new fibres in my muscles, growing new toenails, it was a kind of metamorphosis. Through movement, I could make my body release hormones that would stabilise my mood and ground me, shielding me from the relentless hammering of anxious thoughts. But out here, it wasn't the release of serotonin or cannabinoids, or my brain shutting parts of itself off to conserve energy that quieted my mind. This energy was not inside me. It occurred to me that in this landscape, where the sky scrapes the earth, it was not my body, or any human force that was the main driver of change. It was the wind.

In *The Great Derangement*, Amitav Ghosh describes the 'moment of recognition' of the power of the non-human. Such moments are not a discovery of new information, but the sudden understanding of suppressed knowledge. They can occur during natural disasters, as when a village is washed away by floods. They can also be evoked by (or respond to) incremental human-induced disasters like air pollution as our struggling sinuses and lungs remind us that our bodies are as much part of the landscape as everything else. This recognition is an experience of the uncanny. With knowledge of the climate crisis and what it means for future life, for example, a hot day or mild winter can suddenly become menacing.

As the gale whipped tears from my eyes, I caught sight of a gull in flight, struggling to return inland. Our mutual exertions were juxtaposed for a moment, as the wind bent the gull 'like an iron bar slowly', as Ted Hughes once wrote,[43] then flung it away. As I battled up the hill, the roaring gale

---

[43] In his poem 'Wind', from *The Hawk in the Rain* (Faber and Faber, 1957).

drove understanding into my head: the wind was not a prop in this tale, it was the protagonist. It was a moment in which, as Ghosh writes, 'it dawns on us that the energy that surrounds us, flowing under our feet and through wires in our walls, animating our vehicles and illuminating our rooms, is an all-encompassing presence that may have its own purposes about which we know nothing'.

Like earthworms and kelp, humans are ecosystem engineers, dramatically changing the environment and impacting other species around them. Unlike kelp, however, humans cut down rather than create forests, and we compact and pollute soil instead of aerating and nourishing it in the way of the earthworm. Our influence has become, for the most part, destructive and this human-centric epoch, the Anthropocene, is an age of mass extinction.

As I reentered the pathless peat bog on my way back to the house, I paused to look back at the top of the line of hills and the turbine bases. The valley was filled with prescience, a living space where the turbines themselves would reach into the sky. I imagined it like an installation in a gallery, an exhibition of human arrogance: of a culture which commodifies the landscape, and believes it is the only real agent in the story.

My leggings were soaked up to my shins by the time I got back to Kirkhoose, and I had to lean against the wall to peel off my wet socks before going into the hall. The house itself was still and warm, a striking contrast to the gale outside. There was the familiar earthy smell of wood and coffee. I staggered to the dry room to have a shower and caught sight of my face in the mirror. It had a slightly skinned appearance, bright red and shiny with white rings around my eyes like a scarlet raccoon. But it was my hair that gave me the biggest fright. I like to keep it as low-maintenance as possible, with a short style that generally just needs a smoothing of the palm. The wind had blown it straight out like a brush, creating a wild and cartoonish look I'd never seen before. This was not the kind of transformative experience I had planned and I felt like the butt of a joke, as if the wind was reminding me who was really in charge.

16

On the Doorstep

Standing outside the door, fist raised.

This space – between preparing for an in-person interview and the interview itself – is often separated by a knock. The sound marks a shift in cognitive gear: from the nervous anticipation of what the meeting will hold to a more strategic pattern of thought (both in the present and two moves ahead, a bit like a game of chess) while the real-time information gathering takes place.

This moment is a chance to take a breath, often literally, after the rush of getting to the place on time: to pause and clear my mind.

My return trip to Shetland had been punctuated by many knocks on front doors across the Mainland. This stood in contrast to my visits to relatives. As I discovered early on, I was not expected to wait outside. I was simply to enter, announcing myself as I stepped over the threshold. Once I had done so, there would be a flurry of activity and soon I would be seated on a chair with a cup of tea on my lap. (I still did not have the courage to arrive completely unannounced, and would always ring ahead to make sure they knew I was coming.)

Although this existed in stark opposition to the life I lived down south – where folk mostly turned up at allotted times and texted when they were on their way – it was just a remnant of what I imagined the neighbourhoods were like when Dad was young. When I had asked Drew Ratter about what Ollaberry was like when he was a child, he'd told me people would spend the evenings visiting each other.

'That's just what everybody did,' he said. 'When I was a kid, I don't think there was any house in Ollaberry where we used to knock on the door first. You just wandered in. There was very little of this intense notion of privacy that has developed in recent times.'

I had certainly noticed while living in Voe that far more people seemed to know what we had been doing compared to back in Devon. From putting out washing to pushing the wheelbarrow to the shop, folk would be paying attention. It was ironic that keeping yourself to yourself is far easier in a town or big city than in a rural community. Drew had questioned whether the wind farm had disrupted this equilibrium, but others disagreed. One person I met had found an outlet for people's views on the doorstep.

When Moraig Lyall chapped on doors in her neighbourhood in the central Mainland of Shetland different things might happen:

No one would answer.

If this was the case, she would post her leaflet through the letterbox and walk on.

The door opened.

A hand would extend to take the leaflet and a voice would say: 'Thank you, goodbye'. The door closed and again, she walked on.

A conversation.

The door opened, a hand would extend to take the leaflet. The voice said: 'Thank you' – and then – 'Now, what do you think about the Viking wind farm?'

'I would say, "well I don't think it's a good idea, it's going to be such a monster on the horizon",' she told me as we chatted at a smart café in Lerwick.

This had been when Moraig was canvassing for election as an independent candidate at the council election in late 2019, just around the time Dad had received his diagnosis. She didn't think she'd get in, imagining that people would prefer to go for a Shetlander, rather than someone who had been living in the isles for only seven years. But the result proved otherwise. Since then she had become well known in the local papers as a vocal opponent of the wind farm. Despite her firm stance, by the time she was elected there wasn't much she could do about it. The energy consents unit had already given permission, and in July the following year, the interconnector received the green light too. Within months, construction work had begun.

A lot of people didn't think it would ever happen, she said.

It was only when they realised it was that they felt they needed to do something, but by then it was too late.

'And being so publicly against it, did you receive any kickback? Did it affect your personal life at all?'

Moraig had a very intent grey-blue gaze and I could see her turning the question over and over in her mind to examine it from every angle.

'I think there is a thing in the Shetland psyche that people are not generally very openly critical,' she replied. 'If they don't like something, they'll say nothing.'

I was evidence of this myself, I thought.

The criticism she received online had been along the lines of '"you just see this as a kind of twee holiday place, you're not focused enough on the fact that young people need money and jobs", and that's maybe true to a certain extent,' she said. Money and jobs: words hammered into the heart of the wind farm debate and beyond as the world discussed what our transition from fossil fuels to renewable energy should look like. People specialised in dirty fuel industries couldn't simply be dumped as their professions died out. A just energy transition would mean careers to replace the engineers, geochemists, managers, sales assistants and all the others who work with oil and gas to instead find employment insulating homes, modernising public transport and food systems to build resilience against global heating. As well as the security of feeding one's family, there are other things to consider when thinking about the importance of jobs. Instead of a linear economy founded on extraction, production and consumption, where workers are valued only through their capacity for furthering economic growth, we could have one centred on care: a focus instead on the nurses, teachers, social workers, unpaid carers whose work is currently so grossly undervalued. In *Who Owns the Wind?* David McDermott Hughes writes that to live within our environmental limits, we have to rethink our attitude to employment, away from earning leisure time and finding self-worth in our jobs. There should be provision (a livelihood guarantee) in such a transition for those who do find work or want to work, he writes: 'Perhaps, in order to relinquish fossil fuels, we need to learn to forgive ourselves and others for not working.'

Why should we challenge the idea of endless economic growth? One answer is in our blood.

Growing, growing, gone

If someone drops a plastic water bottle off the coast of California, the current will take it south towards Mexico, and perhaps across the Pacific near Japan, and north and east until it is pulled into the swirling gargantuan mass that is the Great Pacific Garbage Patch. This area, too big and too deep for scientists to trawl, chokes life and threatens ecosystems.

Many forms of plastic do not biodegrade. They simply erode, breaking up into smaller and smaller pieces, tiny grains known as microplastics. Construction, manufacturing, drainage, packaging, insulation – while the industrial use and individual consumption of plastic continues unabated, we can only imagine that garbage patch swelling and swelling and swelling until . . .

But the problem goes beyond the sea. Plastic is so infused

into the food chain it can be found everywhere, in the soil, the rain, even the air we breathe. Recent research has found microplastics in human blood, breast milk and placentas.[44] 'What pearl forms around a grain of plastic in an oyster? / Is it as beautiful? Would you wear it?' asks poet Elizabeth Bradfield ominously in her poem 'Plastic: A Personal History'.

> Would you buy it for your daughter
> so she in turn could pass it down and
> pass it down and pass it down?

*

Fingers together, straight, strike the water like a propeller, pulling through the water – each stroke marks the speed of change. Stronger, longer, faster through the years.

One man gets a boat with a covered deck, the first in the isles; it holds the sea back from filling the vessel and dragging her down with all hands. She can take a few hundredweight of fish per catch. By the time he retires he part-owns a trawler that can take home 250 tonnes of fish in a day.

*

This is one purpose of global economic development: making a perilous profession safer and more comfortable for those living

---

[44] https://www.theguardian.com/wellness/article/2024/jul/09/microplastics-health-crisis

it. This model also makes things bigger, more powerful, pulling more fish out of the sea to feed people and industry across the world. In Shetland fishermen now 'are doing what they think is a sustainable level', Moraig continued, 'but there are foreign boats coming in with these huge gillnets that are kilometres long and basically just entangle everything in their path.'

We'd seen evidence of this along the shores of Voe – nylon threads enmeshed with stems of bladderwrack and kelp.

A common topic when debating the pros and cons of the wind farm was the idea of wildness: the appeal of being somewhere that is not obviously dominated by humans.

'Shetland is somewhere where the natural world has been allowed to maintain a fairly strong hold,' Moraig said. 'The wind farm is going to change that. Folk say there's nothing up there, no one goes there. Sure, you'd rarely meet anyone else up there but I think in some way having places in the world where there's nothing there is important.'

By 'nothing', she meant minimal human interference. For previous generations of Shetlanders, these pathless and remote areas were more than that – they were places where you could die of exposure or drown in a peat bog. They were places of unknown terrors, trows and njuggles waiting to lure people to their deaths. Now, in a world measured by the profits of industry, it was 'nothing' because it had no economic value. For others, who treasured it for the diversity of life that thrived there, it was everything.

But 'wildness' could not survive this era of 'global boiling'. We had to replace extraction with regeneration – and to do this we needed renewable energy. Where, if not the wilderness, would we put the solar panels and the turbines we need to survive?

17

Bird Scarers

Sustainable Shetland's Facebook avatar is a raingoose sitting on the water. In the photo, it stares off to the right, over the head of a fluffy chick, whose black eyes look intently outwards. The parent's expression seems alert and protective, unaware of the distant camera lens.

After floating to the surface, the memory of my conversation with Dad about the wind farm a decade before in his Glasgow flat had never gone away. I returned to it again and again, trying to decipher it from different angles. He had seemed worried about the scale of the project and the rupture it was causing in the community – concerns which had brought him and Frank together. This was in my thoughts as I headed into the rain on the way to Frank's home, where I was also to meet Billy Fox – chair of Sustainable Shetland from 2008 to 2012.

*

A winged shape tugs and flutters in the wind. The size of the body, the length of the tail and pointed head are designed to ignite adrenaline, fear and flight. Potential prey will see the shadow and swiftly change direction, away from the nesting grounds of their ancestors to safer plains. Relentless, hawkish, it patrols the air. But unlike the peregrine and the merlin, the territory of this raptor is only a few inches, tempered by a mooring, a long string that holds it tightly to the ground. It jerks and pulls at its tether that when the wind is fierce threatens to snap. Then it will lift free, into the atmosphere and out of sight.

*

'They are allowed to put bird scarers in to stop the birds nesting, imitation hawks. They have these things on the ground, rotating things, flashing, a significant number of them. I couldn't believe it,' Frank Hay said. By 'they', I assumed he meant the wind farm construction workers.

We were in his sitting room, a soft, cosy space tightly insulated from the weather, his appearance exactly as I remembered from our first meeting at Kirkhoose two years before. Sitting next to him was Billy Fox. He was a few years younger than Frank and was also very neatly turned out. Billy had been reluctant to speak to journalists but Frank had convinced him to meet me.

When I chapped on the door, Frank greeted me with an armful of historic correspondence published in the local newspapers over the years. He also had a folder of official letters with information about the court cases Sustainable Shetland had brought, and some copies of Viking's first public relations material titled *Windy Lights*. As we chatted, he occasionally flicked through the documentation, drawing out this or that paper to show me. It was as if he needed to prove every point he made with additional sources.

'It was in the construction procedures to prevent the birds coming in,' Billy said, referring to the bird scarers. 'It's similar to what they do down south, they net the hedgerows.'

Hedgerow netting is a barbaric practice. In England it is illegal to destroy or damage a bird nest that is in use or being built. To bypass this, some developers have taken to covering hedges or trees with vast nylon nets to prevent birds nesting there, in one swoop destroying habitats for ever-dwindling bird populations and introducing harmful plastic waste. The sight of a hedge strung with nylon netting is a symbol of all that is wrong with our attitude to the natural world.

'It was a very rich area,' Billy said. 'The red-throated diver, whimbrel and many other ground-nesting species like merlin, curlew, grouse, golden plover, dunlin, skylark, meadow pipit.'

I knew the skylark – the tiny bird that parachutes in the air over moors and farmland. In Shetland and out on the Dartmoor hills in Devon, the cascade of chirps from high up in the sky heralded the start of spring. Billy's list was an inventory of treasure.

'And the reason it was rich was because few people went there,' he continued. 'This is the thing that really gets me. The fact that people seldom went there made it a haven for birds.'

For myself, bird scarers were a familiar and benign sight in allotments to protect brassicas from pecky pigeons and in farmland to stop seagulls and starlings from taking seeds. Out on the unfurrowed peat bog, for Billy and Frank the connotations seemed more brutal: to separate birds from their nesting grounds. I asked them how it made them feel, but I could guess their answers.

'Angry and disappointed,' Billy sighed. 'I had spoken with the RSPB and NatureScot about this practice and they said they could do nothing about it!'

'Resignation,' Frank said.

For Billy and Frank, Viking Energy had intruded not only into the landscape of their ancestors and childhoods, but also into their personal lives. When Billy was chair of Sustainable Shetland, he said, he had his identity stolen, the fraudster adding him to online groups he 'never would have joined'.

'There was an awful lot of quite nasty letters that appeared in the local press at one point,' Frank said. 'Unpleasant is what you might say.'

Both men first heard about the wind farm through reports in the local media. Initially concerned about the financial cost to Shetland, Billy wrote a letter to the *Shetland Times* in 2007. 'Viking never got back to me,' he said. His vocal opposition prompted other people to come forward with their concerns. In 2008, he and likeminded critics founded Sustainable Shetland. After chairing the group for its first four years, Billy left when he was elected to the council.

While Sustainable Shetland fired out letters about the wind farm through the local media and held public meetings, the folk behind Viking Energy were also doing their bit to win hearts and minds. Billy attended Viking's first public meeting, which was held in 2007 in Vidlin.

'It was quite a good attendance there,' Billy told me. 'The thing that came out for me was that they were talking about money the whole time, the income for Shetland. It was going to be the second Sullom Voe terminal. Myself and some crofters that came along started asking about deep peat and how they were going to deal with that. Viking Energy seemed surprised with these queries and it looked to me like they had given the peat little thought.'

'We were never listened to,' Frank added.

'Viking held four meetings, why did you feel you were never listened to?' I asked him.

'Because the majority of the people were opposed, about three quarters of the people who attended,' Frank said. 'There was no democracy at all. The people who were against it were ignored. During a protest demonstration the council convener stood on the town hall steps and said: "if the majority of the Shetland public are against it then it shouldn't go ahead": this turned out to be an empty gesture.'

'What should have happened then?' I asked them.

'That's the difficult question,' Frank replied. 'Many people felt that a properly conducted and independent referendum should have been held about the wind farm. That could have helped.'

At this point, Frank's wife came into the room carrying a tray. On it was a teapot, delicately patterned cups and saucers and a selection of biscuits.

After taking a moment to refuel, we returned to the wind farm. Part of the reason members of Sustainable Shetland were suspicious of Viking was how decisions were made at a local level. In two words: the council.

'Councils of old always got involved with everything that went on in Shetland,' Billy continued. 'If there was an organisation that was set up, funding, anything like that, there would always be a councillor involved.'

This began with the oil. Having negotiated their lucrative deal with the oil companies operating out of Sullom Voe in the 1970s, the Shetland Charitable Trust was set up to manage the funds. Councillors automatically became trustees on the board.

'The councillors of the day, particularly from 2007 to 2012, really wanted another cash cow and because this big wind farm was being sold to them, it meant that they didn't have to make big decisions about making cuts,' Billy said. 'They could sit on their hands and say "the wind farm is coming, we're going to be OK, boys". That was in my view where the councillors were coming from.'

I asked them if they thought the main reason people were in favour was because they believed it would solve the short-term economic problems.

'I think so,' Billy replied. 'I think the members of the public that supported it, that was their view. There was no green argument. If you look at the environmental argument, you simply should not be building wind farms on deep peat. I believe Viking Energy exaggerated the erosion of the wind farm area. There was serious erosion on the tops of the Mid

Kame and in Nesting but over towards Scallafield the peat moor and blanket bog was in pristine condition. In other words, the majority of the wind farm site was in very good condition.'

I remembered my run along the Mid Kames the day before and the deep furrows in the black ground. They ran maze-like, taking you off course and into syrupy pools of water. Preserving peat was such an integral part of Sustainable Shetland's argument, I knew I had to dig into the science to get an expert opinion on if and why disturbance to the ground was such bad news. I resolved to investigate it later.

We touched on the events of 2010, where around eighty people gathered in Lerwick Town Hall to hear the council's vote on whether or not to back the wind farm. Not long before, the local authority's own planning department had recommended councillors object to the plan on environmental grounds. But after three and a half hours of debate, with statements from supporters and objectors, the votes weighed in favour of the project. I imagined the large, echoey room stuffed with people and high emotions. If they had voted to reject the application, this would have triggered a public enquiry.

'Most people expected that a public enquiry would be called for anyway, such were the many issues surrounding the application,' Frank said.

It would be two years before Fergus Ewing, then minister for energy at Holyrood, gave the project consent, the number whittled down from the proposal's 127 turbines to 103.[45] Billy was standing for election at the time.

'I think possibly half, or the majority, of the council were not keen on the wind farm at all,' he said. 'But by the time we came in, consent had been given. It was done and dusted. That was when Frank and Sustainable Shetland took it to the judicial review.'

One of the first places I had looked when preparing for our interview was the Shetland media: the online version of the dead-tree press the *Shetland Times*, and the newer online news outlet *Shetland News*, both, in my opinion, serving the role of local media in a consistent and reliable way. As the golden days of local journalism were rapidly fading into the sunset for the rest of the UK, Shetland was lucky to have them.

'While the attention of many will be focused on Lerwick Up-Helly-A' next week, those gathered in an Edinburgh court room will have their minds on a different sort of Viking', Neil Riddell wrote in the *Shetland Times* in January 2013. 'Tuesday will be the first day of the Court of Session's judicial review of Scottish ministers' decision to grant consent for Viking Energy's controversial 103-turbine windfarm.'

Sustainable Shetland was challenging the Scottish government's decision to give Viking the go-ahead on the basis that the developers did not have the necessary licence

---

[45] Ewing was reported as saying: 'Developments like Viking will help us meet our 2020 target, and will make a huge contribution to our target of 500MW from community and locally owned renewable energy by 2020, while benefiting communities, cutting emissions, and helping to keep energy bills lower.'

as stipulated by the 1989 Electricity Act. They also argued that Scottish ministers had failed to pay proper regard to their obligations under the European Union's Birds Directive to protect the breeding grounds of the rare wading bird, the whimbrel. Once widespread across the country, the bird's call was imprinted into many different cultural identities.

Peerie whap

On some shores, she is 'may bird' and 'tang whaup'; she is one of the 'seven whistlers', seven birds flying together at night, and her high call, like a toy machine-gun, is said to foretell disaster.

She is a migrant, a summer breeding visitor. But here in the pools of the cool peat bogs this little speckled brown bird with long grey legs is peerie whap, the whimbrel. Here she will peck her long, pointed beak to pierce worms, shrimps and snails. Here, she and too few others of her kind will listen to the song of the circling male to decide if they will mate and raise chicks together. In a hollow in the lichen and moss they hide their eggs: smooth, speckled, delicate treasure chests.

Fledged, come winter they fly with a white 'V' thousands of miles over Europe to Africa. There, they are of Least Concern in their conservation status. They are still common, safe. Back in the spring to Britain, where they and so many other things with wings and feathers are listed as Red: endangered, in danger.

Swift: skeer devil, screacher.

Linnet: Furze bird, Blood linnet.

*Every year more and more face extinction: Now one in four in
this sad, dried up, dying country.*

Numerical terms

With 290 breeding pairs, Shetland is home to 95% of the UK's
whimbrel population. A rate of 3.7 are expected to die each
year because of the wind farm. In giving Viking the go ahead,
Scottish ministers accepted the loss of 3.7 whimbrel per year
due to habitat disruption. The number was small, they said,
and must be considered in the context of 72-108 annual deaths
from other causes, including predation.

*

The EU directive on Wild Birds states:

> The preservation, maintenance or restoration of a
> sufficient diversity and area of habitats is essential to the
> conservation of all species of birds. Certain species of birds
> should be the subject of special conservation measures
> concerning their habitats in order to ensure their survival
> and reproduction in their area of distribution. Such
> measures must also take account of migratory species and
> be coordinated with a view to setting up a coherent whole.

Member states 'shall take the requisite measures' to maintain
these populations of birds at a level 'which corresponds in
particular to ecological, scientific, and cultural requirements,

while taking account of economic and recreational requirements, or to adapt the population of these species to that level.' For the Scottish ministers, the climate targets outweighed the 'obligation' of maintaining the whimbrel population.

In her lengthy judgement at the court, Lady Clark said she was 'not satisfied' that the Scottish government ministers had complied with their obligations under the Wild Birds Directive. She also found that the developers did not indeed have the necessary licence as stipulated by the 1989 Electricity Act and that 'all parties accepted that this development could not be "operated" without a generation licence'. It was the first time a judicial review of a wind farm in Scotland had been upheld. As the papers reported, it was a 'major victory' for Sustainable Shetland. The court ordered Scottish ministers to pay the group's legal expenses.

'We are heartened by today's outcome, which reflects months of hard work by all concerned,' Frank Hay said in a news report of the time. But the celebrations were short-lived. Ministers did not agree with Lady Clark, and later that year, the government headed back to the Court of Session in Edinburgh to appeal the decision. This time, they won.[46]

---

[46] Around the same time, on the Scottish mainland, another legal battle against wind turbines was being played out, this one involving a pre-presidential Donald Trump. In 2013, Trump started an unsuccessful legal battle to challenge the Scottish government on a decision to build a 'monstrous' offshore wind farm near one of his golf resorts, a controversial project in Aberdeenshire. Trump International's arguments included the failure to hold a public enquiry, and not having the necessary licence as stipulated by the 1989 Electricity Act. He even attempted to become a party to Sustainable Shetland's Supreme Court appeal to support their case, but was rejected. Trump's court cases sprawled over several years, with the wind farm generating its first power in 2018. For some fascinating details

Faced with a 'last chance saloon' to stop Viking, at a meeting in Bixter Hall in Shetland in 2014, fifty of Sustainable Shetland's 800-strong membership voted unanimously to appeal to the Supreme Court in London. In a disappointing ruling for the group, the court found that ministers did have due regard to improving conservation of the whimbrel.

Sustainable Shetland's 'last chance' was over.

'With hindsight, we really didn't have much chance of success at the Supreme Court but it seemed to be our only hope,' Frank said.

'I wasn't involved in that at all,' Billy added. 'I think at the last meeting I attended I was very sceptical about going down the legal route. By that time I was elected as part of the council.'

Both Frank and Billy went quiet.

'You must have raised a lot of money for the legal action,' I said.

'At the end of the day it was in the region of £200,000,' Frank replied. 'That was coming from just the local folk. There were old-age pensioners putting in four-figure sums. There were nearly a thousand people who contributed something. Sustainable Shetland had something like eight or nine hundred members—'

'—it was the largest organisation in Shetland ever,' Billy interjects. 'There are political parties or what have you that couldn't come near that.'

_____

involving former first minister Alex Salmond and a cheese plate, I recommend this article https://www. scotsman.com/news/environment/ defeated-donald-trump-turns-his-back-scotland-1545278

For a community in which strong feelings are generally not expressed in public (at least in my experience), contributing funds must have seemed a safe way to support the cause. To donate life savings, as Billy suggested, would have been a big sacrifice for many people.

'Certainly it was a concentration of people who live near the wind farm,' Frank said.

I looked up at the rain-lashed window. The weather had cast a gloom over the late morning. I had an image of Frank in a few years' time sitting with a cup and saucer on his knee, looking out at the hills. What would the view reveal? Not the wind turbines, at least not from this room, he said.

'But from the kitchen window at the back you'll see the ones at the north end of the valley. They were going to have a borrow pit on the hill there but decided against that.'

Billy sipped his tea. 'If we look at the houses and communities which overlook the wind farm; depending on whether from an easterly or westerly aspect, those unfortunate folk have the prospect of looking at sunrise or sunset through turbine blades for a large part of the year. Imagine that for the next twenty-five years,' he added.

'There are seventy turbines[47] that are nearer than two kilometres to dwelling houses,' Frank chimed in. 'I suppose it's a limited number of homes that are affected but there is

[47] According to Scottish Planning Policy, to reduce visual impact, the guideline separation distance between groups of turbines and the edge of towns, cities and villages is up to 2km. However, this distance 'is a guide, not a rule and decisions on individual developments should take into account specific local circumstances and geography.' https://www.gov.scot/publications/onshore-wind-turbines-planning-advice

no compensation even remotely near mention. These houses aren't going to be easy to sell once the wind turbines come.'

It wasn't just the view Frank was concerned about but the noise and shadow flicker.

I could understand why ordinary folk would be upset about a potential dent in prices. Home ownership provided a major source of financial security for a lot of people in the country as a substitute for adequate pensions, all this against a historical backdrop of exploitation of land users – clearances, meal roads, emigration. Looming above it all, however, was an even bigger issue, one that was already impacting everyone's lives and was set to get far worse: climate breakdown.

Both Frank and Billy insisted they knew global heating was a serious threat to the planet and something had to be done about our insatiable hunger for fossil fuels. So if a giant wind farm wasn't the solution, what was?

'If you don't mind me asking,' Billy said, 'what do *you* think the answer is?'

I paused. I was used to posing the questions, not answering them. I loved listening to people's stories, especially folk from different cultures and belief systems. It made me appreciate the diversity of humanity, our capacity for generosity and connection, but I wasn't entirely passive when soaking up their words. I had views with which I knew not all of my interlocutors would agree. I wondered how much I could reveal here in front of Frank and Billy. Would it put them off sharing their stories with me?

'Will you have more tea?' Frank was ready to pour. The stewed liquid filled the cup. It was this gesture of open hospitality that decided me – I had to reciprocate.

'I think we're facing a climate emergency and we don't have time to mess around,' I said. 'We need to stop burning fossil fuels and we need to urgently transition to green energy.'

What did this mean when it came to the Shetland wind farm? In all honesty, I didn't yet know.

'I don't have an opinion yet on Viking,' I told them. 'But I do think we need more wind farms in general. At the heart of this, we need to stop consuming so much and get back in touch with what consumption means and the impact it has on the planet. We need to be thinking collectively, not as individuals.'

Both men nodded – a gesture I understood to be an appreciation of what I was saying rather than a sign of agreement. I wanted to get back to what they thought.

'Do you see onshore wind generally as a solution to the climate crisis?' I asked them.

Frank replied: 'On a local basis. We don't have a problem with the likes of the farm at Burradale. It's all to do with scale.'

'It's too much, too big,' they said together.

'The scale has always been our main argument,' Frank went on. 'You've got these other wind farms in the pipeline. The council hasn't objected. They haven't learnt anything from this.'

'Beaw Field in South Yell and Mossy Hill outside Lerwick are both consented,' Billy added. 'A third development in the offing is Energy Isles in North Yell, which is proposed on pristine peat moorland, probably the best in Shetland. This still awaits the council's judgement and then the Scottish minister.'

With the capacity of the undersea cable it made sense

there would be more wind farms. I had heard about the two proposals for the island of Yell, and that one of them was sited on an area of special scientific interest.

The preservation of the natural environment was very important to both men. For Billy, this was encapsulated in one of his favourite places, Noss, an isle off an isle, and one of the most important seabird colonies in Shetland. The last human inhabitants left in the 1930s, and since then it has been a designated nature reserve with its 180-metre-high cliffs stained with the white guano of guillemots, gannets and puffins among others. The name of the isle means 'headland shaped like a nose' in Norse, leading many to infer that it was only in the last millennium or so that it actually became an island. If it had been an island when the Vikings added their names to the geography, it would have been 'Nossay', which means 'island shaped like a nose'.

'If you were at Noss now, what would you be appreciating in the landscape?' I asked him.

'I still appreciate the beauty of the island but the reduction of seabirds is very sad,' he said. 'Areas of cliff where large populations of guillemots, kittiwakes, razorbills and puffins nested today contain a fraction of those populations of forty years ago. All seabirds have declined in fact, except for the gannets, but they have now been badly hit with avian flu. There is an irony now with social media extolling Shetland's wildlife. Yes, in relative terms it still does compare favourably with many other places. However, if you took these present-day visitors back forty years they would be amazed at the abundance of wildlife, birds in particular. There are various reasons for this decline but the common denominator is human activities. It is something we must recognise and redress, but I fear there is little sign of that happening.'

For Frank, his connection with the landscape was closer to home. 'The hills around Aith for me,' he said when I asked him where his favourite place in Shetland was. 'Obviously I walked the hills through my youth and fished in the lochs. I have fond memories of that.'

'That's where the wind turbines are to be built, is that right?' I asked him.

'The hills to the east are going to be very badly affected, the west not.'

'So for you it's a childhood connection to the land,' I said.

'Yes, that's right. Memories of peace and quiet, being alone with your thoughts. It's been sad to see the truck tracks and the peat strewn here, there and everywhere.'

Frank added that there had been a lot of coverage in the local press about pollution in burns and water courses. A recent report that had highlighted the absence of trout from the Lunklet Burn was 'very concerning', he said. 'It has been admitted that this has been caused by metals leeching into water courses from one of the Viking borrow pits.'

The Burn of Lunklet was down the road from Voe, a favourite walking spot for myself, Esme and Josh during lockdown.

'You cannot construct a project like Viking without detrimental effects on the surrounding environment,' Frank said. 'We fear that further issues will arise as time goes on.'

Detriment to the environment – but any delay to a complete

transition from fossil fuels would be putting more pressure on other landscapes in other places. Every degree of warming meant changes to delicate ecosystems to which some species did not have time to adapt.

*

The brilliant red eyes and mournful wail – but this is no raingoose. This is another diver; her black-and-white checked wings reflect in the water like a Bridget Riley painting, a black stripe across her neck has the green sheen of shot silk. She is a common loon, a great northern diver.

For the Chippewa of the Americas, her call was an omen of death.

In a Tsimshian tale she restores a tribal leader's sight, for which she receives her distinctive necklace.

In Canada, she has her portrait painted on a 'loonie' dollar coin.

But who can predict the weather on these changing days? Heat causes stress, and too much rain can flood the nest. Fewer birds can hatch their chicks as the effects of climate breakdown bite like no other predator they ever feared before.

With every gas flare, tanker and pipeline that feeds the oil machine, her wail tapers into silence.

*

Shortly afterwards I stepped into the rain, promising to send them a copy of my write-up so they could check they were happy with it. This went against the conventional wisdom of journalism – which was generally to grab someone's story and run – but I was not exploring the wind farm to provide clicks for a media organisation. I was exploring it for myself.

Half an hour later I was sitting in a layby, the car rocking every time another vehicle sped past, scribbling down some notes and highlighting others. As well as the transition from fossil fuels, I had almost mentioned the issue of production and the drive towards endless growth; how our economic system that eats up natural resources had sent society into a death spiral. But I hadn't raised this. I had an uncomfortable feeling that I knew why. In visiting people to find out more about the wind farm and how they felt connected with the land, I was learning about Dad too and the world that had shaped him. In the faces of all the people I'd spoken to so far – Drew, Roxane, Billy and Frank and especially members of my close family – I was looking for something. It was something sweet but not quite satisfying, like a sugar rush. Was it approval?

My takeaway coffee had burnt a layer of skin off the roof of my mouth.

I felt great sympathy for both Frank and Billy. Around them, the landscape was changing beyond their control, in their view for the worse. I could see too how Drew's self-assurance that Shetland was benefiting from the wind farm would not sit well with them. Drew's camp had, after all, 'won' the battle and there seemed to be few thoughts of reconciliation.

But how did this fit into my quest to find out more about the wind farm – was it stopping me from raising tough questions and really challenging people on their views? Unlike Frank and Billy, I did think that fossil fuel exploitation had to end immediately, and the transition to renewable energy had to bring with it a whole new way of thinking: an end to days of extraction and the beginning of a regenerative approach to economics and nature.

Solace + desolation =

Play

'So when you were a kid growing up here. How different did it look?' I ask Dad as we wander around Kirkhoose croft in the summer of 2019.

'It's similar. The boundaries are the same. The main difference is it's not worked in the way that it would have been at the time,' he answers. Even fifty years ago, every farm kept cows, he told me. Usually just a few, maybe three or four for their own use, but a lot of the land use was based around what the cows would like.

'Although my folk had the shop, they still had sheep here and they still worked the place. We used to cut hay and that kind of thing until, I don't know, I was in my mid-teens anyway. They probably gave up the cattle when I was ten or twelve.'

'Is that why you want to start sowing grain in these fields now? Is it a nostalgia thing?'

Pause.

Play.

'Well, partly,' Dad says. There is a kind of formal enthusiasm in his voice, perhaps encouraged by the presence of the microphone. 'It's actually quite good ground. It seems a shame that it's not used much, it's just used for silage. It does look kind of, I don't know. There's something just kind of sad about the land, it's almost as if the ground itself is neglected. It's not used as it was for centuries. You look at old photographs of worked fields with little haystacks. People out doing things. Not that I'm proposing to do that but it would be good to do something even on a bit of it.'

'What are you planning?'

Stop.

Nostalgia is a pain for home, for a time that's gone. But here it's the land that's sad. The connection between humans and the soil has been lost.

So, no. Not nostalgia.

In the 2000s, environmental philosopher Glenn Albrecht coined the neologism 'solastalgia', which means the pain or distress caused by a sense of loss connected to the present state of your home and territory. It is 'the homesickness you have when you are still at home'. In his book *Earth Emotions: New Words for a New World*, Albrecht talked about the importance of place identity for rural people, and 'that rural landscapes were traditionally seen as places of great beauty, with strong emotional attachment running deep in family history'. His research focused on communities in Hunter Valley, Australia, an area transformed by the activities of international mining companies. The valley was a 'piece of paradise on this Earth', yet the industrial scars get bigger month by month. He quoted one resident as saying 'Big corporations have only one plan: to do more of the same and to grow forever like a cancer!' The economy had become chained to coal, Albrecht wrote, and many had become hooked on job security and money. House prices near the sites fell, leaving those who stood their ground for longest with the most to lose.

For those feeling the impact of the mining, the idea of 'home' consisted of 'a rich mixture of ecological, farming, cultural, and built heritage, with perhaps old-fashioned rural notions of community holding it all together,' Albrecht wrote. In these people, he identified a feeling of powerlessness in the face of environmental injustice. 'People were losing the solace or comfort once derived from their relationship to a home that was now being desolated by forces beyond their control.' From 'chronic lack of land care' to rising sea levels, and other changes in weather, flora and fauna, solastalgia is a feeling that is increasingly entering our modern lexicon in the face of accelerating industrialisation and global heating.

While Dad did not speak about feeling powerless in the face of injustice, members of Sustainable Shetland certainly did. In a video shared on the Sustainable Shetland Facebook page, Robert Sandison sings a song he wrote about the wind farm titled 'Hedder Hills an Raingeese'.[48] The video begins with shots of the purple heather-clad moors, and the words: 'unspoiled wilderness area destined to become a huge industrial windfarm'. The sound of his skilful fingers plucking the guitar strings are accompanied by a poignant song, lamenting the

---

[48] https://www.youtube.com/watch?v=exvMrWJov_I

turbine blade that 'destroys the feddered life' with a noise that 'resoonds aa troo' his head. Each verse rounded off with the chorus:

Noo whin I peep troo da aald porch door
Shetland's no Shetland ony more.

18

Cupcakes

The day after my trip to Frank's, I watched the blurred view of Lerwick's morning cityscape recede from view through the reinforced glass window of a ferry. The sea wasn't too rough, which meant I could safely stand without staggering across the saloon with every rise and fall of the waves, and I could also read my phone without feeling too sick. This didn't really matter much as the journey itself would only take seven minutes. Waiting for me on the approaching pier was Jonathan Wills, a man whose name I had kept hearing throughout my research into the wind farm, especially regarding the public enquiry, which according to Frank might have made all the difference to the fate of the project, and according to Drew, would not have made any difference at all. Our paths had almost crossed several times in the weeks before, both in Devon and London, but it was at his home on the island of Bressay that we were to finally meet.

Jonathan had been described as a 'kenspeckle figure'[49] with high-flying experience both in national and local media, local politics and a one-time occupation as the boatman for Britain's most northerly lighthouse, the Muckle Flugga. Keen to help me understand the intricacies of the story, he had forwarded me reams of emails ahead of our interview, some of which referred to conversations dating back over a decade. Through these documents, I pieced together a view of the man. An experienced journalist, he had been hired as a copywriter for Viking's initial PR publication *Windy Lights*, but had later described the project's initial proposal for 154 turbines as 'too big and in the wrong place'. This was an objection that echoed Frank and Billy's concerns.

'There are several Jonathan Willses: student, local politician, islomaniac, SNP convert, boatman,' Alan Taylor, founding editor of the *Scottish Review of Books*, said in a preview to Jonathan's memoir *Reporter on the Rocks*. From what I could gather, he was a complicated and interesting character.

As councillor at the time of the planning decision in 2010, he called for a public enquiry to take place. His motion was defeated. During this meeting he had also raised the issue of the councillors' potential conflict of interest due to their 'multiple and overlapping roles as representatives of this community'. Nowadays he was 'too busy' for politics, choosing instead to focus on his croft and veg patch – the responsibilities of retirement. I was looking forward to a challenging interview.

[49] https://www.shetnews.co.uk/2021/12/13/an-intriguing-account-of-wills-exploits-and-encounters/

There seemed to be a trend among men of a certain age on Shetland, my father included, and that was the wearing of beards. Every one of my male interviewees so far had voluptuous facial hair, some more tightly clipped than others, all with threads of silver around the edges. It gave them a gentle uniformity, and, no doubt, made me unconsciously look for my own father in them. Jonathan was no exception.[50] I saw him as I was waiting at the edge of the pier, my jacket failing to resist all of the water being thrown at it from the sky. A pick-up rumbled into a parking space on the other side of the road, the paintwork looking as weatherbeaten as I felt. A figure popped out of the driver's seat. 'You must be Marianne,' he said. I jumped in beside him.

'I'm not a Bressay man,' Jonathan told me later with a hard-to-place English accent (comparable to my east coast Scottish one). He was moving around the kitchen making coffee. My eyes were still slightly puffy from the early rise and travel, so caffeine was a very welcome idea. As he moved about the kitchen, he staggered a little, as if on the deck of a boat.

'I'm recovering from labyrinthitis,' he said, steadying himself on the counter.

Despite Jonathan's protestations, he had been a resident on this island for over thirty years, raising a family and working a croft. His mother was from Lerwick, but he grew up in the Midlands. In 2006 he was working as a commercial copywriter and Viking commissioned him to write the first draft of *Windy Lights: A Prospectus for Shetland's Viking Windfarm Project.*

---

[50] 'I have had a beard since May 1965,' he told me later. 'It saves electricity and thus CO_2 emissions.'

'They wanted me to put a positive spin on it I suppose. I thought it was factual,' he said. 'They now disparage it, say I was a prostitute, sold out. But actually I was paid about a quarter of the copywriter's daily rate because I thought I was doing a good thing.'

'When you say "they" who do you mean?' I asked him.

'The critics. I've been accused of corruption to my face and behind my back,' he replied.

Viking also paid him to conduct a series of public consultation meetings. When a by-election came up a year later in 2008 he became a councillor.[51] After that, he didn't do any more paid work for them.

I was sitting at the dining table that was covered in a leaf-patterned cloth. On the table Jonathan had placed a green folder full of documents and a stack of books for me to look at covering the time he had been a councillor, when crucial decisions about the wind farm had been made. I had a feeling that many interesting people had sat on this wooden chair before and had felt welcome, a sensation which contradicted slightly the brittle edge to his persona. I had a strong sense that he did not suffer fools lightly.

Jonathan was taking practised care with the coffee, preparing it in a small stove pot, Italian style. A spice rack hung on the wall, packed with small glass jars.

'They said we were corrupt, that we had prostituted Shetland to big industrial interests because we were greedy,' he said, scrobbling about in a cupboard.

---

[51] He was previously a councillor in 1993-95.

'That's a big accusation, isn't it? Where do you think that strength of feeling comes from?' I asked him.

'Well, because they don't like wind farms and they'll do anything, literally anything to stop them from happening. It's just that they don't like the look of them. The problems with vibrations and flicker are all properly dealt with because the Viking Energy wind farm is properly planned. What Viking Energy did was unprecedented. It took all these problems seriously and then mitigated them.'

He poured the coffee and I inhaled the steam eagerly, already anticipating the stimulation of my cognitive parameters.[52]

'Just going back to your involvement in the beginning: what did you think when you first heard about the plan?' I asked him.

'I thought it was a very good idea, much better than oil. Long term. The planning permission was for twenty-five years but no one is suggesting they are taking it to pieces after that, nonsense, because the concrete bases will last a thousand years. Do you take milk, by the way?' He leaned over to pour it into my cup and returned to the other side of the room to get a teaspoon.

I tried to imagine a century from now, the concrete foundations poking out from a subcutaneous layer of soil. What would the land around look like – a dustbowl of desiccated peat blasted by an overheated climate, or a forest of shrubs and life?

---

[52] According to a 2019 study, inhaling coffee does do this https://www.ncbi.nlm.nih.gov/pmc/articles/PMC6881620/#:~:text=Results,the%20mood%20score%20of%20alertness

'There seemed to me a long-term benefit provided that the community can have a big enough share,' Jonathan continued, taking his seat again. 'Then it was a means of perpetuating the charitable trust – forever! When I saw the actual plans, 154 turbines, I thought, woah, hold it, far too many, this is crazy! One of the problems was the size of submarine cables – they came in 300MW sections, three hundred wasn't enough to take all the power but six hundred was too much. That's why all these other wind farms are creeping in, none of which are as well planned or as environmentally benign as the big one.'

Two in Yell, one on a site of special scientific interest, I thought.

'If you look at what was done on bird conservation, the raingeese. Through years of painstaking research, a professional ornithologist found they had very specific flight paths from their nest to the sea and they never deviated from it. They didn't go along the ridge to the hill, so the placing of the individual turbines was informed by the bird studies of the whimbrel and the red-throated diver. Yes, there will be some casualties, but nothing like as many as are killed by domestic cats alone.'

So was the wind farm a problem or a solution? Or was it both a problem and a solution? I knew, following my interview with Drew Ratter, that Jonathan also blamed Sustainable Shetland for the fact that the charitable trust had withdrawn most of its investment, allowing SSE to take the majority share. As Drew had said, if the project had been completed in 2012 as scheduled, the trust would probably have sold half of its share and invested that elsewhere. The dividends from the remaining stake, plus the additional investments and subsidies, would have made Shetland, in Drew's words, 'Croesus-rich'.

The backlash against the wind farm also 'opened a whole can of worms about conflict of interest,' within the Shetland Charitable Trust, Jonathan said. This stemmed from the structure and role of the trust and its relationship with the local council. As a member of the council at the time – and automatically a trustee – he had been at the forefront of attempts to push through reform.

Because local authorities could not be electricity generators, following the Busta House agreement of 2007, the trust agreed to take on the council's interest and invested an initial £7 million into the £500-million project. Critics of the wind farm questioned the integrity of this process, particularly as the council owned a lot of the land on which the wind farm was to be built.

'In effect they were developers as well as council members making a planning decision,' one opponent said.[53]

Between 2008 and 2009 the Office of the Scottish Charity Regulator (OSCR), the national body that regulates charities, received complaints that called into question the way in which the trust was making decisions and how it was managing any potential conflict of interest. Following an investigation, it said the charitable trust's structure 'made it extremely difficult for it to demonstrate its independence from the local authority,' and imposed strict monitoring requirements on it.

---

[53] https://www.slideshare.net/allytibbitt/james-mc-kenzie

'There was no private conflict of interest, ever,' Jonathan said. 'There was in fact a public confluence of interest.'

He compared the decisions of the local planning authority over the wind farm to those made over the compulsory purchase of land for the construction of Sullom Voe oil terminal. The plan had always been, as Drew had said before, to make Shetland a lot of money, which they believed the wind farm would do. Councillors were elected through a democratic process to represent the best interests of their constituents and would serve this purpose also as trustees.

When the court case delays meant Viking Energy would miss out on government subsidies, the trust's investments became 'stranded' (they were not making any money). This meant it was no longer a 'qualifying investment' under HMRC rules and the charitable trust could not put more money into it.

'The point would come when we would have to sell our share or give it to someone else because we wouldn't be allowed to hold that investment, quite properly, by the Inland Revenue,' Jonathan said.

That was why, in 2019, the trust decided to hold their hand at £10 million and SSE took control of the project, promising to provide all future finance required. That was also why the public, through their charitable trust, lost 45% of the revenue when SSE decided some years later to go ahead anyway, Jonathan said.

As far as I could gather, the Shetland Charitable Trust acted like a valve in the heart of the isles' relationship with energy. Over nearly five decades, the charitable body has harvested investments worth over £320 million (originally made with the oil money) to pump into different aspects of island life – from arts and sports to the environment, social care and welfare.

This fact in itself was not too difficult to get my head around. Trying to understand the structure and chronology of the story of the trust, however, was like getting knots out of a thin gold chain. With a history encompassing a stack of acronyms that all seem to borrow from the same hand at Scrabble (SICCT, SCT, SIC), I was probably not alone in my temple-rubbing.

If we command our wealth . . .[54]

Total disturbance payments, paid until 2000 – around £81 million.

The value of the trust's reserves: 2008 – £150 million; 2009 – £170 million; 2010 – £210 million; 2015 – £229 million; 2018 – £284 million.

Due to the 'yo-yo nature of volatile global markets' in 2022, in March that year reserves topped £450 million, and in September fell to £371 million.

*

If the value of the charitable trust's reserves was only £150 million at the time of the Busta House agreement in 2007, how could Shetland afford to commit around £200 million to the wind farm project?

'We had been offered as trustees all that money on loans,

---

[54] For a more detailed chronology, see notes.

not with the trust's capital as a security but only with the trust's share in the wind farm,' Jonathan explained.

This meant that the trust could borrow more money based on the assumption that their share in the wind farm would reap a bumper harvest a few years down the line when they were called upon to repay the debt.

'So that transformed it. It was such a good bet that major banks and finance houses told the trust that they would make that money available upfront. But they (wind-farm opponents) never understood that and they didn't want to understand it because it cut the ground from underneath them.'

He took a gulp of his coffee.

In a community that had grown used to a steady flow of money, the global financial crash left Shetland reeling. 'One thing that few people can doubt is that the glory days of mass spending are gone,' Gavin Morgan wrote in the *Shetland Times* in 2009. 'The amount of money that was available has spoilt the people of Shetland to some extent and now new facilities are generally expected to be of the greatest innovative standards, but this too will have to change as more economical projects will need to be considered, and certain cut backs are going to become essential.'

In this atmosphere, it was perhaps not surprising that folk were suspicious of investing so much public money in such a big project.

'You advocated for a public enquiry—'

'I did. I thought that could sort it out,' Jonathan replied with a dramatic sigh. 'The planning department recommended it but councillors were against it.'

'Why?'

'I don't know. They just wanted to get on with it. It wouldn't have delayed it half as much as the court case.'

I drained my cup, lamenting the small size of the coffee pot. 'Was there any inkling that there would have been a court case?' I asked.

'It came as a total surprise to me, I was a trustee. I think I may have been vice chair at the time. Not that being vice chair was worth a pitcher of warm spit, as Lyndon Johnson said of the vice presidency, because I was not consulted. I was not liked. But that's fine. I remember when it went to court, I was in the station changing trains for Paris, I'd been at a meeting on fisheries, and I got a phone call from Drew Ratter. I said, "What? They haven't." And he said, "This judge says they have a case."'

I felt a surge of indigestion. The image of a pitcher of warm spit was a bit too evocative.

Jonathan described the mood when the court case went to appeal, and how he believed Sustainable Shetland 'never had a legal leg to stand on'.

'What really interests me about this, and the extent of the division, is that quite often people have the same view ultimately. It's too big and it's in the wrong place, you said that yourself,' I said.

'It's been cut down by a third,' he replied.

'Even after that.'

'It's in the right place. It's very carefully chosen to be in an area with no nature conservation designations at all. And the area, where it is, nobody ever went there apart from a few sheep ranchers who were grossly overgrazing the hills. The top of all those hills were going bald, the rock was coming through. Ever since 1947 when the sheep subsidy came in. What the wind farm does is stop that because the grazing will be controlled and the peatlands to some extent will be restored. And the big scar on the side of the hill that you see going north – nothing to do with the wind farm, you could see it years before the wind farm – it was caused by overgrazing.'

The picture he painted was very different to the ones drawn by Moraig, Frank and Billy, like turning a kaleidoscope.

'Nobody ever went there, no tourists went there,' Jonathan continued.

'Do you think a counter-argument to that might be that nobody went there, and that's why there was thriving wildlife?' I asked.

'You could say that. The wildlife was thriving to a certain extent but it wasn't thriving as much as it could have done because the land was degraded by crofting.'

'What do you enjoy about the Shetland community?' I asked him.

'I'm a half-moother,' he said. 'My mother was from Lerwick and my father was English. I have a lot of friends and relations. My mother was one of forty-nine first cousins in her generation. So one of my cousins once said "if all of your relations voted for you, you'd be in parliament by now". They said "we're not going to do that". No, I like the people. I'm fascinated by the people, the dialect, the archeology, particularly pre-Viking archeology. I'm sick to death of Vikings. I don't know why we glorify rapists and pillagers, no. Do you want a cupcake? My daughter made them. I think there's one left.'

He rose from the table and lurched towards the kitchen counter – the labyrinthitis clearly affecting his balance. Soon the sound of the kettle boiling reached across the room, like a great wave building and then subsiding.

'So what Browns are you?'

'My dad was born in Voe, Brown and Balfour,' I said through the cupcake. It was soft and fluffy, with a slight hint of vanilla. Delicious.

'No relation to Bill Brown, the late potter?'

'That's my dad, yeah,' I answered, wiping a thin film of grease from my lips with my fingers.

'That's your dad? Oh, I didn't know that was your dad.'

'Did you know him?'

'I knew him vaguely, only to say hello to. I admired his work. I've got some of it here. I think my daughter borrowed it.'

'What piece do you have?' I asked, feeling some pride in Jonathan's praise of Dad's work.

'A big round plate.'

He crossed the room with the coffee pot. The mention of Dad prompted me to seek a new turn to the conversation.

'Do you think there are lessons to be learnt from the wind farm as Scotland heads towards 2045 net zero?' I asked him.

He chuckled mirthlessly. 'Stick to the facts, don't confuse public and private interests. You'd assume unless there is evidence otherwise that elected public officials are doing their best for the community and are not on the take.'

'In terms of Shetland's 2030 net zero goal, do you think that's achievable?' I asked him.

'No, but it's nice to have a target. People can all do their bit.'

Jonathan certainly seemed to be doing his. He and his wife Lesley, who was vegetarian, had two greenhouses in which they grew half their food. It was easy to grow vegetables in Bressay, he insisted, but unfortunately they couldn't yet grow wine. It felt like the conversation was wrapping up and Jonathan kept looking at the clock. It occurred to me suddenly that I didn't know when the ferry crossings were.

'You'll stay for lunch?'

The invitation took me by surprise.

'I need to pick Lesley up at the pier now, she's been in Lerwick this morning. I'll be back in about ten minutes.' And after a moment of rustling coats and jangling keys, he was away.

In the empty room, I had a chance to look properly at the pictures on the walls. One of them in particular caught my attention. It showed a large wave crashing against a cliff. A boat with a red sail rode the spume. The oil brushstrokes captured the movement of the waves and, combined with my tiredness and recent trip on the ferry, looking at it I could almost feel the rocking of the bow. I learnt later that it was a painting of the Shearwater in the Bardastrom and that Jonathan had painted it.

It wasn't too long before the door burst open again, releasing a gust of wet wind into the kitchen. Lesley greeted me as she shook off her wet coat. She was small and had a kind of energetic bounce about her. I noticed her accent wasn't local.

'This is Bill Brown's daughter,' Jonathan said.

'Oh,' Lesley replied, leaping lightly to a cabinet by the door. 'We've got one of his plates here.'

'I thought Katie had it.'

'No, no,' Lesley said, delicately removing items of crockery. From a stack at the bottom, she removed a large round plate with an abstract pattern on stoneware that looked like one of Dad's early designs, probably from the 1970s.

'I love this one. It's a miracle it's still in one piece having been in this house.'

Lesley had just returned from a trip to Lerwick to visit her elderly mother, who was in sheltered accommodation. She told me about her father and her roots in Alloa, in central Scotland. Her manner was warm and open. Jonathan bustled about in the kitchen, poaching eggs and warming some beetroot soup – 'almost entirely homegrown', Jonathan said. It was a hearty meal that left me with a calm feeling of contentment. After we'd eaten, I continued to talk with Lesley while Jonathan uploaded more documents onto a USB stick. I learnt that their daughter Katie was not only a skilled maker of cupcakes, but also set up the parkrun on Bressay – the most northerly parkrun in the UK. Their son worked for Nova Innovation, the company behind the expansion of tidal power in Shetland. The Wills were certainly an interesting clan.

I sat back in the wooden chair, relaxing into the scene. As Jonathan chatted with his wife over which family photos to save or not to save, I could see a much mellower version of the public face. When it was time to catch the ferry back to the mainland, Lesley gave me a hug and I felt like a friend of one of their children who had popped round for a natter.

The wind and rain had not improved and as soon as I'd thanked Jonathan and slammed the truck door behind me, I made a run for the covered seating on the ferry. As the boat pulled away, I realised how much I had enjoyed speaking to them. Not just Jonathan and Lesley, but all the people I'd met so far. As I'd been invited into people's homes, different hands had placed my name on a twig of the great Shetland family tree. But was my sympathy towards all the characters a weakness or a strength? Should I have been leaning one way or another by now in my unfolding of the wind farm story?

Back at the Lerwick ferry terminal, I started the car. I was looking forward to a moment alone with my thoughts, but first, I had another call to make, to one of the families right on the frontline of the wind farm debate. Next stop was to Weisdale and the home of Evelyn Morrison and her husband Donnie.

Yours sincerely

Viking wind farm project all wrong for Shetland
I refer to J. Wills' letter (Indignant or gloating? *Shetland News*, 10 June 2019) and can assure him that neither I nor any of the Sustainable Shetland members are gloating or are likely to gloat about Viking Energy wind farm . . .
– Frank Hay, 2019

Indignant or gloating? (Viking Energy)
It's hard to tell whether Frank Hay, the chairman of 'Sustainable' Shetland, is indignant or just gloating about Scottish and Southern Energy taking on the responsibility for funding most of the Viking Energy wind farm project . . .
– Jonathan Wills, 2019

Council has nothing to do with Viking
Mr Ian Tinkler asks why there isn't a lot of stuff in my election statement about Viking Energy. The answer is very simple . . .
– Drew Ratter, 2012

Sticking with Billy
Labour candidate Jamie Kerr made his support for the Viking Energy project quite clear on the Radio Shetland hustings and at the Althing . . . I think I'll just stick with the only candidate who, in my opinion, has shown any integrity, and vote for Billy Fox . . .
– Evelyn Morrison, 2011

The Kames giant[55]

A vast bulk stretches out under the night sky near Voe: a body of landscape that has broken off to walk and talk as a separate-yet-connected being. The veins are quartz, the hair is moss, the skin is living stone. It is a great solid mass almost

---

[55] Retelling of a folk story published in *The New Shetlander*, Issue 31.

indistinguishable from the lichen, grasses, and the whimbrel nests under the moonlight. A piece of a mountain that is dwarfed by the stars but looks down at humans and all other small creatures. The giant stretches out across the skyline, testing the quiet with its fingers and toes, and sighs. Perhaps the day has come at last when it can rest. Perhaps it can rest in peace. It closes its huge yellow eyes.

A tiny pinch.

A little tug.

The giant groans. Not again. Oh, not again. Wee hands tweak its lugs and tickle the soles of its feet. The giant turns onto its side. Go away, it rumbles, leave me to sleep. But these are relentless, remorseless little hands. They will nip and scratch like miniature needles, pluck his nose hairs, and backcomb his eyebrows. These are trows, tiny things that live in mounds and play fiddles and dance and steal babies and marry human women. They are mischievous beings that bite like midges. They will lure a man under a mound and play until he is old. They love to bother a giant.

But this time is different. This time the giant has had enough. This time the giant has come prepared.

Slowly.

Slowly.

It reaches out a clay-grey hand to catch something with a finger – the reed-woven strap of a kishie.[56] Slowly, the giant draws the basket towards it. Until.

With a great roar that fractures the stillness and sends a

---

[56] Traditional Shetland basket made to sling over the shoulder.

landslide of peat and rocks down the slopes, the giant gets to its feet, and plucks off the trows dangling from its body, stuffing them, squeaking, into the kishie. At last, with one final thunderous bellow, it tightens the top so they can't get out. It pauses, fingers feeling the taut promise of the knot. The giant intends to throw this kishie far away. Far, far away to Norway, where the little beasties can't get him (trows are not strong swimmers). Slowly, the giant's face cracks open in a wide, wide grin. Now it can be free. Free of all the scratchy, itchy, nippy little things – and at last enjoy a well-deserved retirement in Voe. A sigh of relief shudders the hillside and a small shower of pebbles tumbles down into the valley.

The giant braces its bulk to lift the basket. It heaves, and heaves again. The bundle of trows is surprisingly heavy. They squirm and screech with every swing. The giant can't propel the kishie quite far enough to hurl it. Again it swings the basket and again the arc is too short.

This is not going to work.

Determined, the giant drags the basket along the ground, not sparing the trows a dunt or dip in the ice-cold peaty water when a boulder or a soggy ditch lie in its path. They squeal and chirp with distress. The distance isn't far, but it takes a long time. Giants do not move quickly, and the moon is still up when the plans begin to fall apart. The basket is tough, but the ground is rough. Rubbed together, tough and rough can cause friction, fraying and, ultimately, holes. So it is with the kishie. There is now a hole, big enough for a trow to wriggle free. One trow, two trows, three trows, four. The giant doesn't notice, distracted by a vision of a not-too-distant horizon of *undisturbed rest, quiet and deepest slumber. Five trows, six trows, seven trows, more.*

The giant reaches the brow of the hill. It stands, tensing its body. Then it stretches down, creaking and cracking like the ghosts of trees in the wind in preparation to lift the kishie that should weigh so heavily with trows. With a thunderous rumble, it transfers all its force into lifting the basket. It anticipates resistance. But there is no resistance for this is an empty basket. Yet all that energy has to go somewhere. So, up flies the basket, high into the sky, falling against the backdrop of a dark close to dawn. And up goes the giant, propelled by its own power, only to fall again, reaching out its great foot for balance and crashing to its knee. Where the knee falls, it forms a dent in the hill. Groundwater floods into the footprint. The trows scatter across the bog, leaping and laughing with glee.

The giant's troubles become mapped into the landscape: The lochan Petta Water, and the hollow in the hill that is known as Kneefall. They stand as monuments to those best laid schemes that 'gang aft agley'.

*

The closer you looked, the more you could see. Tiny lights illuminated the moss and miniature fly agaric mushrooms, the pine cones and the fairy figurines. Behind it, the window pane defended the cosy room against the battering rain. In the near distance, a new road led to the ridge of turbine foundations.

'They wouldn't allow this somewhere like Iceland, with their hill trows there. Over the back of the hill there is a very trowie place, if you believe in that kind of thing. I don't disbelieve it but you know. They've got away with digging it up anyway.'

Evelyn Morrison sighed and took up her knitting again. She was always knitting something, her husband Donnie told me, the points of the needles tucking away stressful thoughts into neat and regular rows. I was sitting in their conservatory near Sandwater. It was around 4 p.m. and the dark outside was already mature. We sat by the wood burner; I could feel my skin roasting slightly. Evelyn and Donnie lived right on the edge of the wind farm development. Donnie's grandfather bought the land in 1917, but had not followed in his ancestor's crofting footsteps as he 'hated sheep'. The house looked like a traditional croft house – low, white-washed stone walls – but Donnie had only just finished building it.

Evelyn had a brain tumour, which affected her hearing in one ear. She'd first fallen ill around twenty years ago. The couple had moved up the valley for some 'peace and quiet', but this hope was interrupted by the arrival of the wind farm. They thought about moving but never really believed the project would go ahead. The disruption of the landscape was mirrored in Shetland society too, Donnie said. The isles were once a place where folk looked out for each other; now friends were turned against friends, even families were divided over it, he said.

Despite attending public meetings and writing letters to the newspaper, the couple said they never felt listened to. The first PR material the wind farm published, *Windy Lights* (edited by Jonathan Wills), was a case in point, Donnie said. *Windy Lights* was a word used to describe a tiny generator that people would make themselves to charge the car battery, he said, adding: 'Folk in Shetland were always ingenious at making things.' Like Da and his waterwheel, I thought. To call an information booklet about a wind farm the size of Viking 'windy lights' was cynical, Donnie said. So they took their views to social media and the local papers. It was Evelyn who wrote letters to the editor.

'I light the gun, she fires the bullets,' Donnie said.

As we chatted, Evelyn left the room, returning with a tray of homemade butterfly cakes – fragrant, sweet and soft – a delicious tribute to the old tradition of hospitality.

That night, I returned to Kirkhoose to eat my usual meal of packet soup and frozen peas, tipping an egg into the boiling water for extra protein. Without my child, I wasn't very good at looking after myself. I thought again about the cupcakes I'd eaten that day: the hands measuring the flour, sifting in clouds over the bowl, creaming sugar and butter, cracking eggs and watching the gelatinous mixture turn the batter a deeper shade of yellow. These cakes contained more than their physical ingredients. They were gifts of time and generosity, and the welcoming of a stranger.

19

Personal Best

The crowd gathered on the starting line was mixed. Some were very fit-looking folk with proper Lycra; a wiry man sporting a 'Shetland' tank top who looked like he was in his eighties waited for the signal. There was also a young family with a pushchair, and someone with a dog. Some wore Shetland toories (woollen caps) as insulation against a vicious wind that seemed intent on blasting directly into our faces. As we waited, I became painfully conscious of all the cakes and coffees and teas I'd been consuming over the course of the week, and the 800-mile journey I'd spent crammed onto various forms of public transport. Even after a careful stretch, my muscles felt stiff and unyielding. But it was too late to change my mind now. Despite the upbeat feeling of collective excitement these events so often provide, I felt a cold edge of nerves. Not only did I feel obliged to prove myself in front of these strangers, but I was here for another reason too – to find information.

I'd been running 'seriously' for about a year after finally

joining our local club and moving up a set to the second-fastest group[57] – an achievement about which I regularly bragged to Josh. I had never liked team sports, always aware of how my own inadequacies might be letting the side down. I had tried cold water swimming, but my inability to really master the front crawl, despite best efforts, put me off. It wasn't until the dawn of middle age that I finally discovered that running at a moderate speed and in a group was actually really good fun. Aside from the convenience and the reliable feeling of 'going somewhere', I found something comforting about being in a pack. I shall always treasure the sensation of ascending the lanes around Okehampton on a clear winter's night, the head torches of my fellow runners sending beams of yellow into the dark, gilding clouds of condensed breath; the only sound that of trainers pounding on the sparkling tarmac, the occasional warning shout of 'ice!' or 'car!', and an owl hoot or two. It conjures, for me, a deep and soothing sense of kinship and the reassurance that if you do fall on your arse, there will be someone nearby to help pick you up.

Inspired by my conversation with Jonathan, I was taking part in the Bressay parkrun – the most northerly race of its kind in Britain – which had been set up by his daughter. It followed a 5km-route from the ferry terminal car park, past a play area and shop, and eventually ending at the old primary school-turned-café.

'Ready?' said a volunteer in a hi-vis vest.

We were ready – or as ready as we could be.

---

[57] There are only three groups.

'Go!'

Soon I was straining my muscles against a wall of wind and rain as other runners, similarly buffeted, slowly edged their way along the tarmac in front of me. The force of the gale felt like it was inflating my lungs with every gasp. As we turned back on ourselves for the final stretch, with my back to the wind, I managed to pick up some speed, but the effort was gruelling. I found myself longing for the finish line. Around thirty minutes later, I staggered into the old school playground, brandishing my barcode so my time could be recorded.

Soon most of the runners were steaming and sweating around a cluster of tables bearing plates of bacon rolls, cakes and pint glasses of water. After replenishing my energy levels, I fired out some small talk to break the ice. Along with the usual niceties, I threw in that I was looking into the story behind the wind farm, wondering what such a potentially divisive topic might do to this camaraderie of runners.

'I think the wind farm is great,' one said. He was an 'incomer', having come to the isles decades before. Probably in his early fifties, his physique suggested that he was more serious about running than me.

'People complain about the roads they're building, but no one goes out there.' It was a point of view I'd heard often. 'When I go up, there's no one else around. With these roads, we'll be able to cycle and walk in places you just can't get to now.'

Another runner from a different table turned around to join the conversation. 'There will be some really good cycling when the thing is operational,' he said.

'What do you think about the impact on the peat?' I asked them.

'The peat is quite degraded up there,' the first man said. 'They're restoring it.'

On this occasion, the consensus among the small group appeared to be in favour of the wind farm. But there were other runners not there that day who were definitely not in favour, one said, including a local councillor.

It was nearly time to return to the ferry so I thanked them and got up to see if I could have a word with the organisers. I explained that I was a journalist with family connections to the island, and my interest in the wind farm. One of them pointed me towards a man sitting in the corner – he worked for Viking and would be a good person to speak to. David McGinty looked up from his cup. I recognised him from the ferry and when he overtook me on the run. He was a cheerful-looking man with a strong Glasgow accent.

David was enthusiastic about his work on the wind farm, answering my questions with a friendly informality. When I asked about the impact on the peat bogs, he gave an outline of the process: construction was taking place on areas of the hills already skinned by erosion. Any peat they removed to make room for tracks and other necessities was then used to infill degraded patches of bog and levelled in a way that would benefit regrowth. After that it was reseeded using locally sourced moorland mix to help the new vegetation thrive. This restoration was fundamental to the project's existence.

There was also the issue of birds, and my lugs perked up when he mentioned the red-throated diver. The team had spent a lot of time mapping flight routes, watching as they flew from nest to sea and back again, and these paths had been factored into the planning of the placement of turbines.

'Our work on the raingoose habitats will concentrate on improving existing lochans and making others which are sub-optimal for use into potential habitats by altering the water tables and height of banks. Possibly even some man-made islands,' he said.

Work hadn't started on this yet, but was slated to commence in the autumn and following spring before the breeding season.

'We've constructed some nesting areas away from the turbines, and some of the birds have been seen there,' he said.

Giving nesting birds a chance of successfully raising their chicks kept the project in line with wildlife regulations, David said. He gave me the example of a local contractor who went on leave and left his excavator open, providing an attractive prospect for a pair of starlings, who built their nest there. Workers weren't able to use the machines until the chicks had fledged.

By this point we were already aboard the Bressay ferry, steadying ourselves against the swell of the waves. It wasn't until we had disembarked that I remembered to ask him about a site visit. I'd be very welcome, he said.

20

Cutting Edge

'The story of peat isn't simply cut and dried'
— Dr Ian Tait[58]

This fossil fuel has sustained countless generations on the Shetland islands, with folk cutting, stacking, and burning it for thousands of years.[59] Folk might drag the peats home on sledges, in boats or on Shetland ponies.[60] This dependence started to change from the nineteenth century with a switch to imported coal which gave better heat. First businesses, townspeople, schools, and fishing boats. Then, to paraphrase Drew Ratter: in 1974 everything changed. Instead of peat and coal, Shetlanders

---

[58] shetlandmuseumandarchives.org.uk/blog/why-burn-peats

[59] I highly recommend this for more information on peat cutting: shetland.betweenislands.com

[60] Shetland ponies played an important role in the exploitation of fossil fuels. Being small animals, they became valuable workers down the coal mines in lieu of children, who were banned from underground mine work by the Mines Act of 1847.

were opting for oil and electricity, warming their homes with central heating and boiling stew on gas-ringed hobs.

Peat is almost solid carbon and burning it releases harmful levels of CO_2. But in an article for the Shetland Museum, Dr Ian Tait argues that the question 'why burn peats?' is a complicated one. Today, instead of burning peat to create building lime, we now use imports from France, and scrape away the surface of the hills to build roads.

People still take pride in the work – for the honouring of tradition or simply as a cheap back-up fuel in hard winters. In 2018 a video of one particularly dandy peat-cutter went viral as he sliced and stacked blocks of peat onto the bank. Dressed in tweed and a deerstalker hat, Bruce Wilcock was a master blacksmith and had been the islands' farrier after moving to Shetland in 1975. The video ignited 'huge curiosity' as well as 'amazing appreciation of someone as old/young as him doing such a manually hard job'.[61]

*

'If the peat grows 1mm a year, then you are cutting into five thousand years of it,' Sue White told me as we faced into the stinging wind, picking our way over tussocks. We were in an area of hill land off the main road in Girlsta, a small settlement on the A970 about halfway between Voe and Lerwick. The area was part of a traditional peat-cutting bank and had been harvested in this way for millennia.

Sue knew a lot about peat. She was the Peatland ACTION

---

[61] According to his daughter, who filmed the video.

officer for the Shetland Amenity Trust and was also on the environmental board for the wind farm.[62] She had arranged to meet me at a pioneering project site where a family of crofters had agreed to restore the peat in two of their fields. She led the way, glowing against the gloom in a bright purple jacket, flying wisps from her white pigtails bringing to mind the islands' Viking heritage, although she herself had settled here from England. As we walked, her black spaniel (appropriately named Paddy) padded alongside us, reflecting back some of Sue's own brisk energy.

'Shetland has degraded peat,' she said.

'Because of the sheep?' I asked.

'Partly – also the climate. The wind and the salt erode the surface and dry it out,' she replied. 'There are forty-eight hectares of degraded peat here emitting twenty tonnes of carbon a year. The average family car is five tonnes.'

These hills did not look like the moonscape of the ridge near the Kames, they were much more even, and with far less of the crisp, bouncing heather.

'A lot of heather is a sign that the bog is drying out,' she shouted as I struggled to keep the pages of my notebook from being torn away in the wind. 'Shetland peatlands should be a dynamic patchwork blanket of different species of sphagnum mosses. Some like it a bit drier, others wetter so the different "patches" expand and contract but always form a blanket. We need to stitch some of it back together.'

Walking over this patchwork blanket, with Sue as my guide, I felt like I was on a bog safari. Every now and then she would

---

[62] The Shetland Windfarm Environmental Advisory Group (SWEAG).

pause and show me points of ecological interest. One of these was a tiny delicate bush of pale green tendrils sprouting from the moss.

'This is Cladonia, sometimes called reindeer lichen,' Sue said, squatting next to it. 'You know a field isn't grazed too heavily if this is around.'

Sheep were not the only animals to enjoy a nibble on it. Apparently it was also a favourite snack for reindeer, moose and caribou in the Arctic regions, but a slow growth rate of 3-5mm per year meant it was not to be found in high abundance.

There was another sign of a healthy bog: cotton-grass. The plant was more identifiable in the late summer, when the dowdy brown flowers develop fluffy white seed heads – an ageing process of which I could only dream. The plant had a variety of uses throughout history, from stuffing pillows in Suffolk and Essex to candle wicks in Germany. It acts as a companion plant to sphagnum, its roots helping to stabilise the peat.

We paused at the edge of a pool. Sue wheeched out a dog-poo bag from her pocket, and proceeded to pluck a handful of sphagnum moss and stuff it into the bag.

'I'll show you why in a minute,' she said in reply to my puzzled face.

'Moss wants to hold water in a water-filled area,' she said, holding up a strand for me to see. 'It's similar to bubble wrap.' I looked closely at the soft, almost furry leaves. 'When you walk on it, you burst the cells. It's a bit like walking on stacks of blueberries.'

I recalled the moss in the field at Kirkhoose, and how my boots could sink inches into it like a sponge. I wondered how much destruction myself and Esme had caused roaming about there, lifting our wellies out and marvelling at the footprints we had left behind.

'That's why too many sheep can cause a lot of damage,' Sue said. 'A sustainable level of sheep on this land is one sheep per seven hectares.'

Stitching the blanket bog back together meant readjusting the balance of vegetation, Sue explained. That involved more than just letting things regrow. Over the crest of the hill, she showed me where her team had been raising the water table to keep the peat wet and the moss healthy. To do this, they had reprofiled the hags and created pools and dams.

'The edge of the hag is dry and dead so we use it to make the dams,' she said, her voice quieter now we were away from the wind. 'We reprofile and peel back. It's not construction exactly, more a kind of sculpture.'

We were on the edge of a pool thick with vegetation. Sue took the poo bag out again and placed the moss in the pool for it to take root.

'I always have a poo bag on me to do this,' she said.

Keeping the bog wet would mean the peat would store carbon, rather than emit it. That was why plants like moss were so important. Not only did the moss hold carbon, but its effect of increasing the acidity of the environment made it an ecosystem engineer. Natural solutions like this were such an easy way to bring down carbon emissions, but so far they seemed too low down on the list of priorities. For now, in the 'race to zero' many more onshore wind farms were being proposed for Shetland, thanks to the interconnector that would zap energy to homes across the sea in Scotland.

'Drop a rock in a pool and you have ripples. It's the same with peat,' Sue said. 'There is impact for about fifty metres. There will be cracks forming, gullies.'

A 'black art'

To the engineer, the peat is a foundation on which to build a structure.

To the ecologist, it is a living system.

A floating road doesn't actually float. It sits, the weight of the road finding an equilibrium with the strength of the peat. A separation layer is there only to provide a working platform. This 'dark stuff' is not universally recognised as a foundation for building roads, and 'the construction of roads on peat has all too frequently been considered to be a "black art" by some authorities', one report said.[63]

*

'Yes, the peat on the hills is in a poor state, but it doesn't mean you should dig it all up,' Sue said, venting her frustration over some of the arguments used in defence of the Viking wind farm. All the calculations for the project were based on the Scottish government's carbon calculator, but environmentalists have raised concerns that the science behind this was flawed.[64]

---

[63] *Floating Roads on Peat*, published in August 2010 by Scottish Natural Heritage and Forestry Commission Scotland.

[64] For more details, read Jen Stout's report: theferret.scot/wind-farms-peat-climate-pollution/

'They could be restoring all the hags and gullies. At the moment they are excavating the peat as a waste product, clearing the degraded areas, and backfilling those areas. From an ecological point of view, it's organic waste.' The project was a 'big experiment', she added.

We were back at the car park; the safari was over.

Sue opened the boot for Paddy to jump in, pausing to look out across the fields, dots of sky glinting from pools in the wet ground. I leant against Jen's Honda, swapping my cumbersome wellies for my 'driving shoes' – I was nervous adjusting the pedals without them.

'A lot of the environmental people were opposed to the wind farm because of the damage it would do but are now actually involved in the ecological side,' she said. 'It's like a climate anxiety thing, it's their way of dealing with that. They can't stop the wind farm but they can do their best to mitigate the damage.'

'Is that what you're doing?' I asked her.

'Yes. I've had a lot of conversations with the people who are very strongly opposed to the wind farm, but do you want someone to come in from elsewhere and not be invested in the same way that someone from Shetland is? I find that really quite hurtful. You are a professional environmentalist – you are answering to the environment.'

Being answerable to the environment meant rearranging society's human-centric view of the world. Instead of always taking, there would need to be reciprocity. Her words made me think again of my run over the Kames and how the wind had transformed me into a scarlet racoon. It had been a reminder of the control that non-human forces could have over our lives.

21

A Gift of Cabbage

Beads of light glanced off the raindrops that had caught on the thinning remains of autumn vegetation. I was standing in Green Knowe, over two years since I had last been there, and I was looking for a cabbage.

Where Dad had raised a generation of Shetland cabbage in Green Knowe, Jen was carrying on the tradition. She sowed and transplanted and nurtured them until they stood strong and solid, thrusting out lustrous purple and green leaves, the white venation reminiscent of capillary systems full of blood cells, a river spreading across a floodplain, or the cable network of a wind farm. They were ready to eat and Jen, via text message as she made her way back to Ukraine, had implored me to do just that. I snapped off a couple of the fibrous outer leaves and peeled away some of the more tender inner ones. Already I felt like I was holding more than I could eat so I retreated inside to cook them.

Preparing vegetables from a shop can be a chore. Consumer

is separated from the seed, the soil and the hands that tended them by a suffocating film of plastic. We scan the barcode at a self-service desk without even a human face to whom we can say 'good morning' or 'thank you'; we simply pay our money and go. It is only at home that we can rip the bag open and actually touch it. Preparing a meal from vegetables fresh from the ground is something else: messy with dirt and nibbled by insects, rich in smell and texture and satisfaction. In *Braiding Sweetgrass*, Robin Wall Kimmerer talks about the gift of strawberries. She describes collecting these fruits in jars for her mother to make strawberry shortcake to celebrate Father's Day.

'It's funny how the nature of an object – let's say a strawberry or a pair of socks – is so changed by the way it has come into your hands, as a gift or as a commodity,' she writes.

The kale in Green Knowe had no price tag on it. It was a gift from the land to Jen and from Jen to me. This chain of connection set it worlds apart from the limp specimens tagged and bagged on supermarket shelves.

'The essence of the gift is that it creates a set of relationships. The currency of a gift economy is, at its root, reciprocity,' Kimmerer writes.

I sawed through the thick stems, slicing the leaves into thin shreds. There was mackerel in the freezer that a neighbour had delivered to Jen after a fishing trip – the same neighbour who had taken Dad out in the boat on occasion and later supplied us with fish in the months we lived in Kirkhoose. For once, I made the effort to defrost it and prepare a proper meal to honour the life, toil and generosity these gifts represented.

It felt like a small act of rebellion to put my instant soup and frozen peas to the side for just one night. The resulting stir-fry was a little too tough in parts, in others a little too crispy (certainly not my finest culinary hour) but it felt like it was doing me good. As I chewed and crunched my way through the meal, I looked out at the view of the voe. My thoughts had again turned to kale: from those tiny cannonballs Dad saved from his crop to the mushy stalks left after he died. An image, too, of cold kale soup that no one had the heart to finish, poured into the grass like a tribute to the soil itself and the many lives lived on it. I let the flavours flood my mouth, bitter, sweet and tangy flavours released with every grind of my molars.

22

The Cup

A handful of clay slaps against the surface of the metal wheel which revolves with each pump of the foot pedal. This motion has a rhythmical resistance, which after an initial input of force takes on energy of its own. After a while, thumbs enter the wet material and create a hole. Fingers stroke and pinch the outer edge as it grows into a thick tube, small ripples forming with each turn of the wheel like the rings in a tree trunk. Soon it is finished. The foot lifts and the wheel slows to a stop.

*

I have big hands and long fingers, like my father. That's why I like cups with substantial handles. The one I rescued from the workshop at Kirkhoose was just right: big enough for a decent cup of tea and the stoneware provided good insulation. Every morning and every afternoon on returning from my adventures around the isles I would sit at the dining room table drinking tea or rehydrated cream-of-vegetable soup from it.

Skilled craft-making is an act of connection. To craft an object, makers must have a deep understanding of and respect for the material they use: grain in wood, the melting point of metal, the length of fibres in wool, the consistency of clay. They also have to think about the person who will use the object they are creating: the circumference of a ribcage, the shape of a hand around a mug. The craftsperson is the bridge between the material and the object, stretching out a hand, offering deep appreciation and understanding as well as beauty. It is such a close relationship that materials can change the bodies of these craftspeople, through the skin, the eyes or the lungs (calluses, splinters, asbestosis) re-forming the maker themselves outside and in. Unlike flesh, crafts are designed to last, to be handed down the generations long after the name of the maker is forgotten. Craft is antithetical to a single-use consumer culture in which the hands that make things are exploited and abused and the things themselves are tossed into poison-oozing landfill or vaporised in an incinerator after minimal use.

Dad's cup was probably over thirty years old, made around the time he had taken photos of his daughter climbing the hill, Sneugie, at the back of Kirkhoose. It was this image which, after draining the last of my tea, forced me out of my seat in the direction of the door.

There was no path to the top of Sneugie. It was hard going, and I made slow progress. The breakfast light was still just a stain slowly breaking up the October night. Rain looked unlikely, but just in case, my strides were accompanied by the squeak-swish of waterproof trousers. I passed the evergreens Dad had grown near the boundary with his neighbours' croft, stout and confident trees poking out of the ground like arrows in a bow. Someone had told me Dad knew they would outlive him and that he wasn't planting them for himself, but a wood for his grandchildren.

At last I reached the fence and a gate which marked the boundary between the Kirkhoose croft and common land on the crown of the hill. Some of the fencing demarcating this land had come loose, the wire no longer tight, the posts no longer straight. It would cost a lot of money to replace them, something me and my sister were responsible for now. It was a difficult thing to manage from so far away.

Square posts, round posts, half-round posts, strainers.
Stock wire, plain wire, barbed wire.

It is only recently that wire fences have become a regular feature of the Shetland landscape. Increased economic prosperity meant more crofters could enclose their portion of the scattald (common grazing) for private use. It is an expensive task, about £20-£45 per foot, depending on multiple factors – length, height, number of posts and materials. The labour required to remove the old fence costs extra.

After my walk with Sue in Girlsta, she had taken me to see two crofters who were trying out a very different approach to fencing. Father and son, Magnus and Steven Johnson, were not using wire and wooden stakes. They were using their phones.

Nofence is a system developed in Norway that allows people to control grazing using satellite data. On a mobile app, farmers can demarcate the area in which they want their beasts to feed. The animals wear a collar which tracks their position, and emits an auditory warning when they go over the defined line.

As we sat around their kitchen table drinking tea, both men still in their grizzled boiler suits and toories, Magnus had got out his phone to show me. There was a picture of a field and a line of dots where the collar had triggered an alert.

'It starts off with an audio warning,' he said. 'Then, if they carry on, they get the shock. They do learn fast.'

Having the collars saves the family the expense of putting up a physical fence and also means they can change the perimeters with the tap of a finger. However, the collars are not cheap. For thirty, the price was around £8,000. The Johnsons managed to get theirs through government funding. The reason for trialling this expensive system was to find a more sympathetic way of grazing the land that would allow other life to thrive, particularly the peat.

Nofence would keep the stock in areas where the sheep would not disturb their work creating dams and levelling hags to store water. It would be helpful in other ways too. If a breeding merlin was sighted, for example, the virtual fence could be altered to keep the sheep from trampling the nest.

Sheep were the only way to make the patch of land economically viable, Steven had said. To make it work, the Johnsons would have to put extra value on the wool.

Hent – (Scots) to grasp or lay hold of
Laget – (Norn) a loose wisp of material such as wool

Hentilagets are the scrappy clouds of fleece found snagged from a sheep's back on fences or dykes, or perhaps a rare tree. Every piece was precious, and folk would collect these delicate gifts and spin them into lace. The work of one artist in particular pays poignant tribute to this practice. In 2011, local craftswoman Helen Robertson knitted panels for fences using thin aluminium wire. Photos of the delicate woven patterns hint at something warm and comforting, a shawl or a scarf, which stand out in contrast against the line of sharp barbs above.

'The project is tribute to the Shetland knitters of the past who in their struggle for survival designed beautiful, delicate lace knit patterns,' Robertson wrote. Shortly after installation, a strong gale blew 'as it only can in Shetland' and tore the wire away.

As I climbed, I chose my tussocks carefully, remembering to select the more substantial islands of rush and grass to save my feet from a cold peat dip. I was on common land now, where deep gullies wound through the damp ground. This was the territory of sheep, those woolly maggots who shoulder worm holes into the black butter to escape the abrasive force of the wind. These shelters left the skin of the peat exposed and turning to dust.

The patch of land Steven and Magnus were piloting with Nofence was like this.

'There was so much bare black in it, so much poor foliage,' Steven said. 'It wasn't productive for the sheep to go on and graze. In better land the sheep come off much cleaner, they don't get so dirty in the peat and it's easier to reach them.'

After attending a volunteer day restoring peat with the Shetland Amenity Trust, Steven's son Logan had suggested they do something with the ragged hill. Magnus and Steven decided on a plan: to form a company with another crofter and put in a bid for funding from the Scottish Government's Peatland Action programme to restore the hills in Girlsta. By piecing the hills back together, the Johnsons were adopting a different way of putting value into the land, one that combined profit with reciprocity and would benefit generations to come.

My feet were soaked. Sneugie was one of those hills that keep tricking you into thinking you're near the top. The ground gets stonier and the hags thin out, but actually the peak is still some distance away. Just over 200 metres from sea level you finally reach it: a concrete trig point marked with a small cairn. As soon as I stepped towards it, the wind smacked me in the face and I felt like it was trying to toss me in the air.

With my eyes watering, I looked out across a blue and brown panorama, from the edge of the Loch of Gonfirth right around to the opening of the Olnafirth. The viewpoint seemed to loop me into other moments in time when I had stood on that spot: a tea break from work while resident in Kirkhoose during Covid; an hour away from the family heartbreak at the time of Dad's diagnosis; and thirty years before when Dad had led me there as a child. I'd played in the gullies and bounced on the crispy heather. While I did so, Dad called for a pause as he took out his camera to capture a series of photos, piecing together a moment with his hands that would go on to live without him.

23

A Matter of Perspective

$$KE = \frac{1}{2}mv^2$$

The energy used to boil water for your cup of tea might have started as a gust of wind.

What is the wind?

The wind is air in motion. It moves for different reasons. One of them is pressure. Atmospheric pressure is a measure of the density of air pressing down on the Earth; air wants to move from high to low pressure to equalise the difference. When air rises there is lower pressure, when air sinks there is high pressure. This movement is the wind, the 'Wild Spirit' of Percy Bysshe Shelley's poem, 'which art moving everywhere'.[65]

---

[65] Percy Bysshe Shelley, 'Ode to the West Wind' https://www. poetryfoundation.org/poems/45134/ode-to-the-west-wind

Rotation

Warm air rises near the Equator and flows towards the poles, but another factor directing the wind's journey is the turning of the Earth. The planet's rotation means winds tend to blow west–east rather than north–south. This is known as the Coriolis effect.

Friction

Wind speed increases as you go upwards away from the friction caused by the earth's surface: the higher you go, the windier it will be. The sea causes less friction than the land: the further away from land, the less friction. This means that far-flung Shetland, out in the North Sea, has a higher than average wind speed.

Energy

Kinetic energy is anything that is moving. The calculation is half the mass times the square of its velocity. When the kinetic energy of the wind – the force of its movement – flows across the blade of a turbine, the shape of the blade causes uneven pressure. As the blade moves, this creates both lift and drag, and as lift is stronger, the wind pushes the blades around. Inside the turbine, the blades are connected to a rotor shaft. The rotor is connected to a generator, which converts the aerodynamic force into electricity. So, the force of the wind, this 'Destroyer and preserver', is captured and transformed into a flow of energy that can be harnessed to serve homes hundreds of miles away.

*

'Thirty years ago we put up anemometer masts to measure the wind speeds at Burradale for over a year. The two boys that put it up slept on our kitchen floor in sleeping bags. The data showed that the level of wind was exceptional.'

I was sitting across the table from Angus Ward, who, along with two other shareholders, set up Burradale wind farm on the outskirts of Lerwick over twenty years ago. It was Drew Ratter who had put me in touch with him, but despite this personal introduction, our initial exchange had been tentative.

'With respect, given the amount of "bad press" we have got these last 15 years, I am cautious in discussing complex issues with people who may have a bias against wind farms,' he had replied via email. 'Therefore will you please send me a list of your previous published work.'

By chance, the most recent (and final) issue of the magazine on which I had been editor was all about community projects producing renewable energy, so my lack of bias was easy to prove. It wasn't long before Angus invited me to his home in West Burra. The house was sparkling clean, with new electrical appliances and a fancy extractor fan. Angus had planned the building himself, along with the two adjacent buildings, the façades facing the smashing waves of the North Atlantic. When I commented on how cosy it was, he said it was funny that folk complained about the cold in modern houses. His grandfather would sit in the house in woollen underwear from his neck to his ankles. He had been brought up in a council house nearby where in winter ice had formed on the inside of the windows.

Perhaps it was this experience of hardship that had whetted his business sense and a desire to create a more comfortable life. Thanks to his entrepreneurial skills, and a talent for not letting chances go by (much like Drew), he had reaped a bounty from the wind. It had been a tough slog, and he'd risked a lot to do it. It was this story that he wanted to tell me.

He was giving me a detailed history of the beginnings of Burradale. After proving the viability of the site, the three men planned to build three turbines on the hill.

'Then we had to think about how to get the money together to build it,' Angus said. 'We were spending money of our own. It was high risk. It caused a few strains in the families, but anyway we managed to carry on.'

I could imagine the intensity of these family conversations. Money had been an issue in our house too but as a child I'd only had a small window onto what Mum was going through as a single parent. My memory snags on small details: evenings with a neighbour while Mum worked, never being allowed to finish a packet of something or open a new one without warning her first; a collection of soggy soap ends on the bathroom sink, placed in a special mould so they could be used until the last bubble.

For the Burradale boys, there was a lot to pay for: the turbines, the civil works, the roads and more.

'I think it would have been around £1.7 million,' Angus said.

Angus found a banker willing to cover 80% of the debt. They also received the bulk of the equity through a loan from the Shetland Leasing and Property, an offshoot of moneys from the oil fund. But at 12%, the rate was very high.

'So we're putting in close to £100,000 between us all. I think I was £50,000 down. Hence I dived in salmon cages for fifteen years,' he chuckled.

One of the things he put up for security was his own house. It showed what kind of man he was, I thought, that he was willing to gamble his home in order to build a better one. Putting his house in the mangle was 'frightening' he said.

As well as the flow of the wind, the business plan also depended on the flow of money. The first pot was the project finance, then there was the debt service reserve account to make sure they could pay the warranty on the equipment, the operating costs and when every account was full up 'then it spills over to the dividend'. It took the men about three years before the project started to produce dividends, which they used to pay the loan back faster.

In the meantime, they had constructed the second phase of Burradale: two more turbines.[66] The financial success of the project meant that when the crash came in 2008, the Burradale boys had enough in their pots to pay the debt off.

---

[66] Angus said: 'These were built under the Renewables Obligation Certificate mechanism – the ROC – which at the time offered a £3 subsidy on each kilowatt hour you produced. Then you could sell it on the market. They insist that you sign a counterparty – who you sell your electricity to. In those ten years of counterparty (because we had a ten-year debt) the price of electricity went up from about £60 a megawatt hour to about £100 a megawatt hour on the market – that was inclusive of the ROC.'

'Now, how did that relate to Viking, is the question you are probably most interested in,' Angus said.

SSE had applied for connection to the UK mainland for 250MW as far back as 2002, he told me. After that 'various developers were marching the hills of Shetland', approaching the council and landowners.

When Burradale expanded in 2003, people started to seriously ask if Shetland could connect itself to the UK mainland. Angus wasn't sure about this, but he and the other Burradale boys prepared a paper, which they presented to the council.

'They could see the money was flowing in, they knew that it was a possibility. They also knew that it was probably going to happen anyway. The people who were in this game were watching the results from wind farms.'

As Shetland claimed the title of 'windiest place in the UK', the efficiency of the turbines was a winning factor, Angus said. So they set up Viking Energy Shetland LLP, 90% owned by the Shetland Charitable Trust and 10% by Burradale.

The intention had always been to have an undersea cable and work with a utility company who could run it, he said. This ambition progressed with a 'beauty contest' between the big energy suppliers: Scottish Power and SSE among the contestants. With a green light from the Scottish government, the project leapt another hurdle, and they looked forward to successfully applying for the Contracts for Difference (CfD) in order to secure good returns for the council.

Then came Sustainable Shetland's court case.

Although Viking won the courtroom battles, a change in

government heralded a different attitude to renewables and the subsidies dried up.

Drew Ratter, Jonathan Wills and Angus blame Sustainable Shetland for delaying the planning process with their legal action, which meant the charitable trust had to withdraw a substantial amount of investment. But Frank and Billy argued that the reason the project was challenged in the courts was because of a sense of powerlessness, and a lack of democratic decision-making. In my search for the 'truth' behind the wind farm, I was going around in circles.

Ownership

I had never imagined myself as a landlord, but I couldn't bear the idea of selling my share in Kirkhoose, so after Dad's death I became just that: the official recipient of a rental fee each month, profiting from Jen's hard-earned wages through no graft of my own. Private ownership is at the heart of capitalism, allowing one to exclude others from the benefits of assets and resources. In the words of Adrienne Buller and Mathew Lawrence in *Owning the Future: Power and Property in an Age of Crisis*: 'Ownership is thus indivisible from politics and the collective ordering of our unequal world. It both reflects and reinforces power and class relations at any given moment and in any given place.' Ownership was deeply ingrained into the story of Shetland's relationship with energy, from beached whales to deep bays fit for oil tankers and peatland with the right weather for wind turbines.

'Where Shetland gained its ability to influence the oil industry was the 1974 Oil Act, which was done by the Labour government,' Angus said. 'Shetland Island Council was allowed to compulsory purchase the land around Sullom Voe and force the companies to come to one area with the pipelines, which was a national project of significance.'

It was a theme that spilled over into the wind farm debate: a perception that only people who owned the land would get direct benefits from the wind farm.

SSE Renewables, a subsidiary of multinational company Scottish & Southern Energy PLC, was now the main investor of Viking, and SSEN, also a subsidiary of the company, owned the interconnector. Shareholders of SSE included BlackRock, the world's largest asset manager and one of BP's largest shareholders.

'It seems that the challenges of wind farms lie not only in the technology, but who owns that technology, controls it and profits from it, and the sensibility that surrounds its application,' author James Marriott wrote.[67] SSE is 'oil thinking made manifest', he says, pointing out that the chair of the company is a former employee at BP.[68]

---

[67] https://platformlondon.org/cambo-viking-energy-the-common-wealth-of-wind-in-shetland/

[68] The issue of who profits from the wind farm erupted onto social media feeds again in the summer of 2024. Viking had received over £2 million in just a month in what are known as 'constraint payments' – compensation paid to wind farm developers to reduce output during times when supply exceeds demand and the transmission network can't cope. This eye-watering sum was more than the figure allocated to the community benefit pot for the entire year. The figures were published by the Renewable Energy Foundation, a charity which 'appears to spend most of its time campaigning against onshore wind' and has strong links to climate science sceptics, according to the *Guardian*.

What if the company reaping these profits were publicly owned, with the money fed back into sustaining life for everyone here, instead of a privileged few? What if a publicly owned electricity generator used the revenues to hasten the transformation of our homes and transport to help us survive global boiling?

Outside, the wind whipped up waves in the Atlantic Ocean. There was a brief pause and Angus changed the subject, asking where Dad's croft was in Voe. Like Dad, Angus had been the first in his family to go to college.

'It wasn't common,' he said. 'Your father was four years older than me. He was the generation that just missed the oil boom,' he added, appearing to relax a little.

'I have a cousin that lives out in Roslin. He's seventy-eight now but he went away to Aberdeen in '64 then came home to the fishing then went away to become a teacher in Edinburgh. He likes to play and sing, he played in a little band in his time. He had this musical do, I'm not sure when it was, maybe six years ago. He'd have them every now and again. Sandra and I went down. And all these far-flung Shetlanders appeared about your father's age. About fifty or sixty people. Quite a number. So basically Shetland exported its educated people, of which your father was one.'

I imagined the scene, dozens of women and bearded men in woollen jumpers, sharing stories and having a grand carry-on. In my mind I zoomed in on one figure, a tall, broad-chested figure blinking back tears of laughter as he rolled a cigarette between his fingers.

It was getting late. Not only did I have another appointment, but it was approaching dinner time. Before I left, Angus insisted on showing me around the house. I followed him up a short flight of carpeted stairs to Sandra's art studio. On the way, we passed a connecting window. I stopped to look at the design: a sandblasted picture of a neat line of hills, on top of which stood a row of elegant wind turbines that glowed with the last of the afternoon sun.

*

As I followed the narrow road back to the Mainland, the setting sun spilt orange and pink over the bank of grass and filled the strip of white sand below the road. I stopped the car in a lay-by to take a photo on my phone – an attempt to capture a piece of the scene and take it with me. Before inviting me into his home, Angus had taken me to a small graveyard nearby. Sprouting from a carpet of clipped grass were rows of stones, most softened by lichen and moss, but some still shiny and sharp.

Lichens are a symbiotic relationship between algae and fungi. The algae transform sunlight, water and carbon dioxide into oxygen and sugars via photosynthesis; the fungi feed on these sugars, and in return absorb nutrients and moisture from the environment. It's always a joy to see these tiny communities sharing life together, especially in a place that commemorates the dead.

After a few minutes trying to locate what he was looking for, Angus led me to one of the stones. It read:

Grace Pottinger
wife of William Ward
died 23rd April 1937

'Grace was my grandmother,' he said. 'She had six sons. Two were killed in the Second World War by direct enemy action.' Four sons and a daughter were listed below. Jerry was 'a peerie boy,' Angus said.

'He died when he found some unexploded ordnance on the beach just over there.' He nodded to a point beyond the church. 'That was in 1941.'

There was another name beneath it. 'Samuel A.' The initial stood for Angus. This uncle, after whom Angus had been named, had been in the merchant navy and was torpedoed during the war. We stood for a moment in silence.

'Seven people. There are seven people here. This is what incomers don't understand,' he said, his tone hard. 'They don't understand what it's like to live in a place like this and survive. We're living in the best of times right now.' He looked at me. 'Do you want to live in modern times or in the past? Incomers have literally bought their view.'

We took a minute to look at the names. Under the last one, Angus's Aunt Grace, there was room for more.

As I left Burra behind me and headed for Lerwick, I considered everything that he had said, and felt the edge of his disappointment at seeing a project he had risked so much and worked so hard for fail to reach its full potential. It was a disappointment matched by that of those who had fought against the wind farm and the risks they had taken in going to court. Angus had criticised Sustainable Shetland for their decision to go ahead with the court case: 'How can it be a democratic decision? Who gave them the democratic power "thou shalt not"?' It was an interesting point. What made a decision 'democratic'? Was it a voting system, like the one that elected representatives to local and national government? But this system had fruited an unelected prime minister currently caught in a descending spiral of U-turns, and closer to home, the local council had been challenged on conflicts of interest. On a more personal level, what was behind the division between 'incomers' and folk descended from generations of Shetlanders? Was the only foundation stone in a person's Shetland identity the one engraved with the names of ancestors, spotted yellow and grey with lichen? Could you come from a long line of Shetlanders and still be considered an outsider? Who gets to decide?

'I hope that you can break through some of the ice,' Angus had said earnestly as we stood up from the table. 'I hope that you'll tell the truth.'

The dream

On the eve of my tenth birthday I was given a copy of *Marianne Dreams*, Catherine Storr's fantasy novel for children published in 1958. The novel opens with Marianne on the eve of her own tenth birthday, not knowing that she is about to fall ill and will spend several months in bed. It is during this period of convalescence that she embarks on a coming-of-age adventure. She finds a magic pencil, and the drawings she makes with it come alive in her dreams. First she draws a house, which she then explores in her sleep, then a figure at one of the windows, whom she meets and befriends. At one point she gets angry with this new friend and scribbles bars across the windows and draws a circle of towering stones around the house, each with a sinister eye. This is the point at which the story takes a dark turn. As a child with a leaning towards the macabre, this story took up residence in my imagination, returning to me every now and again throughout adulthood.

It was the work of artist Paul Bloomer that brought the story back to me nearly three decades later.

*

Black shapes crowd the landscape like a crop of blades. Their bulk and their pointed tips dominate the skyline so only peeks of sky are visible.

('Windfarm Vision 1', woodcut, 2008)

The distant skyline is hatched with shafts and blades, their forms suggesting a constant motion that breaks apart the light. In the foreground, the shadow of these forms stretch out towards the viewer like fingers on long arms. It takes me a moment to see them: tiny shapes at the angles of the vast shadows. Then I realise they are houses.

('Shadow Flicker', woodcut, 2008)

*

Paul had also had a dream. He dreamt that he had gone for a walk in the hills and lost his bearings. He wrote:

> Amongst the broken glass and beer can filth I looked around and found myself in an industrial landscape with wind turbines stretching as far as the eye can see. Suddenly I heard a truck driving up the giant road that cut into the hills, then men and boys unloaded motorbikes and screeched around the track they had made into the heather.

Instead of spiralling lapwings, he saw the spiralling blades of wind turbines. There was peat run-off, the birds were gone, save the bonxies that feasted on the birds' corpses beneath the turbines, and folk had abandoned their homes.

> I started to run as fast and far away as possible but no matter how far I ran in any direction I could still see the turbines.[69]

Paul's woodcuts were 'an expression of anger' over the wind farm, he told me as we chatted in one of the studios of the University of the Highlands and Islands, where he worked as a lecturer. It was nearly 5 p.m. and the corridors had a feeling of exhaling after a long day. 'There was a sense that it was unjust. I think there's going to be a lot of loss of identity.'

Paul was born and raised in the Black Country. After leaving school he worked in a metal-pressing factory,

---

[69] https://www.wind-watch.org/news/2008/03/24/i-had-a-dream/

experimenting with woodcuts as a way to express his ideas. At that time he never used colour because 'my worldview didn't seem big enough to find colour and beauty among the smoking chimney stacks.' He moved to Shetland in 1997 after coming to the isles to look after someone's dog. 'I had a powerful connection to the landscape, a sense of belonging,' he said.

He opposed the wind farm from the early days. 'Art for me is my voice,' he said as he scrolled through images of his series of prints on the wind farms. Over the years he had been documenting the construction site, 'drawing the changes, feeling the vibes,' he said.

'I like to spend time in the landscape, feel and observe. It forces unclear ideas into focus.' Many of his students explored the wind farm as a theme in their work, he said. When it first started 'there was a real sense of secrecy and a lack of transparency, pseudo-listening for public relations,' he added. 'Some people were attacked for speaking out.'

We scrolled through some more examples of his work on his Instagram page. One shows a charcoal drawing of a tiny wren singing while encircled by the grasping claws of diggers. In another, a wild salmon is depicted in a sea of farmed salmon. The caption read: 'Farmed salmon asks wild salmon, how did we get to this place? Sea lice and gill choking jellyfish are also present at the meeting.'

'Life on an island is a great humbler,' he told me as he returned his phone to his pocket. 'Everyone has to survive on an island, you have no choice but to get on with each other.'

That was another reason he felt so angry about the wind farm: because in his eyes it had damaged these community bonds. 'I've tried to accept that we are in a broken age. The wind farm is so big we can't do anything about it.'

Later I considered again what Angus had said about incomers not really understanding Shetland. If someone who has lived on the isles and explored the natural environment for twenty years doesn't understand the landscape, who does? What qualifications does a resident of Shetland need to have in order for them to have a respectable opinion on how to manage the land? Everyone I had talked to who wasn't born on the isles had told me about the sense of belonging they felt. As I had experienced myself, Shetlanders were welcoming and hospitable, generously sharing their stories with a stranger. While some of Paul's observations about the landscape were certainly romantic, did this negate the affinity he felt with the way of life here? Like Billy and Frank, it wasn't just the folk who had moved here who mourned the transformation of the landscape that the wind farm would bring. As Robert Sandison's song said: 'Shetland's no Shetland ony mair.'

I pondered this as the headlights of the car illuminated the road ahead through threads of rain. Throughout my life, I had always passed between tribes too quickly to pledge allegiance to this or that community. I had lots of close friends, but these were scattered across the world, like signposts to past lives. When asked where I came from, I would always reply 'Edinburgh', but it had been so long since I lived there that my connection with the city felt like a fading after-image. I never stayed anywhere else long enough to be called an incomer.

On the outskirts of Lerwick I shifted the car up a gear, coaxing it up the slopes past Burradale, the fifty-metre turbines concealed in the thickening gloom. If Angus was a 'native' Shetlander, and Paul was an 'incomer', what was I? I thought of the two perspectives on the wind farm, the light illuminating the stylish window in Angus' home and Paul's angry black and white prints.

The engineer and businessman could see the beauty in the turbines, but the artist did not. In *Who Owns the Wind*, Hughes notes a similar reaction as he explores the dominating presence of wind turbines from the point of view of Sereno, a small village in Spain. At first the wind farm was met with suspicion and hostility but as the years passed by they became incorporated into the personality of the place. 'To gaze upon machinery in this way – outside the box of what is before us – is a utopian act, a choice.'[70]

---

[70] David McDermott Hughes, *Who Owns the Wind? Climate Crisis and the Hope of Renewable Energy* (Verso, 2021).

24

Flightpath

September 2019

10th Dad and I go to a pub in Devon on receiving news of the death of my maternal grandfather.

20th Millions across the world take part in a global climate strike, the biggest climate protest in history. The Shetland Amenity Trust organises a peatbog restoration day where folk can learn about the role this ecosystem plays in storing carbon.

Viking Energy fails to win a bid for subsidies.[71]

26th An empty coffin burns on Voe pier as part of a Lament for the Lang Kames.

---

[71] Contracts for Difference. https://www.shetlandtimes.co.uk/2019/09/20/viking-energy-fails-to-feature-in-contracts-for-difference-allocations

I imagine these points in different lives like woven lines of colour; threading in and out, they do not show all at the same time, but they hold each other together.

*

It should take about eight minutes. Two folk hold either end of a sixty-foot net of fine mesh – delicate enough to hold but not hurt. They position the net over a lochan so when the bird takes off or dives under the water, it is caught in the net. With a quick and light grip, the bird is ringed and then let free. Most of the time, it will stay on the water, afraid of straying too far from its chicks.

Logan Johnson was one of the few ringers in the country who was allowed to handle red-throated divers. He started when he was only fourteen, ringing wading birds with ornithologist Dave Okill, whose detailed and extensive work on the red-throated diver was used as part of Viking's bird report in 2009. Ringing the birds helped conservationists monitor their movements and habits so they could better protect their homes and feeding grounds.

'I've been part of that for years,' he told me. 'I've really taken to it. I think I'm the only one under the age of forty so I think it's going to get worrying in a few years.'

We were sitting in Mareel, a large venue in Lerwick facing the sea which hosted a number of cinema screens, spaces for classes, exhibitions, events, and – importantly for our purpose – a café. I'd arranged to meet him there after hearing how his interest in conservation had inspired his dad, Steven, and grandad, Magnus, to set up a peat restoration business. Logan, then nineteen, had attended a day at Sandy Loch Reservoir near Lerwick in September 2019 where staff from Sue's team at the Shetland Amenity Trust were restoring the site to reduce carbon emissions and improve the quality of the drinking water. Volunteers were invited to come along in their wellies and waterproofs – 'no previous experience is needed, just a desire to do something positive about climate change.'

Logan spoke quickly and with a lot of energy, and I struggled to keep up with him. He also had a tendency of drifting into a different topic for a while only to pause and ask apologetically what the question had been. I didn't mind as everything he had to say was extremely interesting. Logan was born 1999, and as such had grown up alongside Viking Energy's wind farm, but the presence of this monumental structure had a far bigger impact on the course of his life.

After years of learning how to ring birds with reputed ornithologists, in 2018, Logan became involved in the ecological surveying for the area covered by the wind farm. He joined a team mapping where vulnerable and endangered birds nested and the routes they took to feeding grounds. Like most of the UK's bird populations, numbers were decreasing. Not long ago, up until the nineties, ringers would be catching 15-20 raingeese chicks in a day, Logan said.

'Nowadays you're lucky if you ring five or under in the course of a week. It was a natural progression, I suppose, that

I took this work on the wind farm because I thought I could potentially do a lot of good,' he said. 'In some parts of my job I can look after how we can serve the raingeese on the site.'

Workers at Viking made special corridors through the wind farm for the birds and tried to move the maintenance roads so they didn't affect the breeding lochans. They didn't know where all the nests were as the habits of the birds were still shrouded in mystery. Despite that, Logan did know a lot. For some pairs, he knew which years they had succeeded in raising young, which years they failed; he knew which pairs often lost their chicks to bonxies, and where popular breeding lochans often dried out, forcing parents to move their chicks.

'You could make family trees for them,' he said.

One of his favourite encounters was from around 2015 when he came across a puddle of water 'no bigger than that bar', he said, pointing to the one behind us in the café. He caught the female and discovered a ring dating from 2001 – the bird was at least eighteen years old, making her older than Logan at the time. Another meeting took place in a ditch. It was misty, and the diver couldn't see where it was going so it landed in the nearest body of water it could find, but being such a small puddle it was impossible for the bird to take off again. A member of the public alerted him and he went to release it.

With his passion and experience, he got a job for the Shetland Amenity Trust alongside Sue White as a natural heritage officer and was tasked with finding the best areas to do peat restoration to create functioning blanket bog with the ninety hectares of peat displaced by the wind farm.

The fate of the raingoose was not only tied up in the location of the turbines. It was also entwined with other dominant themes of Shetland life: the weather and crofting.

Peat storm

I'd explored the hags in the peat bogs on the top of the hills near Voe, and I'd heard from Sue White about how wind and overgrazing sculpt these trenches, transforming carbon sinks into carbon emitters. Logan was to tell me something else: how the degradation of these once-rich habitats not only contributed to the climate crisis, but also threatened the habitats of the much-loved raingoose.

Many of the birds' favourite nesting sites are on lochans on the tops of hills, like the one behind Kirkhoose. But up there, where sheep have worn away a protective layer of vegetation and shouldered shelter from the elements in the soil, the peat is exposed and vulnerable. All the water is washing away down the gullies, and in the dry summer months, the peat cracks and dries, causing peat tornados. In these conditions, you can't walk without getting peat blown in your eyes.

In winter, the peat is soaked so water runs through the cracks left from the summer, creating deeper gullies. As the water flows down, it meanders like a river, getting bigger and wider. As the wind blows the hilltops away, it erodes the lochans that sit up here until they become shallower and shallower and shallower, with water running out of the gullies. Then, at last, like the pulling of a bath plug, they run dry.

'In some cases, we've lost very productive lochans that have been known to have birds on them for hundreds of years, but they're being lost because of these erosion features,' he said.

When levelling hags and creating pools for sphagnum moss and other vegetation to store water, the peat restoration team were not only helping the landscape to store carbon, they were also building homes for one of Shetland's most beloved birds.

How to build a raingoose nest

First, find a site like the top of a hill, that will allow the adults enough uplift so they can get in and out to feed the chicks. Make sure this will also enable the chicks to turn around and take off. You wouldn't want a perfect breeding site that's a death trap for chicks.

Second, remove the hags – push them to the side, you'll need natural seepage for the peat and to raise the water level.

Third, dig a deep enough hole – somewhere in the region of twelve metres by twenty metres to be on the safe side.

Fourth, hope they like it.

*

I remembered my sightings of the bird on a tiny island on the peerie loch of Gonfirth, both with Dad and on my own as I laboured through the fog during lockdown. Dad mentioned some locals had built the nest for the birds, so I asked Logan if he knew anything about it. He did, it was a good breeding loch, he said. In a meandering way I had become accustomed to during the course of our interview, he went on to tell me more of the story. It was surprisingly gruesome.

'A couple of local conservationists dug out the island a few years ago with a digger. It's about a metre or so from the side so the sheep cannae jump on it.'

'What's the problem with sheep?' I asked.

'Sheep eating eggs and trampling nests is a big issue that folk don't think aboot,' he replied.

I braced myself for more details.

'A few years ago in Papa Stour, a couple of folk went over and surveyed the tirrick[72] colonies and thought – there's something wrong with that. They walked up and checked and a few of them only had one wing. So, it turned out sheep were eating these chicks alive, chewing off their wings, because they had a lack of calcium. Sheep somehow know when they lack calcium, I suppose it's like humans with cravings. In the seventies and eighties this was a lot more common, folk noticed it a lot more. There's a record fae Hermaness of a flock of thirty to forty sheep going doon one of the old trails to a guillemot colony, eating the eggs of between thirty and a hundred pairs. Sometimes sheep just go and trample the nests, they just seem to get annoyed. A lot of raingeese nest on the side of lochs, there's only so much they can do before the sheep eat the egg or stamp on it. So that's another reason to create islands.'

The ravens I remembered from the quarry near Gonfirth were also a recent feature, but Logan said the birds hadn't nested there recently.

---

[72] Arctic Tern.

'It could have been done in,' he said, meaning destroyed. 'Crofters don't like them. All it taks is someone who knows. We're sometimes very careful where we say our ravens' nests are. I've had at least two where I know they've been done in. I think it's people watching me.'

Shetland's wildlife was facing assault from all angles: habitat loss, warming temperatures, or death by a human hand and the hooves and jaws of hungry/angry sheep.

I wanted to know if the Viking wind farm was one of these threats.

'Wind farms shouldn't be built on blanket bogs, end of story. The one on Yell is going to be built on pristine blanket bog, which is mad to say the least,' he said.

Viking was different, however. In words that echoed many of my other interviewees, Logan focused on the sorry state of the bog at the wind farm site.

'Now we have a chance to restore it,' he said. 'The area is colossal. There's such a chance now that we can get up into the hills and make a change. Before we couldn't get the machinery up there. Now we can. It shouldn't be going up there in the first place, but it's there. We have to be doing what we can with it.'

In 'Rain Gös',[73] Shetland poet Roseanne Watt describes how the bird must be exhausted prophesying storms 'i dese doomtöm days' (in these downpour days) when no one wants to listen. Her short stanzas and the crisp, clear sound of the

---

[73] The poem is part of the collection *Moder Dy* (Polygon Press, 2019), a beautiful and essential read for anyone interested in Shetland.

Shetland dialect add to the precision of the poem. There are storm clouds gathering, a high-pressure front of crises for our times: record hot weather, droughts, wildfires, the end of life as we knew it.

Despite the gloomy outlook, Logan was upbeat, partly because of the work his father Steven and grandfather Magnus were doing to restore the bog and keep water from being washed out to sea. Shetlanders needed to revolutionise their land use – create a landscape that stored carbon, and regenerate a land of scrubby trees where birds rest and nest. It was a big ask, but one Logan felt was possible.

'I feel the change, it's coming,' he said.

25

Seeing the Light

Two hydrogen atoms collide in the sun's core and fuse to create a helium atom.

This nuclear fusion creates solar energy.

Solar energy warms the Earth, creating wind and feeding plants through photosynthesis.

In her essay 'Tallgrass', Robin Wall Kimmerer describes how the sun makes the grasses, the grasses the buffalo, the buffalo wallows, the wallows make flowers . . .

And we
We have unmade it all.[74]

*

---

[74] Robin Wall Kimmerer, 'Tallgrass', in *The Clearing* from Little Toller Books (2018) https://www.littletoller.co.uk/the-clearing/tallgrass-by-robin-wall-kimmerer/

There were two lines of plastic chairs facing the dancers, room for around two dozen people. Slowly, every seat was taken. Most folk knew each other, and called out to this or that friend or relative as they settled down. Naturally, finding myself among such a crowd, I raised the subject of Viking Energy.

'It's got a lot to answer for,' one person said. 'Fewer people are speaking in Shetland dialect now, it's all because of that wind farm.'

Though we all chuckled, I wasn't entirely sure it was a joke.

Earlier in the day, I'd received an invitation to watch a dance performance in a village hall. I'd offered to drive there. The dance troupe were doing a tour of Britain and were performing in four venues in Shetland, funded by Shetland Arts, partly funded by the Shetland Charitable Trust, which channelled investments made from the oil money. The dance piece was an expression of friendship across borders; a celebration of cultures in music, dance and storytelling. Afterwards, the band asked if anyone wanted to do some cèilidh dancing, but it was a school night and most folk seemed too tired or shy (certainly I was). When we stepped out of the hall, our breath exhaled into the cold air in clouds of steam. We drove back the faster way, avoiding the windier and narrower roads in favour of a route that took us to the A970.

Just as we were approaching the crest of a hill, one passenger sitting in the back stretched their hand between the front seats and said: 'Look at dat light yonder.' They were pointing at a faint green glow on the skyline. 'Is dat the northern lights?'

It was a good time of year for the lights, partly because of the geomagnetic activity, the angle of the Earth's axis and increasing hours of darkness. In a particularly moving chapter in her book *The Outrun*, Amy Liptrot recalls seeing these 'Merry Dancers':

> The whole sky is alive with shapes: white 'searchlights' beaming from behind the horizon, dancing waves directly above and slowly, thrillingly, blood red blooms

I'd never seen them, having only been to Shetland in the dark season a handful of times. So the prospect of potentially catching them now was particularly exciting. I pulled in at the next layby so we could look more carefully.

Liptrot describes them as an 'unusual kind of light, the eerie glow of a floodlit stadium or a picnic eaten in car headlights'. In Shetland, they are known as the Mirrie Dancers, which comes from the Norn word 'mirr', which means to tremble or quiver. The light we were looking at was certainly unusual, rising from the hill like an insipid green sunrise, but there was none of Liptrot's 'trembling, shimmering, quivering motion, like a dancing gossamer'.[75] We watched it for a while before someone observed that there was too much cloud cover, which would obscure our view of the Dancers. These lights must be coming from the ground.

We considered our location. We were just on the other side

---

[75] For a wonderful discussion on the origin of the phrase 'Mirrie Dancers', I recommend this podcast on BBC Sounds www.shetnews. co.uk/2023/03/01/history-in-a-wird-the-origins-of-the-mirrie-dancers/

of the Lang Kames, coming up to the junction with the A970. There were no houses over there, no gas flares or the Mordor-glow of Sullom Voe, only Kergord, the site where they were building the converter station for the wind farm.

There was a collective 'oh' from the car.

So that's what it was.

I dropped off my passengers and made my way back up the steep stretch of road to Kirkhoose. The darkness was thick and gloomy, but I did not find the prospect of returning to an empty house daunting. Jen's things seemed to intertwine with the place in a way that was not intrusive. They fit. The house felt homely. Alongside Jen's presence, it still contained an air of Dad's quiet studiousness, Josh's care and Esme's energy. But there was something else that was deeply comforting. All that time we had been settling back into our Devon ways, doing things that would be unthinkable in Shetland – like planting tomatoes outdoors or swimming in the river – Kirkhoose had not waited, static, like a shrine to something lost forever. It had grown too.

26

The Fog

'On entry to the main compound, please switch on hazard lights as instructed by relevant signage. You will arrive at the security gate/barrier where you will be asked to sign in. Please remember to reverse park.'

The day had arrived at last. After two weeks of investigating the story behind the Viking Energy wind farm, I was finally on my way to officially enter the site. But it was hard to concentrate. The voices of all the people I had talked to were orchestrating a cacophony of information in my head.

My first task was to meet Viking Energy's environmental manager, David McGinty, whom I'd met on the parkrun. After a short hunt on which I encountered several helpful young men in hi-vis jackets I entered the visitors' room. It was in a prefabricated building with the kind of hardy carpet that reminded me of my old primary school, bringing with it an uncomfortable, self-conscious hint of childhood. Information boards and posters on the walls added to the effect. A plastic fig tree in the corner contributed some lifeless colour to the room. I settled down at a semicircle of desks under the strip-lighting and dug into my bag for my notebook.

David was busy getting ready for the arrival of a group of local office workers, who were also there for the site visit. They eventually filed in, looking cheerful. We introduced ourselves, and David showed us a map of the site – the lungs and vertebrae of wind turbine locations – and gave us a brief presentation on health and safety.

We sat watching, waiting for David to finish his concise and upbeat presentation and invite questions. I often felt compelled to ask something in these kinds of moments – a hangover from attending press conferences – but now I felt no such impulse. It didn't stop me taking notes, though, which I could see David observing with some trepidation. Soon we were tasked with armouring ourselves for the journey: steel toe-capped white rubber boots, hard hats and hi-vis vests. We stepped out towards the waiting bus, the start of a route that would take us past Sandwater over the Mid Kames.

As the wheels of the bus turned onto the smoother surface of the A970, I caught sight of a familiar view: the former inn Halfway Hoose, looking as solitary as ever, but now positioned incongruously at the edge of a busy construction site. As the coach passed the track that led to the distant white building, I thought of its former occupant, Charlotte Robertson. We had never met, but news of her death at the age of eighty-eight the year before had still saddened me. She'd lived in the house for seventy years, longer than Dad's entire lifetime, keeping a cat and some sheep for company on her small croft. Despite being a very private person, faced with the prospect of eight turbines encircling her home at a distance of two kilometres, she had spoken out against the wind farm. It wasn't just a matter of noise from the construction work and 'the light flickering', she said. A big problem was that she hadn't been offered any compensation, and felt – a sentiment I had come across numerous times – that only certain folk were benefiting financially from the wind farm.

'Some people will make a lot of money from this,' she was quoted as saying in an article for the local group Save Shetland.

Was that the main motivation of the people who had championed the wind farm? I thought about Drew, the shrewd politician and dutiful grandfather; Jonathan, the writer, veg-grower and talented painter in oils; and Angus, the businessman, and proud home-builder. All had deep affection for the land that made them. Certainly there was a desire for Shetland not to return to a former way of life that was gratingly hard. From crofters to oil workers, islanders had been given a taste of economic prosperity and status. Who would choose to go back to such a tough life if they had a chance of something more comfortable? I doubted I would want that for Esme.

I thought about Halfway Hoose, lying empty and gathering mould. How much longer would it remain as it was? Lottie's death was, perhaps, the end of the road for this landmark to journeys half finished. I asked myself the question my meeting with Councillor Moraig had raised – where would the path to progress end, and what were we leaving on the wayside as we marched forwards? But it was impossible to carry everything with us, even if we wanted to.

The coach turned off the main road and up a newly laid track for construction vehicles. If we'd carried on, we would have reached the Morrisons' home, a newbuild constructed to look like a traditional croft house. I peered through the window, wondering if the lights of the fairy house were still burning. The wind farm was painfully personal to Evelyn and Donnie, cutting into the warmth and security of their everyday lives. Like many others, the couple had felt voiceless against what they perceived as a 'done deal'. Frank and Sustainable Shetland had transformed this feeling of powerlessness into action by taking the Scottish Government to court. The loss had cost their supporters a lot of money, and, from their viewpoint, the islanders as a whole had lost out on even more.

Frank, Jonathan and Billy had all sent me reports, emails and other documents that would support their separate cases. They had been keen, like Angus, for me to tell 'the truth' about the wind farm. I had read what they provided and more, trying to piece together a chronology of the wind farm itself; to understand where each point of view began and where it had ended up. As I looked out at the hills, strung with wisps of cloud, I considered where their stories had led me. By piecing together different views, I had been gaining a sense of the bigger picture, like the panorama of Sneugie Dad composed of different photographs and stuck to the wall of his study.

My fear now was that I was still missing something.

We lurched to the right up the track that follows the top of the Mid Kames. The fog was so thick, the driver had to be very careful to steer us away from the wide ditches lined with green and black wires. These linked the turbines together in a vascular network that exported the electricity to the main substation and the interconnector.

Red traffic cones pierced the murk, alerting us to danger.

'The cones symbolise the intrusion of humans in the landscape, kind of like blood,' Roxane had told me.

A digger loomed out of the mist and the coach came to a stop. How were they going to manage this one? I thought. The lip of the ditch was almost obscured by the fog.

I thought about the soil raked through the teeth of the bucket, the layers of skin on the face of the hills – sheep-shorn, wind-rubbed, stripped of trees and strung with fences – a landscape of pain indeed.

Those other layers too:

Clay and kleber – shapers of culture.

Peat – the fuel of survival.

Deep under the sea, the remains of animals and plants, compressed over millions of years into liquid hydrocarbons, became a brownish-black soup which brought economic prosperity to an island community. Revenue reaped from oil insulated homes against the weather and burning gas cooked dinners across the isles, but at the same moment of combustion another kind of heat was spreading across the world. Up in smoke, the release of carbon was boiling the atmosphere to such a degree that living treasures in other communities across the world could not adapt fast enough and began to die.

Mangrove
Sanderling
Sloth

The dying embers of their lives glowed in the low orange light of Sullom Voe.

After some skilful coordination with his colleagues on the track outside, the coach driver reversed inch by inch back down the road. We watched from inside the coach as the digger edged by until, with a collective exhaling of breath, we were on our way again.

On either side of us contours and shapes swam past in the mist: ditches, construction vehicles, the giant reels I had seen during my run there over a week before.

'You can see the banks of peat at the side where they are being reseeded,' David said, and all the passengers turned to look.

The tiny points of grass blades poked through the bank like a faded green aurora in the dark soil. This was an area of reinstatement, where disturbed areas were moved and reseeded using a hydroseed method – a slurry of grass seed, fertilisers, soil binders and mulch sprayed onto the soil – once the track had been laid. A solitary sheep wandered over the soupy bank. I thought of the Johnsons' restoration work with Sue White, reprofiling the hags and bringing life back into earth so dry the wind could whip up tornados of peat dust. The presence of humans certainly did cause damage, but some had found ways to heal it.

The mist swirled like a crowd of wraiths through the ditch. I imagined the stranded raingoose Logan had rescued after it made an emergency landing in the fog. What would such a bird feel like in your hands? The soft feathers, the wriggling legs, the ruby-red eye full of surprise and fear.

Without Viking, would these have eventually washed out to sea, draining the landscape of more than just another species, but also folklore and culture? The importance of the peat bog as a living ecosystem that feeds life into our atmosphere and keeps the Earth in balance – this was now entering everyday conversations in Shetland because of the wind farm. Could the project, as Logan hoped, trigger a land-use revolution in the isles, creating a regenerated landscape that served many more species than just our own?

The coach was cresting the hill, the point at which I remembered turning into the wind, feeling the force of the gale against my eyeballs. The construction of tracks, crane pads and the substation for the Viking project covered around 96 hectares, but this was offset with 272 hectares of peatland restoration, which arrested the pre-existing loss of CO_2 to the atmosphere from the degraded areas of bog.[76] It would take less than two years, according to the Scottish government's carbon calculator, for the wind farm to pay back the total carbon cost of construction and operation. Shetland's weather would be powering almost half a million homes. What was the alternative? To continue generating energy from the diesel power station in Lerwick and the gas-fired power station in Sullom Voe? Without the wind farm, Shetland's carbon emissions per head of population were amongst the highest in Europe. All this while countries like Bangladesh and Vietnam started to drown.

[76] Thanks to Aaron Priest, Viking's stakeholder manager, for this information.

We began to descend at the other end of the Kames. On a clear day we would have been able to see the opening of the valley that led to Lower Voe. In the right conditions, sunlight pooled in the wind-scooped hollows, and ignited flickers in the grass.

Our route was looping back on the A970 to follow another road over the hill to Vidlin to see one of the foundations for the turbines. As we approached the turn-off, I noticed something odd perched on top of a fence post. It was hunched and gnomelike, and as the coach slowed down, I saw it was covered with a thin layer of stour from the track. It was a trow. There were several of these ornaments along this stretch, a local joke, perhaps. The presence of these figurines meant something else too: a testament to a time when folklore helped people navigate a safe route across the deep, perilous bogs and hilltops exposed to the cutting wind.

The coach was labouring up now, and a side of the hill fell away into a view of one of the borrow pits – a great gouge out of the hillside. Stone from the pits layered the roads over which the coach lurched and strained. At last it stopped. This was a point at which visitors could go outside and have a close-up look at one of the turbine bases. We clambered out, pulling on our hi-vis vests and hard hats.

The white dome was vast, 22.5 metres in diameter. When completed, the bases would be backfilled to ground level. All that would be visible would be the top parapet, consisting of a narrow ring of anchor bolts to which the turbine towers were attached.

'The steel cage reminds me of a cathedral roof,' David said.

His words matched the monumental size and intricacy of the construction.

Different teams were brought in for different jobs and it was workers from Romania who had completed the cathedral roof. A Danish company, Vestas, was supplying turbine components. For each turbine, the three blades came from Italy and the four tower sections from Spain. At the top was the nacelle, a box which contained the gearbox and generator, and in front of this was the hub, the cone to which the blades attached – all these were from China.

Farming the wind in Shetland was a global effort, and the switching from fossil fuels to renewable energy will be, generally speaking, for the global good. The peat excavated from the Viking site was retained for reinstatement along track verges and cable trenches like the ones I saw out of the coach window. Restoration – helping the crumbling landscape soak up water in moss, pools and soil again – was an integral part of the project's habitat management plan. But the size of the undersea cable needed to facilitate the wind farm meant that more projects were likely to spring up on pristine peat bogs like the ones in Yell. Balancing the urgency of the transition with destruction of natural carbon sinks of that quality made things more complicated.

Underneath the base, Viking had buried some time capsules filled with work from the local schools. Who knew, in years to come, perhaps the children whose work nestled at the roots of these great masts would be telling stories about the turbines in the way their ancestors shared tales about cairns and crös.

I caught sight of my reflection in the coach window and hastily righted the jaunty angle of my helmet.

A chill was nibbling at my fingertips and I was relieved when David herded us back into the coach. As the engine chuntered along, my fellow tourists (the visiting office workers) shared their impressions of the view sliding past their windows. Having wedged myself into the back of the coach, I listened and observed.

It's much bigger than you think.

I don't think people realise the scale of it.

It's hard to imagine the height.

I'd put a turbine in my back garden if it would keep the leisure centres open and the roads in good condition.

I've changed my mind because I've been up here and seen it.

If they could negotiate a Shetland electricity tariff then that's what will make a big difference.

It's interesting to see how fast things are progressing when you see the scale of it.

'What do you think?' one of them asked me.

'I don't know,' I said, sitting up. 'I don't know yet, anyway.'

I had been on a quest for 'truth', assuming this would lead me to taking a side in the argument, but perhaps this wasn't the point. In speaking to people I was not only learning more about my father, I was also forming an idea of the connections that bound folk together; the giant tree on which hung all of our names as well as all the other creatures who breathed life into these islands.

Raingoose

Plucker

Terrik

In listening, I was placing myself among them.

I sat back in the fuzzy coach seat and closed my eyes. In the clamour of voices I had gathered over the last few weeks, a melody was slowly taking form. It was the sound of the wind as a force outside human control, shaping the surface of the Earth. Such a power demanded our respect and reciprocity.

The coach pulled up at the car park, its door opening with a hiss. I thanked David, waved goodbye to the office staff and returned to the car. Before I got in, I took a last look around: the prefabs, the men in their safety gear. Not long after my departure, workers at the site would pour concrete into the final turbine base. Soon the project would begin the challenging task of transporting the blades and sections of shaft to the site.

Part Three:
The Road Back

27

Embra

'When the hero-quest has been accomplished . . . the adventurer still must return with his life-transmuting trophy.'

Joseph Campbell, The Hero
with a Thousand Faces

A city is a living, thinking thing. Like cells in a human body, bits of it regularly die and regenerate, other parts change completely and a few features and functions stay the same. From the age of two, Edinburgh had shaped my perception of the world, from the words in my mouth to the changing of the seasons in the branches of the street trees.

Although it had been many years since I stopped feeling the city was really mine, it was always gratifying to take the lesser-known shortcuts – those narrow closes and unexpected staircases – from Waverley Station to Mum's house in Tollcross, tramping up the stone steps that have been polished and eroded by centuries of passing feet. Some façades have remained mostly unchanged for centuries – Ramsay Gardens, the old Bank of Scotland headquarters, the National Gallery – while around them the cityscape changes, adding a coffee chain here, a 'golden turd hotel'[77] there.

Tópos (place) + philia (love of) = topophilia: 'the effective bond between people and place or setting'[78]

The word topophilia describes a person's bond with a place, usually encompassing natural features like water or plants or other greenery. When as a child I was forming attachments with my parents, my sense of identity was also being moulded by my surroundings. There was the Meadows and its avenues of cherry trees that alternate pink and white blossom in the springtime; the cobbles on our street occasionally shoogling around like loose teeth; the communal garden where I almost strangled myself racing into a washing line (I was picking the scab on my neck for what felt like weeks after that).

I always say I'm from Edinburgh with some pride – it typically elicits a response like: 'I love Edinburgh' or 'oh, it's beautiful'. It's a fact I cherish, as if I can claim some of its beauty for my own. But I can't. It's not really mine. Even my accent, while formed here, only communicates my origins as

---

[77] For a very funny account of how the Golden Turd appeared on Embra's skyline, I recommend this: https://www.scottishlegal.com/articles/david-j-black-the-curse-of-the-golden-turd-will-edinburgh-ever-recover

[78] Tuan, Y. (1974) Topophilia: A Study of Environmental Perception, Attitudes and Values.

broadly east coast. When I left for university, I left the city's slang – like 'shan' (unfair), 'spraff' (to talk nonsense) or 'hingin' (someone who looks unhealthy) – far behind.

If I were to describe my relationship status with this place (Dùn Èideann, Auld Reekie, Embra) I would say: it's complicated. I'm from here but I wasn't born here. I entered the world in Aberdeenshire. A few years later, our family divided. Mum became an established part of Scotland's capital: elegant and educated. The city was in her, and she embodied the city.

This was my home for my childhood and most of my teenage years, so my connection to this place was perhaps the strongest of my life. But although I could blend in, chameleon-like, nipping in and out of its secret nooks, I still found returning to the metropolis a stressful experience. Now familiar with living in a small town on the edge of a moor, the constant noise and movement of people in the big smoke became oppressive. It was not an obvious feeling, but one which lurks behind you, vampiric, pulling on your mood and sipping on your energy just a bit, then a bit more and a bit more, until all you want to do is hide away in a room with some knitting.

So it was as I climbed the News Steps up from Waverley Station. The effort of ascending the Mound, which always caught me by surprise, forced me to inhale the city's fumes deeper into the tissue of my lungs. Pigeons skittered in and out of the elegant masonry, pecking at crumbs and cigarette ends. Someone had secured a padlock with a painted heart to the railings. It was a gesture of love that spoke to me both of security and imprisonment, depending on my mood.

The gaggles of tourists seemed to grow every time I visited and were present all year round now, rather than seasonally. The once regal Georgian façades of George IV and Princes Streets were riddled with tartan tat shops selling 'hey Jimmy' hats and cheap kilts made by unknown hands in faraway places. Speakers piped out a loop of tinned Scottish classics into the traffic noise. It was another symptom of the extractive nature of our times – to take what is deemed valuable and package it into something cheap and sellable.

I had reached the junction with the High Street, the narrow cobbled road that cuts through the heart of the tourist trail. A lonely bagpipe player dressed smartly in the appropriate regalia wheedled an impressive rendition of 'Oh Flower of Scotland'.

And sent them homeward,
Tae think again.

Well, here I was, I thought, homeward bound.

I was on my way to Mum's to talk to her about Shetland and the wind farm and I was nervous. 'Mum' and 'Dad' were two words which I never said together in one sentence.

Dad/Shetland

Mum/Edinburgh

These were such polarised parts of myself that I had never asked about Mum's memories of Shetland before.

In the third stage of the Hero's Journey, as described in Joseph Campbell's book, the hero returns to the ordinary world with a trophy or boon that they have won on their quest: a golden fleece, a sleeping princess – perhaps an island in the shape of a sword hilt as seen by Norse warriors as they stopped off at a set of islands they would call Hjaltland, Shetland. In wielding this sword, and confronting the other half of myself, my mother's half, I wondered if I might be cut in two.

28

Arthur's Seat

Unheimlich = not from the home / uncanny

The outline of the lion had been a constant presence on my walk to school, just visible if I looked north east, poking up above the treeline. The small head, and rather 'overfed rump'[79] was shaped by the eroding remains of a 350-million-year-old volcano. Arthur's Seat, one of Edinburgh's highest viewpoints, overlooks the city centre on one side and the widening expanse of the Forth estuary on the other. Over the millennia, this hill, with its small loch and the encircling presence of Salisbury Crags, has been the site of human settlement and activity: an Iron Age fort, a twelfth-century abbey, visits by notable kings and queens, writers and poets. An interesting – if perhaps not surprising – fact, as Edinburgh-based journalist Erlend

---

[79] See Erlend Clouston's highly entertaining article for this and later reference to James Burnet http://www.aboutscotland.com/edin/articles/arthursseat.html

Clouston writes, is that King Arthur didn't actually pay a visit here. Instead of a seat for a king, the name is thought to have originated in the Gaelic phrase Ard-na-Said, which means 'height of arrows'. It's a short walk for the reasonably fit from the bottom of the hill to the top. At the summit, Clouston recommends taking a moment to salute the memory of James Burnet, the last captain of the city guard. For a wager, Burnet, who weighed eighteen stone, 'took only 15 minutes to run to the top where he lay on the ground like an expiring porpoise.'

A popular destination for tourists, it has a dark side too, with Salisbury Crags a site of suicides, murders and fatal accidents. The hill is also a place of transformation, where a volcano is a lion, a height of arrows is a king's seat, and a man's exertions up a slope turn him into a porpoise.

We didn't walk to the top this time. Instead we followed Queen's Drive, a path that runs between Arthur's Seat and Nether Hill. Banks of bushy gorse were thickening with buds, and above our heads a parliament of rooks mobbed a kestrel. The birds swooped around each other like ragged needles in a frenzied sewing session. In my usual way of siding with the underdog, I felt a twang of pity for the raptor, but as Mum pointed out, the corvids were protecting their eggs, and she cheered them on with some fervour.

'I'm happy to provide a comment for your research,' Mum had said on the phone months before.

Since then I hadn't gathered the courage to ask her directly. My work of the last year had been a delicate process of weaving bits of me together, and I knew Mum had the power to unpick the stitches.

Of all the visitations that had taken place on Arthur's Seat – from Mary Queen of Scots to Wordsworth – it was a fictional meeting here which stuck in my mind. It took place in one of my favourite novels, James Hogg's *The Private Memoirs and Confessions of a Justified Sinner*, a tale of divided identities, published in 1824, which mirrored the turbulence of the Scottish psyche at the time.

At one of the critical moments in the story, George, the unfortunate half-sibling of James Hogg's anti-hero, attempts to escape the sinister presence of his brother on a morning walk up Arthur's Seat. Beleaguered by fog, he watches beams of sunlight refract a dazzling rainbow from 'the cloud of haze', contrasting with the shadow of the slope cast across the cloud. George relaxes, believing himself to have at last escaped his brother, who had become 'like the attendance of a demon on some devoted being'. Of course he hasn't escaped him, but what he does see emerging from the mist is far worse.

What an apparition was there presented to his view! He sees, delineated in the cloud, the shoulders, arms and features of a human being of the most dreadful aspect. The face was the face of his brother, but dilated to twenty times the natural size. Its dark eyes gleamed on him through the mist, while every furrow of its hideous brow frowned deep as the ravines on the brow of the hill.

The meeting in the fog is reminiscent of Freud's theory of the uncanny: where the familiar is repressed in the subconscious only to emerge later transformed into something similar but unsettlingly different. Hogg leaves the real identity of the vision in the mist for the reader to decide. But whatever the real answer is, the meeting is the harbinger of George's doom.

Unlike George, Mum and I were not navigating our way through sinister mists. We were toddling along on a dull but warmish day, typical of early spring, a steady stream of dog walkers, joggers, and other folk passing by. I was afraid her experience might contaminate my own newfound sense of home, making it something unhomely and sinister, but I knew I couldn't leave it any longer.

'So, Mum,' I said. 'What do you remember about Shetland?'

A rough crossing

The sea rises and falls, as if propelled by the giant diaphragm of the Midgard Serpent, the monster of Norse myth. With every exhaled breath the sea spits a spray of brine at the deck. The boat ploughs through darkness, sending feeble beams into the night.

This is no time to be outside. Even the whales and the porpoises stay safely under the waves. Yet under the electric lighting of the ship, huddled forms lie squished into less exposed corners. The passengers who, for one reason or another, haven't booked a cabin and don't want to spend the night in the bar with the prospect of brawling drunks. Most lie still like the pupae of metamorphosing insects, waiting for the fourteen-hour journey to end. But one prone figure does not. This one fidgets and wriggles in a futile attempt to keep her thin, papery windshield, a copy of the Guardian, *out of the clutches of the elements.*

Perhaps the headlines are about the Troubles in Northern Ireland, or a deadly earthquake, or fights for fishing rights, or a plane crash, or a military coup. Whatever they are, the newsprint starts to disintegrate into pulp with every lash of saltwater until it is of little use as a protective layer against the wind. This only adds to her frustration. She could have booked a berth if she'd known she had needed one, but no one had told her. Not even her fiancé, who has travelled ahead.

*

Anna Small was in her mid-twenties, and ready for adventure. She knew hard living very well; she and Bill were resident in a damp one-bedroom cottage in rural Aberdeenshire, where mould ate the curtains and mattresses and in winter she had to sleep with her coat on. She knew open spaces and pressing skies too, as she spent a lot of time on the west coast, roaming through bogs, feet on the springing heather. Perhaps it was this expectation of familiarity that sharpened her first impressions.

'Even the openness of Shetland was different,' she said as we followed the track along Edinburgh's highest hill. 'People were closed, not friendly as they are in the Highlands. I felt like an outsider.'

The problems started as soon as she opened her mouth. People spoke in Shaetlan, that 'fraught coalition between

English, Lowland Scots and Old Norn', as poet Roseanne Watt described it.

'Shetlanders appeared closed, not as friendly as they were in the Highlands,' she said. 'I felt like a Soothmoother initially, but as I got to know people, I made some good friends and I remember blissful days with Bill's cousin on their boat.'

It was 1976, and the calloused life of crofting and fishing was disappearing. It was the new era of black gold, and villages like Voe, Brae and Scalloway now housed a community of workers brought in to service the oil industry.

Bill's Mam was always welcoming. She asked Anna what colours she liked and knitted her a beautiful fair isle gansey, interweaving rust-brown and burnt orange in complicated patterns. Later Mam knitted baby blankets and booties. She would also give the young couple food to take home. On one visit to her in-laws, Anna found a sheep in the barn, and asked Da why it was there, separated from the flock. He said it was to be slaughtered so they could smoke the meat and take it home. Anna felt so guilty, she fed the sheep some grass, although she admitted it tasted pretty good.

But the chilled humidity of the Aberdeenshire cottage nurtured a skin of slime on the reested mutton, and moths devoured many of the knitted treasures. These symbols of another life couldn't be brought home.

There were moments of beauty: white, black and green.

At New Year there was a white out: a blast of snow so violent it eclipsed everything in the landscape. Only swirls of ice moved in and out of focus against the backdrop of nothing.

Anna was intrigued, excited by the spectral forms, and against the advice of Bill's parents, stepped outside with, 'I may be some time', her baby strapped to her chest.

'How did you know where to go?' I asked her.

'With difficulty,' she replied. 'We didn't go far.'

Once they took a rowing boat out to go fishing and she watched the deep sea-swell, vast and sublime like liquid obsidian. She hauled a huge ling up from the black depths, long and tanned, its swim bladder exposed to the wind like a balloon. As it thrashed its death throes she pitied the life leaking out at her feet. Preserved in the freezer, the giant fish kept them fed for weeks.

One winter's night, a green lace curtain trembled across the sky – the Northern Lights – but in a moment it had fluttered away.

Then in 1983 everything changed. She moved to Edinburgh and after that, never returned to Shetland.

29

Crossing the Return Threshold

'What kind of tea would you like? I got you some soya milk, it's in the fridge. Have as much as you can, I won't drink it.'

Mum had not sat down yet; she was rummaging in the fridge for a rhubarb sponge cake she'd made for my visit. She loved rhubarb, the sweet with the sour, and if her allotment was fruitful enough, the cupboard would be full of jars of pink jam by autumn, the freezer rammed with the crimson stalks.

She placed a plate in front of me. The slight tang was offset by a dollop of double cream. I sipped my tea with soya milk, and ate my rhubarb cake and cream, smiling at myself for my dietary contradictions.

Every time I sat at this kitchen table, my eye was always drawn to the collage of photographs that hung on the wall, a kaleidoscope of images from the last century. Crisp black and white photos of my maternal grandparents on their wedding day, and another of my Great Grannie Esme in a theatrical costume[80] of a striped dress and corset, looking slightly amused – disconcertingly familiar in expression and physique to Mum.

I looked out from the glass, too, as a blurred infant in a rural garden, a sulky teen on a sofa, as a grown woman with partners, holding a baby. There were old friends, family pets – a motley collection of the dead and the living. None contained Dad.

Learning about Mum's experience in Shetland had not cut me in the way I had feared. Her memories were not sharp with anger. They were, if anything, soft with the passing of time, with only a hint of stale bitterness. When I imagined the young Anna Small, wind-beaten and salted after her journey on the boat, I felt sorry that her expectations of life anchored to Shetland would never be realised, but at the same time I did not wish for a different course of fate.

It was almost exactly three years since Dad's death. In that time, his absence had forced me to restructure myself. The space that he once occupied was now woven across with other relationships, a family of former strangers whose open doors had inspired a new feeling of comfort and ease: a sense of belonging. When I left the isles, I imagined myself like a caddisfly encased in the tiny bones of a thousand ancestors. Now I had emerged, and experienced what Joseph Campbell describes as 'the terrifying assimilation of the self into what formerly was only otherness'. Mum and Dad were not separate. In me, they existed in union.

---

[80] She was an actress.

We were still sitting at the table when Mum's lodger entered the room. Dr Dipali Mathur was a postdoctoral student at Edinburgh university specialising in the problem of e-waste. They chatted comfortably as Dipali moved around the kitchen, preparing herself a light meal before going out.

'So you're interested in wind farms?' Dipali asked me, taking a seat next to Mum on the other side of the table.

As I reeled off a short outline of what I'd been doing, she sat back, listening thoughtfully.

She explained how she had spent the last few years looking at how the world's addiction to economic growth had used and abused some of the poorest and most vulnerable. Since the 1970s, when everything had changed in Shetland, global economics had also been transformed, driven by an ideology known as neoliberalism, under which citizens become consumers and the 'market'[81] replaces the state.

'Our economic system has been rigged to exploit and extract natural resources, including human labour, for the cheapest price possible,' she said.

Neoliberalism survives by taking and not putting back. Hand-in-hand with colonialism this has led to governments and multinational companies deliberately dumping toxic materials into the backyards and bodies of the world's poorest.

Efficient recycling had yet to catch up with the problem of

---

[81] As George Monbiot wrote in a *Guardian* article in 2016, '"The market" sounds like a natural system that might bear upon us equally, like gravity or atmospheric pressure. But it is fraught with power relations. What "the market wants" tends to mean what corporations and their bosses want.'

what to do with solar panels and wind turbines after they were no longer usable. In some cases, the resulting e-waste ends up in mountains that mark the skyline of marginalised and vulnerable communities in India, on whom Dipali focused for her research. I thought of the Kames and the battalion of wind turbines towering over the ridge.

It was a 'tricky' problem, Dipali said, because often the human-made chemicals causing harm to these communities were also beneficial to humans: pharmaceuticals, solar panels, wind turbines. Slow decision-making when it came to protecting the people living in these waste landscapes was a kind of structural violence, she said, 'which ensures the poor remain poor to serve the capitalist regime'.

This so-called 'toxic colonialism' is not just about dumping waste, but sourcing materials in the first place – lithium, silicon, cobalt, manganese and rare earths – minerals and elements which are necessary to power the transition from fossil fuels. Bookending this linear process of extraction and disposal, a similar story is played out: pollution of air, soil, water and life, child labour, dangerous conditions, conflict zones.

Community-owned energy groups had raised their concerns, particularly about solar panels and links to human-rights abuses. A statement by Community Energy England had set up a working group to help source the 'least worst' equipment and shout from the proverbial rooftops to drive improvements in the market. It was a start but more needed to be done.

As Dipali and I talked, our hands curled around Mum's mugs (one from my old university, another with a Christmas picture Esme designed), our conversation reminded me of the words of one resident of Brae who had spoken to me about what Viking meant to him.

'Sitting on the fence wasn't an option when the wind farm hove into view, but now – alas – indifference advances, as does the progress of monster capital, desecrating all in its path.'

It seemed to me now that we should all beware of how indifference directs this path of desecration. We were all connected to each other and if the foundation of 'progress' was someone else's suffering, then we needed to find a new way forward.

30

The Crossroads

Convoys are scheduled to leave Lerwick three times a day: on weekdays at 6 a.m.; 11 a.m. and 2 p.m.; and on Saturdays at 6 a.m.; 10 a.m. and noon.
The Shetland Times, 6th February, 2023

Sheep hooves in the moss, starving people with pickaxes, a digger laying gravel, the wind in long grass – new paths are always appearing, heading somewhere, but there is always a point at which we can choose which direction to follow. As I was chatting to Mum in Edinburgh, Shetland's road system was busy. It had taken two years of careful planning, negotiating a safe way to deliver the pieces of turbine through the twists and turns of the landscape.

It started in the harbour, where fifty-metre blades lay stacked in rows as if fishermen had just dragged ashore a pod of white whales. Fringes on the blades gave the impression of baleen, serrated to improve airflow and minimise noise. From there a convoy of vehicles, including bespoke trailers with extra axles, would carry the giant structures along the A970 to the site of the wind farm, escorted by specialist police officers who went ahead to warn oncoming traffic to pull over in rolling road blocks.

As well as the blades, there was the nacelle, the tower sections and more. Altogether over the next six months, a thousand components would make the journey north.

By the time you read this, the turbines should be turning, each blade capturing the kinetic energy of the wind, transferring it to the rotor shaft and generator, converting this force into electricity to be channelled from Kergord and Caithness. Perhaps the kettle you just boiled was powered by a gust of wind in Shetland and Britain's most productive onshore wind farm.

But the road goes on and on, and elsewhere in the isles, other work was underway.

A rate of knots

Just a year into the productive life of the Viking Energy turbines, Shetland has another milestone in its sights – an ambitious plan to become a 'world-leading green energy island'. It is called ORION, and the vision is big: to produce 'clean' energy from the wind, tides and hydrogen as well as carbon capture.[82] The plan also includes the decarbonisation of oil extraction, powering operations through renewable energy to reduce the carbon footprint, a process known as 'electrification'.[83]

---

[82] Opportunity for Renewable Integration with Offshore Networks.
[83] Potentially 8 million tonnes of carbon by 2050.

Instead of drilling for black gold, ORION has its sights on a different treasure from the sea: green hydrogen.

> *Grey – mix fossil gas with steam = hydrogen + large quantities of CO_2*
> *Blue – same as above, but capture and store most of the CO_2 underground*
> *Green – pass electricity produced by renewable sources (like wind) through water to split it into oxygen and hydrogen*[84]

Hydrogen can be compressed and stored in tanks for a long time. With the right infrastructure and renewable sources, Shetland will be able to produce the gas at an industrial scale, keeping some for local use, exporting the rest to Scotland via a pipeline and Europe via tanker. Instead of being the UK's largest carbon emitter, by 2030 the vision is to be net zero, supplying 10% of the UK's hydrogen needs by 2050.

None of this, according to some, could have taken place without the Viking Energy wind farm. Around the time Josh, Esme and I were preparing to leave Shetland for Devon after nearly eight months living in Kirkhoose, Shetland-born Daniel Gear, who worked in the analysis of global energy sectors, sought to counter the 'misinformation being shared' about Viking. In a lengthy Facebook post, he wrote about why he

---

[84] Grey and blue hydrogen are also known as 'fossil hydrogen'. For a deeper look at blue hydrogen, I recommend this *Ecologist* article by John Szabo and Gareth Dale https://theecologist.org/2023/jan/13/hiding-behind-hydrogen

believed the wind farm was necessary for Shetland's transition from fossil fuels. He covered all the bases, detailing the real and present danger posed by global heating and the little time we have left to mitigate the worst of it.

'We need to look at this project first in the context of climate change, which means taking a global view first, then a national view, then a local one,' he said.

Daniel put Shetland's role in fossil fuel extraction, and the benefits it has reaped for the islands, into sharp focus. He also talked about 'negative externalities' – an economic term used to describe a situation when those who neither consume nor produce a product, like the Dalits in India, indirectly have to pay a cost for it, like landfill, plastic waste and carbon emissions.

'Make no mistake, we have been beneficiaries of this negative externality for as long as we've prospered from the production of hydrocarbons through our shores,' he wrote.

Time was running out to slow down climate breakdown. Shetland had a big part to play – and a responsibility to do it well. So how did Viking fit into this? It was all about the interconnector. Once Viking was up and running, it would be using 443MW out of a 600MW capacity. That left a lot of potential energy for renewable energy projects in Shetland. The grid would also provide the energy necessary to support the electrification of oil and gas platforms, carbon capture, and the production of hydrogen.

'Remember what I said about the human cost of these emissions – we would effectively go from being responsible for the most climate-related deaths of any region in the UK per resident, to being responsible for the most lives saved per resident, in the world,' Daniel said. 'We can develop a world-leading clean energy hub and do disproportionate good because we can. But there is a very short window of time, and it's only possible with the interconnector, which is only possible with the wind farm.'

He later wrote a Letter to the Editor for the *Shetland News*.[85] Unlike other such letters published on the topic of the wind farm over the years, it did not give the impression of being thrown from a trench at an opposing side, but rather aimed to bring the two sides together.

The view from Kirkhoose

As the blades were arriving in Lerwick, Jen Stout was recording a radio documentary about Shetland's energy future.[86] In it she described what she could see from her rented house looking north to the flare stack of Sullom Voe and south down the Kergord valley to the Viking Energy construction site. It was the view from Kirkhoose. Listening to her report, I felt a twinge of the old strangeness, the possessiveness I had over that place, but it soon dissipated. Jen's voice was delivering the significance of Kirkhoose, Voe, and Shetland to a global audience. The view was as much theirs as it was mine.

Kirkhoose seemed to straddle so much of Shetland's past and future. Outside, on the other side of the bay, Jen included

---

[85] You can read his piece here: https://www.shetnews.co.uk/2020/08/22/we-are-blessed-with-abundant-potential-at-a-time-the-world-needs-it-most/

[86] https://www.bbc.co.uk/sounds/play/m001jklx

a clip from an archive of the voice of Ian Clarke, 'Scotland's Colonel Gaddafi', the man celebrated with brokering Shetland's deal with the oil companies back in the seventies. Comparable to Norway's sovereign wealth fund, this was the deal which would see Shetlanders become the wealthiest council in the UK. Clark was giving a sermon from the old church in Voe on his departure from the islands to join the Board of the British National Oil Corporation.

'For love of money is the root of all evil,' came the thin voice, emanating across the room as if from the bottom of a bucket. 'Surely this verse is a very pertinent verse for those of us in Shetland today.'

If we rooted out the economic system that has led to the multiple environmental crises we face today, would this 'love of money' be the final tug we'd need to remove it?

It was 1976 and everything was changing. From that turning point nearly fifty years ago Clark spoke to us, his voice recorded and stored as a magnetic signature on a tape. Around half a century later, it was converted back into sound waves using electricity, into a world where the ripples of that change were affecting further transformation – for good or bad.

When I listen to a podcast or a radio programme, I like to knit. I find keeping my hands busy helps me concentrate, and by knitting I am creating something practical and, at least in theory, nice to look at. That was what I was doing while I listened to Jen's report: colourwork using Shetland wool. I always use this wool. The fibres are short and tough, giving them a 'stickier' texture, which allows them to hold together better. As I absorbed Jen's report, I watched as the pattern emerged from my hands, a traditional fair isle design from a book Dad had given me for Christmas one year. The points of the needles hooked knot into knot into knot, each stitch holding the others together.

As I knitted and listened, my thoughts took me back to the old whitewashed church in Voe, that short stretch of grassy slope, at times beaded with devil's-bit scabious, purple flags and wild orchids, where we used to try to spot the black one in a colony of rabbits, or listen to the oystercatchers as they congregated on the salty silt. The contours of that place were not just rippled by the wind, but shaped by human hands in joy and hardship.

According to a story I'd heard, the current graveyard was once a croft. A tenant family had hacked a living from the rough ground, keeping some animals, growing kale. At the time, wool was big business, and the lairds were looking for ways to reap more profits from the land. So they evicted the tenants, my distant relatives, to make way for a new kind of sheep with more wool and more meat – more valuable than the commodities that could be gleaned from the human residents. But the sheep were not hardy and they died of disease. The plan failed. In the end, the Church of Scotland bought the land for use as a graveyard. Soon crops of headstones sprouted from the grass. The soil already knew them, for they were the descendants of the very same people who had worked the ground with their hands. They had reclaimed their land at last. For that, they had the last laugh.

Settlement, exploitation, displacement, survival.

It was every family's story.

31

Belonging

There was another chapter to explore. For all those folk like Dad who 'belonged' in the Shetland soil, there were others who did not feel this connection despite being born and raised there. Back in Devon I had two calls to make: one to Shetland and one to Edinburgh. I wanted to speak to two women, a mother and daughter, about an event that had taken place years before.

On the day: Collect posters from volunteers in 50 different locations – from Unst to Fair Isle – between 2 p.m. and 3 p.m. Pick up a poster to hold while you walk around the community, following social distancing rules. Upload photos onto social media with the hashtag #ShetlandStaands wi #BlackLivesMatter.

Many remember the horrific events of the evening of 25th May, 2020. He was a Black American and his name was

George Floyd. His dying cries for his mother as he lay pinned under the weight of a white police officer's knee in Minnesota reverberated around the globe.

'When that happened, it just consumed me. After four days, I just couldn't stop greetin'. So I said to a friend, "we've got to do something".'

Joy Duncan was sitting at her kitchen table, looking at me over the rim of her glasses, as we met on video chat.

On one of my returns to Shetland, I had read the names of generations of Wards in a graveyard with Angus, and considered the inspiration behind West Country-raised Paul Bloomer's sketches. Today, speaking to Joy through the opening of two windows in cyberspace, I wanted to find out what the idea of 'belonging' meant to her.

It was perhaps fitting that we could only meet online. Joy and her friend had spearheaded an event to stand up against racism and show Shetland's support for the Black Lives Matter movement. At the time, the islands were only a few months into lockdown. They had to speak to the head of the NHS and the police – but after a week of Zoom calls they finally found a format that would work with the Covid restrictions and the group Shetland Staands wi' Black Lives Matter was born, the phrase meaning 'Shetland stands with' in dialect. It was the largest public protest in Shetland's history, according to Joy, with over 2,200 islanders taking part, around 10% of the population. Proud to be among them, Josh, Esme and myself took our own selfies from the main thoroughfare in Voe.

'It raised a whole level of consciousness about racism for

people to say "that's not OK anymore", partly for young folk like my daughter, Mara,' Joy said.

Joy was a 'born and raised' Shetlander. Her two grandads had been whalers and her mother ran a fifty-hectare croft. Like many other islanders, she was a musician, but she didn't play the fiddle. Over the course of her life, she had found a different means of self-expression: African drums, which she had taught across Shetland in schools and community groups for fifteen years.

'I left Shetland when I was eighteen and came back twenty years later, when my daughter was two and a half,' she said. 'Her dad is Black Cuban. I met him in Havana.'

Selfies

They pose for the camera in front of blanket-green grassland, their feet touching wildflower verges, grey tarmac, near parked cars and the burnished surface of the sea. An old couple, groups of friends, a baby, a toddler in a pram. All smile, the posters in their hands. Though they are standing apart, they are together. In solidarity; they stand against hate.

*

'We've had an incredibly supportive response to our protest in Shetland,' Mara said in a *Guardian* interview at the time of the protests. 'Of course there were still plenty of people who didn't quite understand the movement and what it's about, but the supporters heavily outweighed the non-supporters.'

The isles are overwhelmingly white. Out of a population

of nearly 23,000, only 2.2% of Shetlanders are of Asian heritage, and 0.8% other ethnic groups.[87] In a moving account published in the same newspaper shortly afterwards Mara shared her experiences growing up as a mixed-heritage child in Shetland.[88]

'I was bullied mercilessly in primary school and it took me years to realise that actually happened,' she said. 'Because I didn't realise I was being bullied, I never thought to talk to my teachers about it. I never sought the support I needed. But when issues did come to light, for the most part I was supported by my teachers.'

The then nineteen-year-old went on to describe how she identified much more with the Cuban side of her family than the Scottish side. 'So amalgamating my black and Scottish sides is something I've not quite done yet. But it's definitely interesting,' she wrote. 'I can remember hearing black people with Scottish accents for the first time and thinking I'm not the only one!'

Unlike her daughter, Joy's Shetland identity had remained strong throughout her life, even in the two decades she spent away from the isles. Exploring countries with different languages and cultures could be very daunting, but being a Shetlander gave her confidence.

'Part of the thing wi' growing up in Shetland is, I have a big family here, I grew up in Scalloway. Here, you ken who

---

[87] According to the 2011 census.

[88] I recommend reading Mara's story here: https://www.theguardian.com/uk-news/ng-interactive/2020/jul/29/young-british-black-voices-behind-uk-anti-racism-protests-george-floyd#4

everybody is, and you always feel secure,' she told me. 'I'm not shy to speak to folk, wherever I go I feel happy and confident to try to connect. I think one of the things with going to Cuba, they have a really similar family structure, and a first cousin once removed, they're just family, that's it,' she said.

She described going to her daughter's grannie's house in Cuba.

'It was just like my mam's hoose, there was family coming and going all day long. But of course Grannie was the provider, there was always rice and peas on the go, as opposed to mince and tatties. So it just felt easy and normal even though it was a different language and a different culture.'

Born in 1966, Joy had seen big changes in Shetland society. Before 1974 (when 'everything changed'), if you walked along the side of the road, folk would stop to see if you wanted a lift.

'After the oil came you couldn't get a lift even if you stuck your thumb oot,' she said. But that was the same story everywhere. 'Things develop and things change,' she added, and I couldn't detect any notes of nostalgia in her voice. 'In the countries I've gone to, I've always felt so welcome. I always wanted to make sure that people visiting here would feel the same.'

When Joy returned to Shetland with her daughter, she encountered something else.

'In Shetland people like to think of themselves as warm and friendly, but there's a level of ignorance there that they don't realise they are being racist.'

Racism manifested in different forms, from thoughtless comments on the street to online trolling. After one incident,

Joy published a post on Facebook condemning the use of 'blackface' in Shetland's fire festivals, Up Helly Aa.[89]

'The aftermath was just . . .' her voice tapers off. 'Afterwards I made a point of bringing the issue of blackface into the classroom, the staffroom; it made people uncomfortable at times.'

It was the death of George Floyd years later that tipped the scale, she said. 'It woke people up to what racism is.'

In the wake of his murder, a resident of Brae, Ellie Ratter, wrote a letter to Up Helly Aa committees asking them to ban blackface. 'Some squads will not know where blackface originated from and simply want to portray a character,' Ellie said. 'I think it's important to educate people on where this trend originated and why it is still harmful to people of colour today.'

The letter prompted Member of the Scottish Parliament for Shetland Beatrice Wishart to issue a statement calling for islanders to 'do better' in the face of racism.

'Some may have been party to things that seemed harmless, but in fact have never been acceptable,' she said. 'As individuals we should call out racist remarks or so-called jokes when we hear them. Seeing blacked-up faces at some local events needs to be a thing of the past.'

For Joy, the shift in public awareness affected her too. 'I've been promoting African cultures, getting African musicians here in Shetland for fifteen years, and I think this influence

---

[89] For some background on the history of blackface, this is an interesting read https://nmaahc.si.edu/explore/stories/blackface-birth-american-stereotype

has been with the children throughout their schooling. But I realised there was a hell of a lot more I could do.'

Things in Shetland were changing, and generally for the better, Joy said. She welcomed the fact that in recent years, incidents of racism in Shetland have been dealt with sternly in court. 'Racism has no place anywhere and it has no place in Shetland whatsoever,' the local judge (known as a sheriff in Scottish law) said when a teenager was fined for shouting offensive comments from a moving car. Earlier that year, when another young man used racist language, the chief inspector was quoted as saying: 'People are now clear that this sort of thing is unacceptable, people will call it out now and that is thankfully what happened in the most recent case.'

It heartened me to observe Joy's confidence in who she was and where she was from. So what she said next surprised me.

'I sometimes feel like a square peg in a round hole. Because I've gone off and done different things, and brought it back to Shetland, I never ken exactly where I fit,' she said. 'To be honest, once you've gone off and travelled aroond, I've never really felt settled. There's always something missing. And I've always got itchy feet waiting for the next trip.'

I knew how she felt.

All the same, her ties with the landscape remained strong. 'Some of the vistas just thrill me. There's something about the light, the colours that it brings out. The certain textures of the water. It thrills me to a deep level.'

Her words evoked a scene of open moorland, and the ripples of a lochan breaking a reflection into a thousand pieces. A crowd of scenes filled my mind: the grating call of ravens by Gonfirth Loch, Dad tossing his fold-up shovel into Gossa Water, the feeling of sea-sanded pottery in my palm.

'But the wind farm,' Joy said. 'I drive all over Shetland so seeing the landscape literally getting ripped up like that—'. She didn't finish her sentence.

Our conversation returned to the idea of 'belonging' and Joy mentioned the word 'blyde', a popular term meaning 'glad' in Shetland.

I'm blyde to see dee
A blyde welcome
W'ir hoopin da day fins you blyde an in fine fettle

For Joy, belonging to Shetland meant welcoming folk who didn't come from there, inviting them in and making them comfortable. It also meant standing up for people.

'If you want to promote yourself as warm, blyde, especially at the moment where folk are coming from all over the world, we need to understand what is OK and what's not OK,' she said.

She recalled a moment on the morning of the Shetland Staands protests when she was getting ready. A song came on the radio. It was a Stevie Wonder song.

Hate's goin' round
breaking many hearts
well, please stop it

Love's in need of love today

'I felt myself levitate,' she said. 'People were coming out because of love.'

Cold colours

Apart from some tongue-tapped vowels, there was a clipped softness in Mara's accent that was not dissimilar to mine. She had set aside time to speak to me on video chat from her flat in Edinburgh as she enjoyed a rare afternoon off from her two jobs.

Edinburgh suited her. She liked the activity, the mixture of people, the manageable size and beauty of the city. Unlike those distant isles, where her experience of racism in childhood and her early teens compounded a sense of disconnection, the fine sandstone facades of Auld Reekie[90] felt like home. In Shetland she described herself as British or even English, as she'd spent the first three years of her life in London.

'Now, in Edinburgh, it feels like the right place to be Scottish,' she said, and the warmth in her voice made me feel a new affection for my old hometown.

Being raised on an island didn't define her, she continued. 'I know I grew up there and my mum has a strong Shetland identity, but to me my mum was always global. She introduced me to different cultures. This had a direct impact on how I viewed the world.'

There was another trend too, which affected most of her generation, growing up as they did in the hyper-connected world of social media.

---

[90] The city's nickname means 'old smoky' in Scots.

'Many people my age do not have a strong sense of Shetland identity,' she said. 'There are some islanders, from families of crofters and fishermen, who still have the proper accent, but not that many.'

The proper accent – something that was fading from the lips of so many across the United Kingdom. Although a lot older than Mara, I was also part of that tide, my vocabulary eroded into something uniform by waves of popular culture: TV, film and music. It would be a Sisyphean effort to attempt to turn that back now.

As a child she lent a hand on her grannie's croft, helping with the chickens, sheep and tatties. This kind of traditional activity was the closest she felt to Shetland, but even then, she wouldn't want to be a crofter, but a farmer. Crofting is particular to Scotland, especially the Highlands and Islands, with parcels of land normally held in tenancy and rights and duties of care set in specific legislation. Farming, however, is untethered by location or culture. But with her two jobs in a busy part of Edinburgh, that stage of her life was likely to be a while away yet.

I wanted to know how Mara's connection with the place affected her thoughts about the wind farm. The Viking Energy project was, after all, around the same age as Mara herself, growing from vision to reality just as she had grown from child to adult.

'I'd say I'm more for renewable energy than the preservation of the landscape and wildlife, but I know different biomes are important for sustainability,' she said. 'But I've never had strong feelings about it.'

Mara described Shetland as a 'closed culture', one in which she felt like she didn't belong, despite spending most of her younger years there. I thought about my own desire to be part of this place, seeking a filler for the hole Dad's death had left in my sense of self, but also an edge of hostility I felt from some about what criteria were necessary for an incomer to 'belong'.

'You know how some people associate different colours with different letters of the alphabet?' Mara said as our conversation was drawing to a close.

She paused and started loosening her headscarf so I could see the pattern: purple, red and pink stripes on white.

'As you can see, I feel comfortable with warm colours,' she said, smiling. 'Those are the ones I associate with Cuba. I associate Shetland with blue, green and grey. Cold colours.'

The palette she had picked out was just the right one, and immediately evoked a scene of low-lying cloud, a sliver of sea and stretches of dark peat spliced with improved grassland. It was a beautiful and grim picture. Cold colours indeed.

32

The Blank Landscape

From Shetland to Edinburgh and now to the West of England. As my quest to discover more about the Shetland wind farm was drawing to an end, another newly rural resident with roots in oil islands was on a journey of her own.

Low hills, wet meadows, grids of green, as far from Bath as the commuter drives – this was the Somerset levels, home to wildlife, farmers and people who have moved here to escape city life.

'Some of these areas feel sacred, they feel ancient,' Marchelle Farrell said of the countryside around her home. 'But for me personally, the landscape is marred by a patchwork of overgrazing. It wouldn't have looked like this to the people who lived here thousands of years ago. Back then it was a temperate rainforest. Now it's not the healthiest.'

Marchelle had become a villager there only two years before, making it her home so her partner could be closer to his new job. While taking time off her own post as a consultant psychiatrist and psychotherapist to raise her young children, she served a stint as a parish councillor. Despite being far away from the pollution and stress of big city life, the environmental crisis still pressed on her thoughts. So she did what she could, encouraging people to use sustainable forms of heating in their homes, and by helping set up a climate marquee at the village fair. It was here that she first came across the map.

It was a view of the contours and colours of the downs around their village. As villagers sidled past, a group of strangers appeared, inviting them to look at the map and consider what these places – the hilltops, woods, meadows, all of it – meant to them and why.

'They presented us with a blank landscape,' Marchelle said. 'Then they asked us what we thought might be possible in terms of renewable energy.'

As people visiting the fair paused to consider this, staff from the climate charity the Centre for Sustainable Energy (CSE) gave examples of what forms of renewable energy might work and where – sun, wind, water. Some people mentioned wind. Could ten small machines be placed in this or that area, and if so, how much energy would they generate? Marchelle learnt that they could meet the energy demand of the entire community and more with one big turbine.

'You get that in a real, tangible way with a map,' she said.

There was more to come: a parish meeting with a rough semicircle of chairs around the room. This shape was important. Unlike rows of desks like a classroom, a semicircle invites a feeling of inclusion and equality. Also integral to this was the absence of hierarchy or power structures. There were no authority figures, unlike at the many council meetings Marchelle had attended. Everyone was given a chance to speak and be listened to.

The meeting was part of a CSE project[91] which engaged with communities on how and where renewable energy might be developed around them. It looked at the type and scale of renewable energy which might be acceptable to a local community, the landscape impact they'd accept and how they might benefit. No community was uniform and to get a big enough slice of public opinion, the team would hand out leaflets about the workshops at school gates, and get in touch with groups with a broad range of interests from walking to history and sport.

Once consensus was reached, this would ease forward the planning stage – usually a point at which many hopes for developing green energy projects came and died. Public support for renewable energy was at an all-time high, yet support tended to disappear the moment a planning application was submitted. When senior planner at CSE Dan Stone told me the three grounds on which people typically objected to renewables projects, I felt a twinge of déjà-vu.

1. An individual's bond to a place

Cairns, birds, fishing, trows

---

[91] Future Energy Landscapes methodology started as a research project in 2015 with countryside charity CPRE. CSE has been scaling it up since 2021. www.cse.org.uk/my-community/community-projects/future-energy-landscapes-community-consultation-method/

2. Perceived distributed benefits

   Land rental, crofters' payments, community benefit funds

3. Procedural justice

   'They never listened to us.'

Shetland and the West of England had a lot in common.

'It makes no sense talking about renewable deployment in the abstract without talking about the impact on the landscape. It's critical,' Dan said.

The impact. A farmer might see a hilltop differently from someone who worked 9 to 5 and went walking on the weekend. The value of the land was tethered to its emotional significance as well as its economic worth. But the personal connection was a slippery thing to measure and to tease it out of folk required experience and sensitivity. Central to this was the neutrality of the folk holding the workshop: they were there to provide objective information with no forced outcome. The main goal of the workshops was to engage with people and make them feel heard, no matter what their opinion might be.

'If you're not getting below the skin of why that person's in opposition, and quite often there will be something behind that, something genuine, and you just label them a NIMBY[92]

---

[92] 'Not in my back yard'.

you're not understanding what that concern is, or addressing it,' Dan said.

To get to the bottom of how people felt about local renewable projects, Dan and his colleagues set them a challenge – to think about what proportion of their energy demand they thought they could meet from renewables around them. The CSE team would then give them a kind of menu detailing all the options that could be realistically deployed. If someone said, for example, put some solar panels on the village hall roof, that would only serve a tiny fraction of the community's energy needs. What always came to the fore, Dan said, was who owned and who benefited from the technology deployed.

Anything agreed at the workshop would be written down and distributed to the wider community as a survey. Someone in Marchelle's village might have received a survey question that looked like this:

> People in the workshop expressed support for renewable energy to meet 400% of your electricity demand. Are you happy with being a net exporter of renewable energy? Are there any preconditions you want to apply to that?

Not only did the debate encourage an open floor, rather than a cluster-bomb of angry opinions, it also encouraged people to listen to others in their community and understand their points of view. Putting trust at the centre of development felt like a turning of the tide, away from the shouty world of national politics and social media: yes versus no equals I don't care anymore.

But we didn't have much time. I asked Dan, was empowering the community in this way going to be quick enough to meet the changes we needed before we missed our net zero targets, or did we need industrial projects on the scale of the Viking Energy wind farm?

There was a long pause.

'I don't know,' he said at last. 'I think it's one of those things – there are different approaches that will work in different areas. But I don't know, it's a difficult question, I'm not sure I've got the full answer to it.'

For Marchelle, replacing the use of oil in her village with one big turbine would be a dream come true. Her reasons were not just practical, but also deeply personal. She was born in Trinidad, an island in the Caribbean exploited for centuries under colonialism.

'The big oil economy was how we made our way out of slavery, that's why we're not dependent on tourism,' she said. 'We haven't had the vagaries of having to pander to tourism like other islands, Jamaica for example. But the government is in a chokehold with the oil industry.'

When I organised my interview with Marchelle I hadn't realised that we already knew each other. I had commissioned an article from her for the magazine I worked for, a poignant, quiet and powerful piece titled 'I Am This Place'.[93] In it Marchelle explored the idea of 'native' and 'invasive' through the wildflowers she grew from seed in her garden. She

---

[93] Marchelle won the Nan Shepherd Prize in 2021. Her book is called *Uprooting*.

mentioned speedwell, a perennial plant with tiny blue flowers commonly found in lawns and rockeries. The seeds can live in the soil for up to twenty years – the time it takes for a human to grow into adulthood, or a wind farm to sprout from idea to reality.

'They have made themselves at home here,' Marchelle wrote in the article. 'Yet they are considered alien. What does it take to become native here?'

Marchelle's connection with the landscape went far further and deeper than her wildflower garden in Somerset, or the sacred hills of the downs. It went beyond her personal experience, tapping into something universal. She wrote:

> Can we dream freely in our collective unconscious? We think of ourselves as primarily individuals, but teachings reside in many traditions of the self as a false construct, a mere fragment of the true organism that is the whole. I do not know how easy you find it to think of yourself in this way, as 'no-self', but I struggle to loosen the belief in my 'self' as the primary object.

Throughout my journey through Shetland, making a home in the hole Dad left behind, I was always focused on this idea of my 'self' at the centre of the story. I had grown up with division embedded into who I was, and I thought my attempt to understand the controversy over the wind farm had been partly to mend that rupture. Becoming a member of a tribe made me feel whole, even if the tribe was at war with itself. I desired to be welcomed and accepted by both sides. But just as

I had been powerless to bring Mum and Dad back together, I couldn't arbitrate between Shetland's factions either. I had to let it be.

Instead of a quest of self-discovery, this journey had been about something else: finding the strength to be at peace with this 'no self'. Perhaps from this perspective, as Marchelle told me, we can 'sit up and reckon with the path that our species has taken over the last few hundred years'.

Extinction

At the end of the road, turn back and count the steps it took to get here.

Empty white bags of fertiliser, half-pickled in the peat, fray at the edges into the thick brown water.

Microplastics pass from placenta to embryo.

Glaciers slide into the sea as the planet bakes in sky-high temperatures.

Sweat no longer cools the skin, the heart is too weak now to sustain this thundering pulse.

When did we forget that we are the land and the land is us?

When did we stop listening?

We can't keep taking and not giving back. Renewable energy is not a luxury or a faraway dream: it is the only route we have to a liveable future, and the only way to get there is with a united voice. This wasn't a story about me. I wasn't a flawed hero, an adventurer facing trials and tests, alone against adversity. My journey had not been about allies and enemies. It had been about finding trust – to give people an equal platform and ownership of their words, to understand that we are all – native, incomer, artist, farmer, peasant, landowner, raingoose, great northern diver, peat, mangrove, kale, whale, wind – part of the same 'un-self'.

33

Look Up

'*What, now, is the result of the miraculous passage and return?*'

Joseph Campbell, The Hero with
a Thousand Faces

It was a warm day in late spring and I was standing in our small back garden in Devon when I realised that my collection of voices telling the story of the wind farm was still incomplete. The thought came to me because of the plant that I was eyeing. Kale had accompanied me throughout my journey. From Dad's funeral to the months in Kirkhoose, my return and back here to Devon: seed to root and seedling, leaf to flower, and again to seed. This nutritious vegetable was the gift that symbolised a partnership between humans and nature, around which circular walls were built to defend against the wind and hungry rabbits.

Kale was a staple in my unkempt allotment and I had

planned to plant some rather leggy plugs in a small area of soil cleared in the grass. Last year's plants had already shed their spring spray of brilliant yellow petals under the pressures of a May heatwave and were firming up some thin green pods. Josh had grown the seedlings from a previous crop, but this effort hadn't proved too successful (we were a family of inattentive gardeners). Still, a handful were clinging to life. I reasoned there would be no better place than this to ask Esme, now seven years old, about her Shetland roots.

My efforts were not fruitful. It was too hot to go to the allotment, she said, and anyway, she was busy tending to her new snail farm. I had mixed feelings about this, particularly after a few too many evenings spent accompanied by the wet thunk of slug hitting metal as I picked the orange-brown molluscs off my kale babies. I wasn't always in time to stop the delicate plants being munched into rags of green lace. In the end Esme agreed to be interviewed in our garden as long as she could also play with some salty green dough that she'd made. Our conversation didn't start well.

Play

'Don't ask me what I remember about Shetland because that's boring,' she says in her best hoity-toity voice.

There is a pause while I try to think of a different tack.

'What did you like most about being there?' I ask. We're sitting on the grass. Esme is rolling her dough up into a ball between her hands, stretching it a bit and poking her finger into it.

'Oh, I like living in that house. It gives me a feeling that Grandpa Bill is still there in a way.'

'Why does that matter to you?'

'Mumma. That's an embarrassing question. What would you say if you liked the snails as much as me and I asked you, why do the snails matter to you?'

I watch her thoughtfully, unsure how to answer her retort. This is the problem with raising a strong, independent woman. She likes to practise her critical thinking on her parents.

'Hm, well what about the actual place?'

'I like to see the views from the top of the mountain that the house is next to.'

'Oh yeah, Sneugie. You went up there with Daddy, didn't you? Do you remember what it was like?'

Pause

I had probably been working at the time and had forgotten the trip they had taken together up the hill. It is pleasing to remember it now, another layer of time to add to my collage of the hilltop.

Dad with his daughter.

Daughter just before and then after her dad's death.

Granddaughter and her dad.

Play

'At the top it's stony and there's a kind of tower. It's really funny because Daddy wanted to see the view but it was cloudy. Mumma, look—'

Maybe it's because we're talking about Grandpa Bill, a figure Esme often associates with his Santa-style facial hair, but she has picked up the dough and arranged it on her face like a green beard. We laugh. This lighthearted homage to his memory feels like an appropriate way to end the discussion – one I suspect would meet with Dad's approval – so I let her get back to her snails. Josh is nearby washing the windows. I get up and brandish the microphone in his direction.

'Are you going to talk to me now?' he says, his hands covered in suds. 'Yeah, I really loved the walk up Sneugie.'

'How did you feel about the Shetland community?' I ask him.

'Um. I didn't really feel like I was part of it. But I did feel welcome,' he says, bending to rinse the squeegee in a bucket at his feet then straightening up again. 'I don't know if it was lockdown or Shetland in general but time felt different. There was an intensity there. I loved those moments with Esme. Time seemed to last longer.'

Stop.

Time.

Good – Shared joy distilled in our minds as memories.

Bad – Silent spring, insectageddon, climate breakdown.

Time to act.

In 2014, Kathy Jetñil-Kijiner read out her poem, 'Dear Matafele Peinem', at the opening ceremony of the UN Secretary General's Climate Summit. In it she brings to life a picture of her home in the Marshall Islands, a lagoon 'lounging against the sunrise'. With sweet, sharp words, she describes the drowning, rising seas, climate refugees and the systems that are pushing island nations to oblivion. But there are many who won't let that happen, she says. There are 'hands reaching out / fists raising up'.

'We won't let you down,' she says. 'You'll see.'

*

Look up.

Clouds darken the sky like spilt ink spreading across a blank page. If we can hold together with the equal force of our shared stories, perhaps we can weather it.

Epilogue

The Way Home

They would not stop for 38 miles, traipsing through the night and day, tiny bullets of rain battering their waterproofs. Following in the footsteps of generations of Shetlanders, their legs were aching, full of spaigie, hansper and creeks.[94] Unlike those ancestors who walked from necessity, this group was doing so to make a point. They had set off from Sumburgh lighthouse, south of the airport, to follow a route which mirrored another journey – one trodden thousands of miles away in the Gaza strip as cities of civilians fled their homes to escape the storm of bombs.

'First of all, this was about Palestine,' Alex Armitage, local councillor and consultant paediatrician told me. 'But from a secondary point, it was also about us and who we are as Shetlanders. We are islanders but we are not insular.'

Alex had been part of a group urging the council to call for

---

[94] Shetland words meaning aching legs after too much walking.

a ceasefire, which they eventually won. He organised the walk to capture the attention of people more interested in Shetland news, rather than the wider world.

'The walk really brought it home to people,' he said.

I imagined the Shetland walkers, buttoned up against the cold, snacks in their bags and warm boots on their feet, their minds on the desperate families dragging carts filled with possessions. Over 15 hours, each step would press on layers of history, a past out of which would spring the future and connect lives across the world. Dig through the strata from bottom to top – from routes scraped by hungry hands for meal to bitumen surfaces, refined from petroleum, melting to pitch in record-summer heat. Now also there is a floating road opening deep peat to construction traffic for the wind farm. This new track reflected my own journey, lined as it was with balls of glacial clay heated and fired as if rolled between my potter father's fingers. This lightweight filler that supports the New Road in Sandwater is also found in the M8 in Glasgow, the city where Dad worked, and approaches to the Queensferry Crossing in Edinburgh, the city of my childhood.

As the Shetland party walked, just over the horizon the fossil fuel industry was holding fast its grip on our futures: investors from Norway and Israel received license to drill in Rosebank, the biggest undeveloped oil and gas field in the North Sea. Burning these fuels will produce more CO_2 than the combined emissions of the world's 28 lowest income countries, according to the campaign group *#StopRosebank*. Cambo, another undeveloped oil field (this one owned by the same Israeli firm) promised a similar fate.

Boot prints in moss of a mother and child searching for bones

Sole-shapes of starving peasants who laboured on the meal roads

When writing *The Shetland Way*, I often thought about mirrors: light glancing off glass or still water creating twin images. A fairy likeness, familiar but strange, that presented a different perspective.

*

Alex was speaking to me on the phone from his sofa in Bigton, south of Lerwick. It was a Friday, a day of rest and ideas, as well as the day the weekly *Shetland Times* was published. 'I'm in the newspaper all the time,' he said. 'I wake up with a deep fear about what I'm going to read about next.'

He was around my age, his mother was from Shetland. She, like my Dad, left in the 1970s seeking a different life on the mainland. Alex also grew up in a capital city, this one London, visiting the isles during school holidays. Here we were less symmetrical. Unlike myself, he had always had a strong tie to the isles, braided through his close relationship with his mother and her desire to return. After spending stints working there in his younger years, as a student doctor and also as a cleaner at the hospital in Lerwick, he settled there in late 2020, a few months after I had left, to work as a consultant paediatrician.

Insider and outsider, half-moother, city dweller and islander. With a London accent, he talked about visiting his ancestors' gravestones and asked: 'Who is a real Shetlander?'

It was a word that held so much: like a fragment of pottery on the shore, time-worn into something new but still with some allusion to its former life.

It was April 2024, shortly after Alex had launched a campaign bid for the Westminster parliament: the 50th anniversary of the Zetland County Council Act, an agreement which enabled Shetlanders to do well out of oil and gas.

'There are so many parallels,' he told me. 'Just as in the 1970s and the discovery of hydrocarbons in the North Sea, today it's about wind.' As the windiest place in the country, Shetland had become a land of opportunity for renewable energy developers, who would, like the oil firms, seek to invest as little capital as possible to gain the biggest returns.

'The forces of capitalism, if left unbridled, would put a wind turbine in every possible location in Shetland,' Alex said. 'I support the production of green energy in Shetland as part of my principle of global solidarity and being an outward-looking community, being part of a place that cares about other communities too. The key thing is how we do that; a way that is not just for people but nature and planet too.'

While interviewing some of the many actors in Shetland's wind farm story, I was careful to avoid taking sides and casting judgement. I was there to listen and report. But taking account of all the various angles did not leave me sitting on the fence. People have strong opinions about renewable energy, wind farms in particular. But as Alex said, there's no denying that they need to be built - on land or sea, and sometimes in areas that are bound to disrupt someone's view at some point on the skyline. The matter at hand is not whether they should be built, but how and for whom. If the foundation stones are laid only to support endless economic growth then we remain on a path to ruin. Energy sources like wind, tidal and solar may be renewable, but farming them in the same old way will result in the same old harvest, with all its injustices and exploitation. Shetland may be the windiest place in Europe, just as it had the best access to oil and whales, but renewable energy on its own does not automatically result in an empowered community. Even after Viking becomes operational, the isles might continue to have among the highest rates of fuel poverty in Scotland. We need a different system that builds community, instead of benefiting some and excluding others.

Something has to give.

There are other ways to own energy. Across Europe, community-owned energy projects in a variety of forms allow local people to buy renewable energy projects for the benefit of their community through shares, lower energy bills, funding pots to address fuel poverty and reduce emissions. These projects tend to be small and not enough work is done to diversify membership, but the model challenges that of large commercial developers by putting the welfare of the community as a whole - not that of individuals - at the centre of the story.

In Bristol, England's largest onshore wind turbine empowers a struggling community.

Lochaline, a village on the west coast of Scotland launches its own hydropower scheme, powering 1,000 homes.

Welsh residents club together to save an empty school building in Carmarthenshire, transforming it into an eco-hub with space for socialising, workshops and warm banks, heated rooms for those who can't afford their energy bills.

How could something like this be done in Shetland? When it comes to wind energy, there needs to be democratic control over planning, Alex suggests. 'For example, maybe the council is not democratic enough, maybe a citizens' assembly could be part of the decision-making process. The key part is participatory democracy as well as representative democracy.'

There are, of course, limitations: the framework within which the picture is contained. Zoom out of Shetland's wind-scaped hills to view the seas that connect continents and it's easier to visualise the interconnections between Shetland's relationship with energy and the rest of the world. Community-owned power projects are all very well, but in this global context more needs to be done to stem the impacts of the climate catastrophe coming our way. What is 'community' anyway, but the connections between people who rely on each other to live? Why should we stop at Shetland-owned energy? Public ownership would take these vital resources out of private hands and force the changes we need at the speed in which we need them.

Just as the crö of Basil Anderson's poem, change is inevitable. We are born and we die, and around us the landscape grows and shifts. What was once a defensive wall to protect kale from hungry rabbits becomes a sundial, a landmark and a fairy ring.

'Just over the last seven generations, there have been huge changes,' Alex said. 'There was the salt cod boom in the 1800s and later the herring. There was the whaling, the merchant navy, the oil industry and the age of social isolation and capitalism. Now we have wind turbines. Through all this Shetlanders have always adapted.'

But as human-induced climate change boils the planet, adaptability will be tested to the limit.

As we wrapped up our call, Alex recalled one conversation that had stuck in his mind.

I close my eyes and imagine the scene.

Broonies Taing is a moody place, the old sheds and collapsing pier cold monuments to a time of noise and activity when the area was a fishing station then later an oil industry supply base.

Facing the water are huge concrete prisms cut off at the top, stacked like a giant's toys, with great ropes of rusted steel poking out. Alex has climbed them and is looking out to sea, sitting with his back to the concrete and his elbows on his knees, breathing in the salt and tang of the sea air. Beneath him a fading sign says 'unsafe pier'. He is in a contemplative mood. Something moving snags his attention, a figure making its way through the ruins towards him, an old man. At first Alex is hesitant, unsure of who the man is and what he wants. As a local politician and doctor, he is well known and knows well his opinions voiced in the local press are not always smiled upon. He stops and waits. The figure walks towards him. Who is it?

'Hello, Alec,' says the man, using the Shetland version of Alex's name. The older must recognise the younger from the papers. 'I knew your family.'

'Oh? Who was it that you knew?'

And so the connections are made, ties strung between the branches of family trees. It is a custom among Shetlanders meeting for the first time to place each other on the islands' vast genealogical canopy. In conversation, there are many points on which this yarn might fray, strong opinions on politics, or energy. Alex braces, expecting a criticism or sharp rebuke perhaps on an article he has written or speech he's made about the need for a different way of doing things. After all, old people are often nostalgic for the past.

'We have to have these wind farms,' the man says. Alex raises his eyebrows.

'I remember life before the oil,' he continues. 'I remember when folk went off to the whaling. I've seen more than one cycle of change.'

*

We leave them now, on the remains of yesterday's industry, listening to each other. The past and the present twisted together, ready, perhaps, to weave a different pattern.

Endnote

Shetland Charitable Trust (1976–)

1974 – Construction begins on Sullom Voe oil terminal.

1976 – Born under the tongue-twisting name of the Shetland Islands Council Charitable Trust, this body begins life as a means to administer the proceeds of the Disturbance Agreement, a deal signed with oil companies to compensate Shetland for social and environmental disruption caused by the oil work. Charitable status means exemption from certain taxes. The council is the sole trustee, with all twenty-two councillors taking on the role of trustees.

1990 – Two non-councillor trustees are added to the list: the Lord Lieutenant of Shetland and the headteacher of the Anderson High School.

2003 – Renamed the Shetland Charitable Trust.

2007 – Under the Viking Energy Partnership, signed at Busta House, the Shetland Charitable Trust has a 45% share,

SSE Renewables has a 50% share and Burradale the remaining 5%.

2008 – *The Office of the Scottish Charity Regulator (OSCR), the national body that regulates charities, receives complaints that called into question the way in which the trust was making decisions and how it was managing any potential conflict of interest.[95] In February trustees defer making a decision to invest a further £3 million of the trust's money in the wind farm because so many declare conflicts of interest. In March, trustees pass the decision.*

2010 – *OSCR imposes strict monitoring requirements on the charity.*

2011 – *Trustees agree to reconstitute the trust to 'further separate it from Shetland Islands Council'. This meant rejigging the board to fifteen, with the council appointing seven.*

2016 – *Trustees vote to reduce the number of councillor-trustees to four. Two years later, the number of trustees shrinks to twelve, and from that point on comprises only selected trustees.*

2019 – *The trust announces it will not invest additional funds in the Viking Energy wind farm.*

---

[95] At the time, Jonathan proposed a solution to OSCR that the trustees should all be independently elected by the public. The then chief executive of OSCR said at a public meeting in Shetland that this proposal 'hit the bullseye'. However, her successor disagreed. 'My fellow councillor-trustees caved in when he threatened them and agreed to make the trust a self-appointing, self-perpetuating body with no publicly elected members. I call those councillors the Undemocrats,' Jonathan said.

2024-5 – The SCT's annual report will reveal: 'A first indication of what the trust's investment in Viking Energy will actually be worth to the community is likely to be revealed in the organisation's annual report for the financial year,' reported in local media.

Acknowledgements

Writing *The Shetland Way* has had such a transformative impact on my life that I sometimes feel the book itself has become the main protagonist in my story. It has reconfigured my network of friends and family, and sparked a change of career from journalism to community-owned energy.

I have often questioned what has driven me to write it. The verb I keep returning to is 'listen' – listening to others, human and non-human, and especially to my own inner voice. As the wind farm began to emerge from the hills, I listened, processed, then wrote, and the words gained their own life outside my thoughts.

I've tried to represent the many people I spoke to as accurately as possible. The words I heard have been filtered back to you, the reader, through my own impressions, fears and hopes. This was part of the reason that I decided not to transcribe speech phonetically, giving just a hint of dialect in the text. Also, as neither a native speaker nor a scholar, I felt my attempts to represent Shaetlan accurately could end in disaster. It's a beautiful dialect and I encourage readers to find

some Shetlanders to listen to and/or visit the website www.
shetlanddialect.org.uk for some excellent resources on the
topic.

I'm so deeply grateful to all my interviewees, who not only
took the time to share their personal stories but also read
through numerous versions as the text evolved over time.
Their generosity and kindness have anchored me during the
storm of writing this book. Huge thanks also to the many
others I talked to whose names are not mentioned in the text,
among them Miriam Brett, Graham Fraser, Eric Graham, Paul
Harvey, Laughton Johnson and the team from Transition
Turrifield – also family members who took the time to fact
check and comment.

This project would not have come to life like this, or even
at all, without the skill and understanding of my editor, Ann
Bissell, and agent, Emma Bal. It is a huge privilege to work
with them both. I'm also indebted to the wonderful writers
and friends who encouraged me along the way, including Jini
Reddy, Kathryn Aalto, inspiring workshops facilitated by Lily
Dunn, as well as Josh Stride, Yasmin Dahnoun, and Simon
Flint.

Among the dearest who helped me stitch the pieces together,
I would like to thank, in particular, Brendan Montague for our
chats during those sea swims in North Cornwall, Gary Cansell
for his analytical eye, and Gareth Dale for his unwavering
enthusiasm and support when things were beginning to
fray – this book would never have made it without you. All
the while, Josh Kopeček remained a wonderful and dedicated
father, whose calming refrain 'it will all come out in the wash',

continues to be true. And forever keeping me grounded, Esme, was, and will always be, the joy of my existence.

Thank you, Mum, for your love and belief in this project.

Thank you, Dad, for your love and legacy. We miss you.